Judas

Judas

How a Sister's Testimony Brought Down a Criminal Mastermind

Astrid Holleeder

JOHN MURRAY

First published in the Netherlands in 2016 as *Judas: een familiekroniek* by Lebowski
Publishers, an imprint of Overamstel Publishers
First published in the United States of America in 2018 by Mulholland Books,
an imprint of Little, Brown and Company
First published in Great Britain in 2018 by John Murray (Publishers)
An Hachette UK Company

All images courtesy of the private collection of the Holleeder family

A CIP catalogue record for this title is available from the British Library

ISBN 978-1-473-68511-6
Ebook ISBN 978-1-473-68512-3

Printed and bound in Great Britain by Clays Ltd, Elcograf S.p.A.

John Murray policy is to use papers that are natural, renewable and recyclable
products and made from wood grown in sustainable forests. The logging
and manufacturing processes are expected to conform to the
environmental regulations of the country of origin.

John Murray (Publishers)
Carmelite House
50 Victoria Embankment
London EC4Y 0DZ

www.johnmurray.co.uk

This book is dedicated to my mother. I have written it for my daughter and the children and grandchildren.

Contents

CONTENTS

CONTENTS

Judas

Prologue
The First Attempt on Cor's Life
(1996)

ON MARCH 27, 1996, MY SISTER SONJA HOLLEEDER AND HER HUSBAND, Cor van Hout, picked up their son Richie from kindergarten. Cor parked his car in front of their home on Deurloostraat, and they stayed in the car, laughing with Richie, who was singing along with his favorite song, "Funiculì Funiculà" by Andrea Bocelli, in the back seat, leaning forward between his parents.

My mother just happened to be standing at their kitchen window when a man wearing a dark coat walked toward Cor's parked car. At the same time, Sonja looked at Cor and noticed someone approaching in the background. At first she thought he was going to ask for directions, but the determined look on his face made her uneasy. He approached the car on Cor's side.

Through the window, Sonja looked straight into his face, and it's still etched into her memory. A yellow-brown face, with lots of wrinkles.

"Cor, what does he want?" she shouted. Cor looked to the left.

Before he could answer, the man pointed a gun at Cor and started shooting. At that moment, Cor dove aside to cover.

Sonja started screaming. Richie was in the back seat of the car; had he been hit? Had Cor been hit? She opened her car door and tumbled out. To prevent herself from getting shot, she crawled on her knees to the back door, opened it, and pulled Richie out. With him in her arms, she ran inside. The door was already open as my mother had rushed out to help her.

Cor had been hit several times. He staggered out to chase the shooter, but, unhinged by his injuries, he started walking in the wrong direction. After he had made it a couple hundred yards, the neighbors helped him back to the house.

Numb and bleeding profusely, Cor just sat there in the stairwell of Number 22 until the ambulance arrived.

I was in my office on Willem Pijperstraat when I got a call on my cell phone. My mom was yelling into the phone.

"Are they alive?" I shouted.

"Yes, they're alive, but Cor was hit. Come over now, please!"

"Is it bad, Mom?"

"I don't know. They took Cor away in an ambulance."

In a panic, I closed my office and drove to Deurloostraat, where Sonja was waiting for me. She opened the door and fell into my arms, crying, "Cor was hit everywhere!"

"Where?" I asked. "Where was he hit? Will he survive?"

"Yeah, they took him to VU Hospital. He was hit in his arm, shoulder, and back, and one bullet shattered his jaw. But he'll live; he's in surgery right now."

"What about Rich? Is Richie okay?" I asked.

"Yes," she said, "he's upstairs. He wasn't hit. Thank God he doesn't really understand what happened. Please act as normal as you can."

"Of course." She was badly shaken and hyperventilating.

We went upstairs, where Richie and my mother were. He was playing on the floor. Luckily the child hadn't seen Cor's bloody injuries. Sonja had pulled him from the car quickly enough and taken him inside right away.

"Hi, honey," I said to him. "Are you having fun playing?"

He looked up and, seeing me, exclaimed, "Assie, Assie, flames! Flames!"

I pulled him onto my lap and asked him, "What about the flames? Go on and tell Auntie."

He was just two and a half years old, and he told me in his own way what had happened. A really naughty man had thrown rocks at the car and there were flames. That was his version, and we wanted to keep it that way.

"Such a naughty man! But he's gone now, sweetie. Daddy chased him away."

Sonja asked, "Could you pick Francis up from school? She doesn't know yet and I want to have her with me. I'm not sure what other crazy stuff might go down."

"I'll go over right now."

I drove to Francis's school and told the janitor I was her aunt and she had to come with me to the hospital.

From her classroom, Francis had already seen me standing in the hall and was startled. The janitor went in and whispered to the teacher, and Francis came out.

"Come on, honey," I said. As we walked down the hallway I told her what had happened, trying to remain calm.

She stood still and grabbed hold of me, her face turning pale. "Is Daddy dead, As?" she asked, her voice trembling.

"No, but he's been hurt pretty badly. He's in the hospital. Mommy and Rich are fine. Come on, let's go home."

It wasn't long before Sonja got a call from the hospital. Cor was out of surgery.

"Are you coming with me to see him?" she asked me. "We can leave the children with Mom. I don't want to drive. I still feel pretty shaky."

"I'll drive," I said. "I want to see him."

We walked to the car, but halfway there, Sonja started trembling. I got into my car but she kept standing there.

"Get in," I said.

"I can't."

I got out and walked over to her. "What's the matter?"

"I'm scared. I keep seeing it, that man walking up to us, the sound of the glass breaking, the shooting. Cor covered in blood. I can't get in," she said.

"Come on, Son, you'll have to. You better drive yourself now, right away. Otherwise you won't do it ever again. Come on, now—you can do this!"

I opened the door and ordered her to get in. "You're right," she said. "I have no choice."

At the hospital, we walked straight to Cor's ward. Police stood guarding the door to his room. Cor was just waking up from surgery; the bullets had been removed from his body, and his lower jaw had been wired shut.

"Are you okay?" I asked.

Cor smiled faintly and stuck his thumb in the air. Speaking was prohibited this soon after jaw surgery, but he couldn't have said anything anyway, not with the cops right outside the door.

He gestured about Richie.

"Rich is fine," Sonja said. "It's a miracle he wasn't hit. You just get out of here."

Rage flamed up in Cor's eyes, and he made a gun gesture; he wanted revenge.

We wanted to know if Cor had any idea where this had come from, so we would know where we stood and what measures to take, if necessary. Sonja and I stood on either side of his bed, staring at him, waiting for an answer.

Cor looked both of us in the eye and shook his head repeatedly. He didn't have a clue.

"I guess we'd better not sleep at home for a while," Sonja said. Cor shook his head once again.

"Okay," Sonja said.

We sat by Cor's bed for a bit, but he was tired and his eyes kept falling shut.

"You get some sleep. We'll be back later," Sonja said.

When we got outside, we took a stroll so we could talk privately, away from the police. "Do you believe Cor really doesn't know who's behind this? Or is he just not telling us?" I asked Sonja, knowing full well that women in our situation are never told anything.

"No," Sonja said. "In this case, that would be too dangerous. He actually doesn't know—otherwise he'd tell us from what direction we should expect danger."

"You don't have a clue, either?" I asked.

"I don't know, but I do have a feeling."

"What is it?"

"Never mind. I can't tell you when I don't know for sure."

"You know you can tell me anything, right?" I asked, slightly offended.

"Nah, leave it. I just don't feel comfortable accusing someone just like that. Can we please change the subject now?"

"Sure," I said.

"But I'm not going back home. I'm too scared. For all I know, they'll come back," Sonja said. "Can I stay at your place with the kids?"

"Of course—we'll go get your stuff right now."

Back at home, I sat down next to Sonja on the couch and finally took a good look at my sister. I noticed tiny feathers falling out of a hole in her coat. I put my finger in and picked out something hard. I was holding a bullet in my hand.

"Looks like you were hit after all," I said.

"Really? See, I told you I have a sore back!"

"Let me have a look," I said, and I lifted up her sweater. An abrasion caused by a grazing shot ran across her entire back.

"I can see why you were in pain," I said. "You were hit. But it's superficial."

Sonja had been extremely lucky. When Cor ducked to shield her, he changed the bullet's direction. The bullet had entered his body first and, after leaving it, had grazed her back. Cor's body had slowed the bullet down enough that it came to a stop in the sleeve of Sonja's coat.

Cor had quite literally caught the bullet for her.

"I could have been dead, Astrid," Sonja said.

"You could all have been dead, Son," I replied.

Just thinking about the danger my family had been in, I was engulfed by rage—what dirtbag did this? What cowardly dog of a man would shoot at a woman and a little kid?

Over time, Cor recovered, under the watchful eye of the police in the hallway. It was their duty to protect every citizen, but they weren't too keen on this particular citizen, a notorious criminal who'd undoubtedly brought this upon himself. As for Cor, he wasn't too keen on protection from the people who were once after him.

"These fuckers, they think it's funny when I get scared shitless every time they cock their weapons," he said, smiling.

As soon as he could, he left the hospital and vanished to France with Sonja, Richie, and Francis. Cor's best friend and our brother, Willem, nicknamed Wim, went along with them, bringing his girlfriend, Maike.

For protection, Cor brought his friend Mo, an Afghani man he knew from prison, down to meet them. The two had kept in touch and because of the war in his homeland, Mo was used to violent situations. He came armed, ready to protect Cor and his family if necessary.

They made their first stop at Hotel Normandy in Paris. From there, they continued on their way south to the Hotel Les Roches in the village of Lavandou on the Côte d'Azur.

Cor and Wim discussed every possible motive for the attack over and over. Things between the two of them were becoming tense, and they'd gotten into an argument more than once.

After a few weeks, Wim and Maike came back to Amsterdam to find out what was going on.

A short time later, Wim brought back the message that Sam Klepper and John Mieremet, two seriously bad guys they knew from their crime circles, had been behind the murder attempt.

Cor found it hard to imagine. Why would they be after him? He wasn't involved in any conflict with them.

But Wim thought it made sense. He reported that Klepper and Mieremet had demanded that Cor and Wim pay them a million Dutch guilders. The only way to resolve the conflict was to pay this amount.

The attack was over, but the danger hadn't passed yet. It wouldn't be passing, either, since Cor told Wim right away he didn't intend to pay anything. He refused to be extorted. This enraged Wim, who said he'd been put under huge pressure in Amsterdam. He had to make sure the money got paid or what happened to Cor would happen to him. Wim claimed that not paying would initiate a war that would end in a bloodbath. Our families would be exterminated without hesitation, all because *Cor* wouldn't pay up, because *he* wanted a war.

Cor still refused to pay. Wim thought he had no choice but to do so.

While this was going on, I flew to meet Sonja and Cor to pick up Francis so I could bring her back to school in Holland.

Sonja picked me up at the airport. "Are you tired?" I asked her.

"Why? Do I look that bad?"

"A little bit," I said cautiously.

"I guess I do," she said, and she filled me in about Klepper and Mieremet and the disagreement about paying up. "Now Cor and Wim won't stop arguing. It's keeping me up at night."

"Is Cor scared of what will happen if he doesn't pay?" I asked.

"No," Sonja said. "I wish he was. Cor says it's pointless to give them the money, that they're at war now anyway. He won't let his wife and child be shot at like that. Wim claims Cor is to blame for all of it because he gets drunk so often and probably insulted someone."

"And what is Cor saying?" I asked.

"He thinks Wim should be supporting him instead of giving in to those two like a wuss. They're in a real fight this time."

"So the shit has only just hit the fan?"

"I guess so," Sonja said.

"I know it would be great if you paid up and that were the end of it, but I think Cor is right. Do you believe it will actually end once you pay? Klepper and Mieremet know that Cor knows it was them. There's no question that they'll just think he's waiting for a chance to get back at them. They'll want to stay ahead of Cor no matter what."

"That's what Cor keeps saying," Sonja said. "He doesn't understand why Wim's pushing for the money."

I could think of a reason, but I kept it to myself.

We drove to Le Lavandou's harbor, where Cor and Mo were having drinks.

"Good to see you, Cor. That jaw of yours doesn't look half bad," I said.

"Come join us, Assie. Have something to eat. We've ordered already."

After joking around a bit about his injuries, Cor said to the others, "Why don't you guys take a stroll. Assie, you stay here for a minute."

He looked worried. "Did Sonja tell you yet?"

"Yeah, we know who they are, and that you're in an argument with Wim."

"What do you think about all this?" he asked.

"I agree with you. Why should you be shot at, and have to pay on top of it? How does that make any sense? I don't get Wim, though...nobody ever tells him what to do."

"Yeah, he's running to the other side a bit too quick for my liking. Make sure to keep a close eye on Francis when you get home. Keep her away from Wim if you can."

I had loved Cor as a brother since the day Wim brought him into our home. He treated us and those around him completely differently from the way Wim did. Cor was warm and friendly. Wim was cold and heartless.

I didn't see why Wim would surrender to the enemy this easily, why he wasn't backing Cor up, after all they'd gone through together. Even if Cor had done something wrong, what did it matter? We'd never abandoned Wim despite all the misery he caused, had we? Why would he do that to Cor now? Of course, I was aware that supporting Cor could have serious consequences, but what about principles? Surely you wouldn't have your spouse, or even your sister, shot at and then pretend nothing had happened, right?

It shocked me to think Wim didn't seem to feel that way.

★ ★ ★

The next day, I flew back to the Netherlands with Francis and tried my best to keep her away from Wim. Cor moved to a small French farmhouse that lay hidden away in the woods and was rented out as a holiday home. The interior was described as "authentically French," which turned out to mean outdated and seedy. The outdoor swimming pool was the only thing that fit the description of a holiday home. It was not the kind of place Cor would normally take for a vacation, and at this moment that was crucial. He didn't want to be anywhere he'd usually go. Nobody could know where he was.

By "nobody," he meant Wim.

Sonja and Richie were there on and off. One evening, Sonja and Cor were sitting on the terrace outside when Cor said, "If anything should happen to me, I want us and our children to be buried together in a family grave, and I want a horse-drawn carriage."

Maybe Wim was right—maybe it would be better to pay up, she proposed timidly.

Cor exploded with anger. He took her remark as treason. "Are you going to forsake me, just like him? That Judas! If that's the way you feel about it, you may as well join your brother, and I'll never have to see you again!" he yelled.

Sonja was struck by the ferocity of his reaction. She hadn't meant it that way, she said, she was just worried about his safety and that of the children. What good was money compared to their lives?

Cor remained steady: paying wouldn't solve anything.

Sonja was stuck between her husband's will and her brother's. All she could conclude was that she'd better stay out of it. Cor had always been the one to decide what was best, and she'd leave it to him this time, too.

Cor left for Martin's Château du Lac, in Genval, Belgium. Sonja kept traveling back and forth, but it was hard to keep up with the kids having to go to school.

Whenever Sonja returned home, Wim would be on her doorstep, asking the same question.

He wanted to know where Cor was staying.

With Cor's instructions not to tell anyone in mind, Sonja pretended she didn't know.

Part I
Family Business
1970–1983

Mom

2013/1970

My mother called me at seven a.m., which is quite early for her. She usually gets up at eight sharp and starts her daily routine by feeding the cat, making breakfast, taking her heart and blood pressure pills, and giving her daughters a call. The fact that she was calling me this early meant something was wrong.

"Hi, Mom. Up this early?" I asked.

"Yes, I've been awake since six thirty. Your darling brother stopped by this morning."

This seemingly humdrum remark was her way of telling me that, once again, there was a problem with Wim.

"That's nice," I replied, thus implying I understood the visit had been anything but nice.

"Are you coming by today? I got you some dried pineapple," she said, really meaning, Come over now: I have something to tell you and it can't wait.

"All right, I'll drop by today," I said, meaning, I'm coming over right now because I know you need me.

"Good. See you later."

We've been communicating this way since 1983: every conversation is layered, every "regular" interaction harbors a completely different meaning known only to our family. This manner of speaking originates from when Cor and Wim were first identified as Freddy Heineken's kidnappers.

Ever since that moment, the Justice Department has put our family under a magnifying glass, and for decades all our phone calls were recorded via wiretap. To communicate safely and without the Justice Department knowing what we were talking about, we developed our family code.

Apart from the veiled language we used with Wim, we had developed our own coded way of discussing him. Just as the authorities were a danger to Wim, Wim was a danger to us.

I drove to my mother's house. After living for a few years in the southern part of Amsterdam, she had moved back to her old neighborhood, the Jordaan, where we had lived as a family and where my siblings and I grew up. We lived there from my birth in 1965 to when I was fifteen and we moved to the Staatslieden neighborhood. I knew every paving stone around here, from Palmgracht to Westerorten.

The Jordaan used to be a working-class neighborhood, a depressed neighborhood, in fact. Its inhabitants called themselves the Jordanese, a willful bunch wearing their hearts on their sleeves but respecting one another—live and let live. From the seventies on, the neighborhood's historic character and picturesque looks began to attract young and more highly educated people, and the neighborhood became extremely popular. Many Jordanese disappeared and "outsiders" arrived, but my mother enjoyed living there, still finding a few friends among the people she knew from the old days.

I parked my car on Westerstraat and walked to her house. There she stood, already waiting for me at the door. I was touched at seeing this sweet old lady. She was seventy-eight now, so fragile.

"Hi, Mom," I said, and kissed her tender wrinkled cheek.

"Hello, darling."

As always, we sat down in the kitchen.

"Would you like a cup of tea?"

"Yes, please," I said.

She rummaged around the kitchen and put two mugs on the table.

"So, what's going on? I can tell you've been crying. Has Wim been pestering you again?" I asked.

"Very much so. He wants to get himself registered at my address, but I just can't do that. This is communal housing for the elderly and children are not allowed. If I did it I could get in trouble, I may have to leave my house, and I'd be out on the street. He was outraged when I told him and went off the deep end again. He called me a worthless mother, said that I didn't do anything for my own child. Child?! He is fifty-six years old!

"I should be ashamed for not even wanting to help my own son. He kept on screaming, so loud I was scared the neighbors would hear. He's *just* like his father, just like his father," she repeated, as if she had to hear it twice to believe it.

She was worn out by the terror that had passed from father to son. Wim had been terrorizing her ever since he was a little boy, and she had always attributed it to his lousy father. That's why, even in old age, she let him treat her like garbage. That's why she never abandoned her son, despite the gravity of his crimes, and kept visiting him in prison after his first conviction, hoping he would change, and even after his second conviction for the extortion of several real estate tycoons—after all, he was still her child.

All in all, she visited him in prison about seven hundred and eighty times. Seven hundred and eighty times she waited in line, seven hundred and eighty times she went through security, took her shoes off, and put her things on the belt to be scanned. From 1983 to 1992, when Wim was locked up for the Heineken kidnapping in La Santé

Prison in Paris, she traveled a thousand kilometers to France and back every week. After he was extradited to the Netherlands, she visited him here. Nine years in all, and six more years later when he was imprisoned again for several extortions.

"Wouldn't you like to get some peace and quiet, Mom?" I said, taking her hand.

"I don't think I ever will," she sighed.

"You don't know that. Who knows, maybe he'll go back inside and never get out."

"I won't visit him then," she said right away. "I'm too old for that. I can't do it anymore—it'll be too much for me." Every visit he humiliated her and blamed her for all *his* mistakes.

I realized if he were to be jailed because of my own betrayal, she *couldn't* even visit him anymore because he'd use her to track me down and kill me.

No, if I went through with my plans, she couldn't ever see her son again, and only then would she find real peace.

As much as I wanted to tell my mother about my plan to finally take a stand, I couldn't run the risk of her slipping up. As long as I hadn't made up my mind yet, I shouldn't tell her anything, and I should keep behaving normally, meanwhile doing what I've always done in our family: protecting whoever didn't comply with Wim's raging demands.

And so I reassured my mother: "Listen to me, Mom. You're not going to register him here. He can find another address. I'll talk to him. It will be all right, don't worry."

I finished my tea, got up, and kissed my mother goodbye. "I'll find him. It will be okay."

"Thanks, honey," she said with relief.

I walked to my car, but instead of getting in, I walked the route I had taken homeward during grade school, to the house I grew up in. I saw the green lantern hanging from the facade. It marked a gloomy place, and the closer I got to the house, the colder I felt. The chill that used to prevail there still made my body freeze.

I stood across the alley, and the sight of the house brought back a flood of memories, of my childhood, of our family living there— my mother, father, Wim, Sonja, my brother Gerard, and me. As the oldest, Wim was always "brother," whereas Gerard was demoted to "little brother," even though he was older than I was.

My mother met my father at a sports event where he was taking part in a cycling race. He was a couple of years older than she, handsome and extremely charming. He seemed sweet, friendly, and attentive to the people around him, and was a hard worker. They dated for a while, then got engaged and moved in with my mother's parents.

Mother Stien and Willem Sr. (1956)

When my father found work and a house near the Hoppe factory in the Jordaan, they got married and moved there. My mother was over the moon with having her own home and her position as a married woman.

Soon, however, her thoughtful fiancé transformed from Dr. Jekyll into Mr. Hyde: a fickle and unpredictable tyrant, a side of him she had never seen before and which he displayed only after she'd been caught in his web and couldn't get away.

He quit cycling and started drinking heavily. He began hitting her and forced her to give up her job and all her social connections.

My maternal grandmother had offended him by saying once that he "probably didn't want any coffee." He interpreted this as *her* not wanting to *serve* him any coffee, and my mother was no longer allowed to stay in touch with her parents; after this, my mother didn't see my grandparents for fifteen years.

My father had succeeded in completely isolating her. He imprisoned her within her marriage, and he set the rules she had to follow. From his perspective, he was "boss": boss of her, boss of their home, boss of the street, boss at work.

My father was a megalomaniac. Every day he'd scream, "Who's the boss?" and my mother had to reply, "You are the boss."

After he had isolated her, he brainwashed her. She was "just" a woman, and women were inferior beings, their husband's property, and whores by nature. To prevent her from "whoring and harloting," she was forbidden to encounter other men. She had to stay home all day and was not allowed to go out. When she had to get groceries, she had to leave a note letting him know exactly where she was going.

He was pathologically jealous. He'd come home during his lunch break, and if she happened to be out, he'd hide in the hall closet to spy on her. She never knew if he was in there and she didn't dare open the closet because he would then conclude she was planning to cheat on him. Surely, if she wasn't planning to cheat on him, she wouldn't have to check for his presence in the closet. Even a necessary visit to the doctor would be followed by cross-examinations and torture to determine whether she was "fooling around" with the doctor. He dominated and controlled her entire life.

And he scared her to death. She wasn't allowed to talk back to "the boss" or she'd get hit.

The first time that happened, my mother was taken completely by surprise. How could this sweet and sympathetic man suddenly have turned so cruel? Surely she had done something wrong—she had to have. He confirmed this during lengthy monologues: how lousy she was as a housewife, how happy she should be that he still wanted her as his wife, how she didn't actually deserve him because she was worthless. He made her believe that she deserved the abuse because she was a terrible wife and messed everything up on purpose just to make his life miserable.

She responded by trying even harder to live up to what he wanted, hoping she would do better and thus prevent him from abusing her. The beatings weren't even the worst part; it was the continuous threat that terrorized her into obedience, and she was much too scared to leave. The ceaseless terror had shattered her identity and willpower.

When she was pregnant with her first child, she hoped becoming a father would change him, but it didn't. During her pregnancy, his abuse continued as it did with her subsequent pregnancies and deliveries. My mother had four children with this man.

We called all of our Jordanese neighbors "auntie" or "uncle," so our next-door neighbor was always our Auntie Cor. She took my mom's situation to heart. My mother never said a word about it, but these houses were so flimsy that everyone on the block knew my father attacked her at night.

Auntie Cor told my mom about birth control pills. "Stop having these kids," she told my mother. My mother wasn't allowed to use the pill. According to my father, birth control was for whores and women who wanted to fuck around without getting pregnant. But after the fourth baby, Auntie Cor couldn't stand to watch it any longer and personally got the pill prescription for her.

"Enough is enough," she'd said when she came to visit, and handed her a box of pills. From then on, my mother was secretly using birth control.

That made me the last kid in line.

Stien, Willem Sr., and Astrid (1966)

My father treated his children the same way he treated his wife. He beat us, no matter how small and defenseless we were. As with my mother, he didn't need a reason—he made one up on the spot. That was how he justified his actions. It always was "our own fault"—we made him do it. My mother protected us from him when she could. Whenever he started hitting us, she would jump between us and catch the blows. The morning after, she'd often have trouble walking or moving her arms.

Left to right: Stien, Sonja, Gerard, Willem Sr., Astrid, and Wim (1966)

From the time we were little, we all tried our utmost not to draw my father's attention, for his attention included the risk of scolding, shouting, and beating. We were well aware that none of us could risk having a schoolteacher or neighbor going to my father to complain about our behavior, for then all hell would break loose. Not just for ourselves, but also for my mother and the other children in the family, who'd have to suffer my father's fury. Our behavior at home was exemplary. At school we were obedient, paid attention in class, and worked hard. In the street, we were never cheeky or wanton. We were all compliant, good kids who never broke any rules.

Left to right: Wim, Gerard, Astrid, and Sonja (1966)

After the beer brewer Heineken took over the Hoppe factory, my father worked in the company's advertising and promotion department on Ruysdaelkade. My father was so devoted to his boss, he worked Saturdays, too. Sometimes he took us with him. We'd play among Mr. Heineken's parked cars.

While we were at the factory one day, I discovered a large wooden tub covered by a tarpaulin. I was just four years old and thought I could sit on it. When I did, I immediately fell through. The tub turned out to be filled with some kind of liquid, and my trousers got soaking wet.

After a while, my legs started to hurt more and more, but all I was worried about was whether I'd been a bad girl, and refused to tell my father. The pain got worse by the hour, but I didn't show it. As the day went on, my trousers dried and my accident was no longer noticeable. That evening, my mother set me on the sink as she always did to wash me. We didn't have a shower. When she pulled my trousers down, skin fragments from my legs peeled off, and my skin had been soaked off in some places. It turns out I had fallen into a tub of caustic soda, but I hadn't made a sound all day because crying was forbidden.

Astrid (1970)

During the day we could escape to school or play outside. But there was no getting away from evenings.

Every night, he'd come home drunk, sit down in his antique armchair, and keep drinking all through the evening and much of the night. My mother was to supply him with cold beers. *"Stien!* Beer!" he'd keep shouting. He'd easily finish a case of half liters in a night.

Each of us tried to be as invisible as possible in the living room, and we all wanted to go to bed as soon as we could, just to be min-imize our time in his presence.

Once in bed, you might be out of sight, but you still weren't safe. Every night we'd lie listening to him shouting and raging. We were experts at guessing from the tone of his voice or manner of speech how badly things would get out of hand that night. We'd lis-ten carefully in case one of us was mentioned in his tirade, fearing the moment he'd come into the bedroom.

Once he was standing in the bedroom, the best we could do was to all pretend to be sleeping, hoping he'd leave. The evenings and nights crept by. Every half hour I could hear the Westertoren bell ring as I waited for the shouting to end, for him to go to bed.

It's left me with a profound hatred of ringing bells.

Evenings were bad enough, but Sundays were truly horrible. On Sundays, he was home. All day long.

Filled with the smell of booze and my father's unpredictability, those days seemed endless. Only one thing was certain: there would be shouting and hitting. Sometimes it started early in the afternoon, but with a little luck, it could start a bit later.

Above all, I feared dinnertime, because on Sundays he dished up the food. And the amount he scooped onto your plate had to all be eaten. If you didn't clean your plate, you were an ungrateful shit and would most likely be spanked. Trembling with fear, I'd watch him fill my plate. It would always be a huge amount, way too much for a little girl, and I often couldn't eat everything.

At some point, I'd developed a range of tactics to get rid of the pile of food unseen. Depending on the clothes I was wearing and the type of food, I'd put it in my pockets or stuff it into my cheeks and then I'd ask if I could go to the bathroom. There I would get rid of it or spit it out.

You were never asked whether you liked something—you just ate what was served. There were two things I truly loathed:

spinach, and gravy on my food. One night, we were having spinach, the snotty kind that was impossible to hide anywhere without getting it all over my hands and having liquid run from my pockets. As always, there was gravy, and my father poured so much of it onto my plate that it made the food float around in it. It was hopeless. I could never eat it all. I started to feel full and began to eat slower.

My father noticed and yelled, "Finish your plate! You wanna get a good spanking?"

Of course I didn't, but I didn't know how I was going to finish that huge plate of food and the greasy gravy.

"Eat it!" he screamed, and gave me a spoon to eat the gravy as if it were soup. I felt sick and tried to hide my gagging. If he saw that, I'd *really* be in trouble. But I couldn't keep it down, my stomach pushed the disgusting spinach and the nasty, greasy gravy back up into my throat. I tried to hold it down, but the food squirted straight back onto my plate.

He lost it. How dare I spit out my food? I was a fool to think this dramatic scene would get me off the hook: now I would have to eat my own vomit. I stiffened and stared at the disgusting substance on my plate. At his order, I hesitantly scooped up a spoonful.

"Eat it, ungrateful bitch—you will eat!"

I closed my eyes and put the spoon in my mouth. The world around me faded, and everything went black. When I looked up, I saw my father beating my mom. She'd pulled the plate from under my nose and was being beaten for it. When she was lying on the floor motionless, my father summoned me, "Look what you've done! This is all your fault!"

It wasn't just what he did to me that was my fault, so was what he did to others.

He was never to blame.

★ ★ ★

For years I thought my domestic situation was normal and all fathers were like mine. It wasn't until I was eight years old that I realized that wasn't true.

One day, I went to play with Hanna, my best friend all through grade school. She was the shortest girl in class, and I was the tallest. Every day I'd pick her up to walk to school together, to the Theo Thijssenschool on Westerstraat. We usually played outdoors, but this time she'd asked me to come play at her house. Her mom, grandmother, and little sister were there, too.

We were practicing a dance routine to show off on the playground when the doorbell rang. All four of them chanted, "Daddy's home!" I grew pale and looked around for a hiding spot, but couldn't see one. They didn't understand why I started running around the room and told me to stop being silly. "Sit down," Hanna said, and pushed me onto the couch. "Dad's here."

That's right. Dad's here. That's the problem.

Hanna's grandmother put her arm around me and said, "Isn't that nice?"

Nice? Not at all! I heard footsteps coming up the stairs, saw the door swing open, and noticed a man with a happy face standing there. "Hello, my darlings."

He kissed his wife and children. They seemed to genuinely enjoy it. What was going on here? To make matters worse, he walked straight up to me.

"Hello, dear. Are you having a good time playing?"

I was speechless, and Hanna said, "Yes, Daddy. Look, we can dance!"

She danced around and spoke to her father with such glee, and he replied so happily. I had never spoken directly with my father. I can't recall ever having a single conversation with him. All there had ever been were raging monologues.

It was in that moment that I realized things could be different. I saw with my own eyes that dads could be kind, too. From that day on, I knew my father wasn't what a father should be, and every night I prayed to God, asking Him if my father could please die.

My prayers weren't answered.

We all wished him dead, hoping for a fatal accident or lethal encounter with the wrong person, but it never happened. We were all prisoners of my father's madness.

We treated each other the way my father treated my mother and us. If any one of us aroused his rage, they shouldn't count on any sympathy; on the contrary, they had inflicted misery on the rest of us, too. "Your fault!" we'd yell, even though we were well aware that my father's behavior was completely random.

My dad's violence seeped through every layer of our family and soaked us all. Since getting angry at my dad was not an option, we fought among ourselves, blaming each other for a hopeless situation. We were tense children, and the continual threat looming in our home left no room for tolerance or mutual understanding. Aggression and violence became a communication strategy.

That's just the way it was.

We didn't know any better.

So the violence was passed down generation to generation.

My dad hit my mom. Following his example, my brother Wim hit my sister, Sonja. My "little brother," Gerard, hit me. I never started the fights because I knew I'd never win. Not against my dad, not against my brothers. I was the smallest one, and a girl at that. Regardless of my efforts to be like a boy, I always lacked strength.

As soon as my parents left for their daily after-dinner stroll,

Gerard would start with me. It was a daily ritual; we played family every night. He—unconsciously—imitated my father, and I had to tell him he was the boss, the way my father had my mother say he was the boss. If I didn't, I got hit, just like my mom. But I never told him he was the boss. I couldn't. I took the blows, but I did get back at him. He may have been stronger, but I was smarter.

Gerard was a shy kid. He hardly ever spoke. He'd shut down the second you looked at him. I was two years younger but much cheekier, and I always took the lead. I fixed everything for him, thus swapping my physical disadvantage for mental domination. I used his weaknesses. In exchange for information about a girl he had a crush on, I'd demand his pocket money, fifty cents a day. He paid because he was afraid to talk to her. Holding his fifty cents in my hand, I enjoyed the power I had over him.

I'd rather be perpetrator than victim.

Walking through my old neighborhood, I turned off our block and continued toward Egelantiersgracht. I thought of Wim, and how it had all come to this. Around the corner was the house we had once moved into temporarily because ours was registered as a monument and had to be renovated, as many of the Jordaan's houses back then did. This was a spacious mansion along one of the canals of Amsterdam, a light-filled dwelling with large rooms and high ceilings, completely different from our house on Eerste Egelantiersdwarsstraat, which was a workers' house with tiny, narrow rooms with ceilings only just allowing an adult to stand upright. Three of us shared a room, and I slept by the window overlooking the canal. Wim was the only one who had a tiny room to himself.

As a family we didn't have a social life. My father didn't have any friends, and my mother wasn't allowed to. We never had any visitors, there were no parties, every birthday or holiday was hell, and there was nothing to look forward to. There was no laughter in our home, and fun was forbidden. When we were merry, he'd ruin the mood.

Wim reached high school. He'd grown into a tall, handsome guy with his dark brown hair highlighting his big, beautiful blue eyes. He started going to the gym, built up muscle, turned into a man. His world expanded out beyond our block and he started meeting all sorts of people, which changed the way he saw our father.

He started rebelling against his rules. The world outside our family was increasingly attractive to him, as he discovered fun and good times actually did exist out there. He claimed the right to a personal life and went his own way. He'd often come home late and knock on my window.

"Assie, are you asleep?" Wim whispered softly into my ear.

"No," I whispered back.

I'd been awake all night until finally the shouting had stopped and my father had gone upstairs. Even then, I couldn't get to sleep.

"Has Dad gone to bed yet?" he whispered.

"Yes," I said.

"Did he go crazy again? Was it about me?"

"Yes, he was yelling that you were late, but Mom turned back the clock so he wouldn't catch you."

"Good."

It wasn't the first time my mother had adjusted the clock, and it wouldn't be the last. Thanks to her, Wim had been lucky yet again. He hardly ever went to school, but he managed to make money anyway. "See, As," he said, "this is how I do it," and pushed a brownish, greasy chunk into my hands. I didn't know what it was, but Wim made money off it, so it had to be good. I was happy for him. Earning money increased his independence, which enraged my father, and Wim kept getting hit.

My mom also had a rough time with her son, who, even as he defied his father's rules, started to resemble him more and more. Now she was being assaulted from two sides. She didn't know what to do.

Ever since he'd started secondary school, her son had changed. He was bad-tempered and unfriendly to be around and just as unpredictable and aggressive as his father. She couldn't correct his behavior; he couldn't care less what she thought.

He knew she'd never ask for my father's support. She'd never turn her son over to that lunatic. To protect him from his father's beatings, she covered up all his misbehavior.

Wim knew Mom was caught between them, and he used it to his advantage. He did what he felt like and was always asking for money. It was never enough. If my mother refused, he'd become violent and punch holes in the doors and walls. Like his father, he was pathologically jealous and beat up all his girlfriends. If my mother confronted him about this, he'd get even more aggressive and start hitting even harder. She learned to simply shut her mouth. His fury scared me, and I tried to avoid him the way I did my father.

Starting in middle school and continuing into high school, Wim would bring his school friend Cor home during the day, when my father wasn't there. They would eat Hema sausages for lunch. I always liked having Cor around; he liked to joke around, and he was sunny by nature. When Cor was around, the tension lessened and the atmosphere at home actually became pleasant.

Cor had a completely different outlook on life than Wim. He took everything lightly and always came up with solutions. He was able to enjoy life; Wim imitated him. It made him a happier person.

When Wim was by himself, I'd avoid him, but when he was with Cor, he was okay to be around.

Cor affectionately made fun of our imperfections and nicknamed us all. He called Wim "the Nose" because of his big nose. My father was called "the Bald" because he had practically no hair left on his head. Soon this turned into "the Bald Madman" due to his bizarre behavior. Rather cheekily, he called by mother by her first name: Stientje. Sonja got named "the Boxer," because she practiced kickboxing and used to fight him off when he tried hitting on her. He called Gerard "the Dent" because of the scar chickenpox had left on his nose. Predictably, I was called "the Professor" because I was a good student.

My dad hated Cor, who wasn't impressed with him and laughed at his shouting and scolding. The Bald couldn't get to Cor, and so the Bald's power over Wim began to wane. He couldn't deal with this and kicked Wim out of the house.

After Wim left, we saw him only when he and Cor had lunch at my mom's. I thought he'd played it well. He'd escaped my father. I wanted that, too.

I had almost finished primary school and was going to secondary school. I was a fast learner and I devoured books. At school, I was praised for being "intelligent," but at home this was a cause for endless teasing. According to my brothers and sister, I was "weird" and always acting "smart." When I made thoughtful remarks, they'd say, "There she goes again!" and I was dismissed as a bookworm.

To ease my hurt, my mom explained to me that I wasn't weird and that I was "intelligent like this because I had been held by a university student immediately after birth." He had passed his learning skills on to me. I shouldn't listen to all the teasing, for it couldn't be helped.

My brothers and my sister had a different explanation for my behavior. They thought I was a foundling. I wasn't my parents' child or my siblings' sister.

They said I wasn't an actual member of the family.

Astrid in elementary school (1973)

Maybe I should have felt hurt by this, but it made perfect sense to me. Of course I didn't belong to this family. There had to be a family out there that was smart and loved reading, one that would accept me. So as a little girl, I waited for my real parents to come get me. In vain. In the meantime, I had to deal with this family. A family in which a girl became a housewife and wasn't expected to get an education.

My headmaster, Mr. Jolie, registered me at the athenaeum—a specialty school in the center of Amsterdam—and told my mom it would be a waste to send me to domestic science school.

The headmaster had assured her it would be easier for me to find work after the athenaeum, and Mom, knowing that turning me into a housewife would be impossible, agreed. She kept this a secret from my father, who didn't think girls should be educated at all. My mother waited to tell him until after a night when he had been "really bad."

"Really bad" was her phrase for nights when she was abused so badly that he couldn't deny it in the morning: the proof would show on her arms, legs, back, shoulders, and face.

Not that my father minded beating the hell out of her, but it bothered him if the whole neighborhood could see the evidence. He liked to keep up the image of good father and devoted husband. The mornings after these "really bad" nights, he'd be a bit less prone to violence.

On one of these mornings, my mom casually mentioned I'd be going to the athenaeum. She knew he probably wouldn't really take it in, and he didn't, but at least she could honestly claim later that she had told him in case he tried to make trouble about it.

I was twelve years old, and before I went to the athenaeum, Headmaster Jolie called me to his office and said I should start practicing my speech. I spoke one hundred percent Jordanese slang, which would not be done at this new school. I would have to learn to speak decently.

It was the first time anyone had ever pointed my speech habits out to me. But where could I learn any other way? Everyone around me spoke this way, and I never left the neighborhood. My world covered the area from Palmgracht to Westertoren. That's as far as we got.

That summer, our neighbor Pepi happened to invite me to come with her to her summer house. It was a huge villa in Noordwijk, in the dunes near the beach, and, ironically enough, right across the street from one of Heineken's homes. Miss Pepi wasn't a real Jordanese but an outsider, imported. She'd originally come from Wassenaar and spoke Dutch without an accent. She wasn't called Auntie or Auntie Pepi, just Pepi.

Pepi—the name alone was fabulous. Pepi could drive a car, she had a child but no husband, she had a job and enough money. All this made her an oddity in our Jordaan neighborhood. A single mother, working outside the house at that—it was a scandal. But she was everything I wanted to be. She became my main role model.

I spent a couple of weeks under her wing that summer, and when I called my girlfriend Hanna at the end of my vacation, she almost hung up on me, thinking someone was prank calling her. When I'd convinced her it was really me, she was in shock. "What's happened? What have they done to you? You talk funny! Get off it! Who do you think you are, the queen? Did your upper lip stiffen?"

Without being aware of it, I'd taught myself to speak without an accent, and I didn't stand out at the athenaeum.

I loved being at this school, where I met people with a rational outlook on life, as opposed to what I was used to at home. Nothing was arbitrary; cause and effect prevailed. You could influence what happened to you, and what happened to you was of your own doing. Being in this environment was a huge relief to me. I didn't have to feel ashamed for wanting to learn the names of all the human muscles by heart, for enjoying studying the dictionary, for wishing to learn the species of birds, trees, and herbs. Here, it was perfectly normal to hunger after knowledge. Everybody had the same "abnormality." Having an opinion was appreciated, and people listened to it. You were even allowed to argue with an adult, as long as your argumentation was solid. Everything I got ridiculed for at home was appreciated here.

During the day, I had a great time at school, but the evenings were still dominated by the Bald Madman, as we privately called him.

He sat in his large antique armchair, with his wife and children lined up before him on the couch. He could take his pick, and one day it was my sister's turn. Like Wim, Sonja had reached an age at which my father feared losing his grip on her. Unlike me, she had turned into a "real girl," with manicured nails, makeup, and a hairdo that could easily compete with Farrah Fawcett's.

I loved the way she looked, and I used to watch in awe as she transformed her straight hair into luxuriant curls in front of the mirror. Much to my father's dismay, she had turned into a beautiful young lady. She worked in a shoe store on Kalverstraat, and that day her boss had given her a bouquet of flowers as a reward for her efforts. She was proud.

My father didn't allow her to feel this positive emotion. He assumed the flowers meant she was having an affair with her boss. She was a whore like all women. My sister wasn't having an affair with her boss, but refuting his assumption was futile.

Sonja was sitting on the couch. He walked up to her, grabbed her by the hair, and said, "You're just a filthy whore!" He pulled her arm and slapped her across the face, but she managed to get away and tried to run upstairs to her room. He chased her and got ahold of her again. I could hear Sonja screaming and pleading, "No, Daddy, no! Don't!" I ran after them and stood in her room, watching.

In the bedroom was a marble-top antique dresser. I watched my father drag her to it by the hair and slam her head against it. I was sure her skull would crack. I saw her eyes roll back, and at that same moment, my mother and I jumped on my father to pull him off her.

When we'd managed to get him away from her, he suddenly stood in front of me.

I looked him straight in the eye and asked, "Why are you doing this? Don't we do everything you say?"

He answered my question by slapping me across the face left and right.

I thought, Go on, hit me, asshole. I had stood up to him, and I knew I'd have to suffer for it.

I was so afraid that I couldn't feel any pain. That ruined the effect of his beatings, increasing his rage.

"Get out!" he screamed eventually. "Get out and never come back!"

Suddenly I was thirteen years old and homeless.

By rebelling against my father, I had put my mother in an extremely difficult position. Because I wasn't allowed to come home, she had to choose between accepting the existence my father determined for her and turning away from her child, or taking her destiny into her own hands and leaving her husband without a penny in her pocket.

My mom chose the latter.

Providence—or just good timing—helped her in taking the step. Auntie Wim, our neighbor from across the street, had just found love with Uncle Gerrit, and he moved in with her. My mother could move into his house on Lindengracht.

"It was meant to be," she said. She started working as a caregiver for an old lady, and I had a job at the marketplace and handed all my earnings to my mom, and that's how we got by.

The four of us lived in the house on Lindengracht: Sonja, Gerard, my mom, and me, less than a mile from my dad. Not far away, but at a safe distance. My mom slept in the living room on a foldaway bed, and we slept in hospital beds given to us by Louis the Scrapman, an acquaintance of my father's who felt sorry for us. He ran a demolition company and had taken the beds from a hospital that they knocked down.

The shower was on the balcony. The place was tiny and freezing, but to me it was paradise. No more fear, no more screaming, no more violence.

I loved every minute of it. But it wouldn't last long.

Through the neighbors, my father started pushing for my mother's return. They felt so bad for him—he looked so feeble and neglected, and he told them he couldn't live without his wife. He'd do anything if only she would come back.

The neighbors took this story to my mother. She felt responsible for her marital duties and went to speak with him. He assured her he would change. There would be no more drinking, shouting, and hitting. My mother was all too keen to believe it. Besides, we had to leave the Lindengracht house: Uncle Gerrit and Auntie Wim were having issues, and Uncle was moving back to his house, and it was best if we left.

My mother went back to my father. I was forced to live there again. I hated her for it. She hardly had any money, nowhere to live, and young children to take care of, but back then I didn't sympathize with her at all. I only understood her when I became a single mother myself.

My mother had barely crossed the threshold when the terror

started again. After my "rebellion," I had become his main target. I tried to be away from home as much as I could, but if I didn't sleep at home, he took it out on my mother. Wim had left the house years earlier, Sonja hadn't returned with us but lived on Van Hall-straat, and Gerard spent most of his time at his girlfriend Debbie's. I couldn't leave her alone with the Bald Madman. Out of fear he would beat her to death at some point if I didn't, I slept there.

Like before, the terror often lasted through the night. He'd walk in and out of my bedroom, screaming and scolding. I hardly got any sleep, and still I had to perform at school and in basketball. I played in the National League (well, I sat on the bench, but at fourteen I proved quite promising). Everything I had accomplished for myself was in jeopardy, just because my mom had hoped this man would actually change.

I got so run-down that I wasn't able to feel any fear, only hate. I looked for a way out of the situation and found it in a large, sharp kitchen knife I hid underneath my bed. I intended to murder him.

"It's nothing but self-defense," my friend Ilse said when I told her about my plan to stick the knife into his belly. Ilse knew just how bad my father was.

"You think so?" I asked.

"Sure," she said. "You should just do it."

Ilse said it would be better to stab him straight in the heart. But to me aiming at his belly seemed easier, as it was the size of a bouncing ball and protruded a good deal. The question was, could I make a deadly hit that way? I could see that stabbing him in the heart would be more effective, but it also required more precision. What if I missed? It had to be spot on. What if he took the knife from me? He might kill me. I spent many nights pondering how best to kill my father. I even practiced in my dreams. Yet I couldn't find the right time to take action. He was never drunk enough, he stood too far away, and he moved too quickly. I couldn't succeed in killing him. Not because I didn't want to, but because fate decided otherwise.

From the time I was thirteen until I turned fifteen, my father was stationed in the village of Lage Vuursche for work. He had become impossible to work with. He was always drinking during working hours, in a perpetual state of drunkenness, having conflicts with everyone because his megalomania led him to believe he was in charge of the entire company.

After years and years of misery, they'd finally gotten fed up with him. He had to leave the advertising and promotions department. My mother, brother, and I wondered how bad things might get if my father was without a job and my mom couldn't pay the bills.

The Heineken company came up with an elegant solution for the man they could easily have fired on the spot for misbehavior in the workplace. He was transferred to a place where he would run into few people and his terrible conduct would cause as little trouble as possible. He was given a second chance—another job, at full salary, in a beautiful wooded area.

It goes without saying the Bald was deeply hurt by this move. In his mind, he was the most devoted employee a company could wish for, and he should have been rewarded with respect and a promotion. In reality, he was a boozed-up, aggressive, quarrelsome subordinate who was lucky not to have been fired long before, and we knew all too well that he should be thanking his lucky stars that he was still employed by Heineken at all, given his record of troublemaking.

Meanwhile, my father's change of job didn't interest Wim in the least, and he didn't take any notice of it. He didn't want to be drawn into our misery—once *his* misery, too. He'd never discuss the Bald, and he'd come by only when he wanted his washing or ironing done.

★ ★ ★

At his new workplace, my father rapidly began displaying his mega-lomanic territorial instincts again. When he had started at his new location, he had taken two geese with him for company, who had reproduced into a huge, annoying colony.

Everyone in the area was bothered by the noise and shit they pro-duced. Management ordered him to get rid of the geese, but my father didn't comply.

Out of rage, he wrung all their necks and dumped some of the carcasses on his direct manager's doorstep. This was not appreci-ated. My father came up with the idea of blaming me.

Every day when I got home, I had to sit in front of him and he'd ask me why I'd put those geese on his manager's doorstep. When I replied I hadn't, he told me not to lie, for he himself had seen me there, in a tall black coat—*his* coat!—carrying the dead geese. He'd never do anything like that, but the blame was being put on him.

I might be getting a "higher" education and all that, but I was still a retarded brat, and I couldn't make him pay for my deeds. He tried his hardest to brainwash me by repeating the story over and over. He got my mom involved by saying she'd told him she'd seen it, too.

He was so convinced of his own story, I'd almost start to believe him by the end of these sessions.

Once, when I was fifteen years old, I came home from a training camp. I noticed our front door was boarded up. While I stood look-ing at it, Auntie Wim called out to me. "Come in before your father sees you!" she said, and pulled me inside.

She told me my father had kicked in the door, and Gerard and my mom had fled because he'd gone completely out of his mind again. They had found refuge in a house on Bentinckstraat.

At Auntie's, I heard what had happened. The Bald had come home drunk again. I wasn't there, so he started pestering my mom by doing a cleanliness inspection. Our house had a ground floor, two stories above that, and an attic. On each floor, he'd swipe two fingers over the surfaces of all tables, cupboards, every spot that could be dusty, to check if my mother had dusted properly.

Of course, being a devoted and terrified housewife, my mom always had.

Since he couldn't find any dust, he continued on, looking for ways to make her life miserable. He didn't mind creating a domestic failure by pulling the bed linen out of the closet and then asking why it was such a mess. My mother could never win this game.

"What's that, in the ashtray?" he'd asked her sharply.

In our household, no one smoked, and because this ashtray was unused, my mom had put a savings coupon in it. He screamed that that ashtray wasn't meant for these things and started opening all the cupboards and throwing their contents down the stairs, from the second to the first floor. Crockery, cutlery, side tables, chairs, anything he got hold of went down because she hadn't cleaned up the house neatly enough and now she had to do it again.

Gerard, who had been in bed upstairs, came running down at the sound of my father, my mother's screaming, and the noise of breaking crockery. He saw my father trying to throw my mom down the stairs, and something snapped inside him. He stormed toward him. The Bald made an attempt to lunge at him, but Gerard hit him right in the chin.

He fell backwards, slamming the back of his head, and lay motionless for a few seconds.

With one blow, Gerard had put an end to his dictatorship, and shockingly the Bald seemed to accept it. No one in our family had ever dared to go at him physically. Not Mom, not Wim, not Sonja, not me.

Gerard, the quiet, timid boy, had stood up to my father.

Honestly, I'd never have expected this from him, and I was eager to get all the details of how he had taught the Bald a lesson, but, quiet as he was, he just said, "There's nothing good about it." That's all I got, and all I needed. Gerard was my hero, and I was glad I hadn't been home that night. I might have grabbed the kitchen knife from under my bed after all, and who knows how that might have ended.

Gerard didn't just save my mother from my father, but me from myself as well.

After that, Gerard, my mom, and I fled my father once again. My mother would never return to him. I had finally escaped. Peace, at last! That's how it seemed. But this long-awaited peace and quiet brought its own issues.

I had gotten used to tyranny. The abuse at home had been a daily routine. I didn't know any better. Constant vigilance was my normal, and crazily enough, I had grown comfortable with that state. Such continual stress shapes your mind, your senses, your emotions. The coping mechanisms I had been using since I was little to survive in my family were all I knew; they were who I was. Now the family order had dissolved and I didn't know how to function.

After he'd left the family, Wim had found a new home in the criminal underworld. Here was a warm nest in which he could bask in what he was used to: tension, aggression, violence. A world that called on his urge for survival and self-preservation.

Sonja, too, had managed to continue her life in the old way. She had learned from the Bald that a husband has complete control over his wife's existence, and she saw this teaching confirmed in her evolving relationship with Cor. Her life revolved around him. She was at his beck and call all day long. Gerard coped in his own prudent way. He'd been accepted into his girlfriend Debbie's loving family.

I wasn't suitable for crime like Wim was. All the fringes of society had to offer me was a role as prostitute or gangster moll. And the subservient female role Sonja played held no appeal for me.

Not knowing what to do with myself, I got aggressive. I'd burst into a rage over nothing. After once locking up my mother in the hallway closet in a moment of panic, I realized I couldn't go on like this. I had turned into my dad.

I was sixteen years old, and I ran away from home. Away from the situation that brought out the worst in me. I ended up in a crisis facility, got in a severe accident, went back home, and in 1983, I left for Israel to work on a kibbutz, the only way to stay abroad without having any money.

In Israel, far away from home, I felt at ease. The constant threat of war caused a pleasant sense of suspense, an alertness I was familiar with. I worked and played basketball, but when I discovered I couldn't compete unless I was Jewish, I went home at the end of summer to start the new basketball season there.

Now that my father was gone from our lives, Wim had taken over the regime. He was calling the shots. We had all come "home" again.

No one in our family had been able to escape from the past.

I walked back to the house on Eerste Egelantiersdwarsstraat, peeked through the window to see if anything had changed in there at all, but it looked just like I remembered it. The door opened.

"Are you looking for someone?" a friendly young man asked. "You're looking so intently."

"Oh, no," I replied. "I was just looking around. This is the house I grew up in."

"How nice—would you like to come in for a bit?"

Go in? Never again did I want to set foot in that nursery of horrors.

"No, thanks, that's really kind of you, but I have to go!" I hurried back to my car.

First thing was to handle Mom's problem. I got my phone out and sent Wim a message. "Cup of tea?"

"Okay, thirty minutes" was his reply.

We didn't discuss locations over the phone. Doing so would be easy for an observation team to track down and monitor us. That's why we used code names for certain meeting points. "Cup of tea" meant the Gummmbar, a coffee joint near my office.

Wim arrived on his scooter, dressed all in black as always, looking sullen and offended.

"Ridiculous!" He was set off right away. "Won't even register her own child. Bloody shame! Now what do I do?"

"Wim, listen. Calm down. Our mother is almost eighty years old. If you register with her, she might get raided again, or have trouble with the housing association. Mom can't cope with the stress."

"Yeah, whatever—and what am I supposed to do? Fucking egoist. Something has to be arranged, or—"

"We'll figure something out," I reassured him, and we talked until we thought of an address that would be more suitable for him to be registered at than Mom's. When Wim saw things turn to his advantage, he usually calmed down quickly.

After talking to Wim, I got in my car and phoned my mom right away.

"Hi, Mom."

"Hello, dear," she said.

"Everything all right?"

"Yes," she said.

"Same here. Will you be eating soon?"

"In a bit. Thanks, honey."

"Bye, Mom."

This was my way of telling Mom that things were dealt with. Wim didn't have to be registered at her place.

Now I could finally start my workday.

Sonja and Cor

1977

SONJA WAS SIXTEEN YEARS OLD WHEN SHE MET COR AT OUR HOUSE. HE was twenty. After being friends for a while, they started a relationship. Of course, my father wouldn't allow it, and so they'd see each other only in secret, at our house when the Bald was at work or away from home.

Like my mother, Sonja wanted to be a housewife. Every woman from the Jordaan became a housewife. Women with jobs were either pathetic, or married to worthless men who couldn't even support them. A husband's quality was measured by the wealth he could offer his wife. Sonja had been training to be someone's wife since childhood. She taught herself to do domestic chores at a young age: making beds, cleaning house, and doing laundry. I still marvel at how my sister magically turns her kitchen countertop from a dull, dirty surface into shiny black marble. Or how she transforms my living room from a junk shop into a room out of an interior design magazine. It's a profession, and Sonja loved it. Her life revolved around taking care of Cor; she doted on him all day long.

I, on the other hand, refused to do any domestic chores from a young age and never really learned how. Even in adulthood, I have panic attacks about a full laundry basket, messy kitchen, or dusty living room. I saw my mother taking care of these things every day;

to us they were part of womanhood. But womanhood also meant being beaten. Running a household is a valuable skill, but one I will never master.

When Sonja and Cor got together, Cor already had a girlfriend, but he broke up with her when Sonja got pregnant, and the two moved in together.

Throughout their relationship, it was only natural for Cor to do as he pleased and tell Sonja nothing about it. He used to laugh at any question she'd ask and say, "What you don't know won't hurt you!" This often made Sonja suspicious. She didn't mind if he was involved with criminals; all she wanted to know was whether he was cheating. So she followed his every trail like a bloodhound.

She'd often take me along and sometimes we'd find him and drag him away from all kinds of brothels downtown. He'd laugh it off: of course he didn't cheat—didn't he honestly tell the prostitute he was married before he stuck it in?

Cor wasn't the type of man to let his wife in on anything. She was there to take care of him; that was all he asked for. Discussing work was for men, not for women, who were clueless anyhow. Which was all for the best, since they couldn't tell anyone what they didn't know. Women are always risky to have around, especially when they have children. Cops will use their weaknesses to get them to spill the beans. They'll tell a woman her husband has other women on the side, which often makes her crack. No, women weren't told a thing, and Sonja didn't have a clue what Cor was up to.

It was November 1983. I had recently returned from Israel and was spending most of my time at Sonja's. The year before, she'd gotten pregnant with Cor's child and had moved from Van Hallstraat to Staalmeesterslaan to live with him. There, she had given birth to their beautiful daughter, Francis, in February 1983.

Astrid with newborn Francis (1983)

Cor loved his daughter but was too busy to spend much time with her. He and Wim were working day and night, and in between, they'd go to Sonja's to eat and to cuddle Francis. Sonja was used to it; if Cor was on the road with Wim, he'd come home only for food and sleep. I used to have dinner at Sonja's all the time, and I'd meet Cor and Wim there.

One night, we were all seated at the table when Wim said, "Here, this is for you" and handed me a hundred-dollar bill across the table. What was this? Wim giving me something? He'd never done that, apart from a stuffed toy at a fair once. Wim wasn't a generous person. His pockets were always full of cash, but never for us. My mother was toiling away in other people's houses, but he wouldn't think of handing her any. And here he was, giving me money. A hundred dollars? Why did I deserve this?

"Are you feeling okay?" I asked him.

"If you're gonna be smart about it, you can give it back," he snapped.

"No way. It's mine now."

It seemed odd to me. He used to hold up banknotes in front of me and ask, "Want some?" Then if I said yes, he'd pull the money away and say, "Get a job, then!"

Something was off. Something was wrong with him. There had to be some reason why he was suddenly being nice to me.

Something was wrong, all right, I was about to find out what. I may not have been an obedient wife, but when it came to what the men were up to, I was just as clueless as Sonja. We'd both be taken completely by surprise by what was about to happen.

The Heineken Kidnapping
1983

IT WAS THE BREAKING NEWS OF THE DAY: FREDDY HEINEKEN AND HIS driver, Ab Doderer, had been kidnapped. Heineken, the man around whom my father's life revolved. For more than twenty-five years he'd worked for the Heineken company, and night after night I'd heard him talking about his plans for "the Brewery," how he wanted to contribute to it in his own crazy manner. I'd always felt ashamed of his bizarre devotion to the company, but I could sympathize with his respect for Mr. Heineken. And now the man had been taken right off the street, in front of the Heineken headquarters in Amsterdam.

A few evenings later, Wim came over for dinner at Cor and my sister's, and I was there, too. The television was showing the latest news on the kidnapping.

"What d'ya say about that?" Wim asked.

"It's extremely stupid," I replied. "Who would kidnap Heineken? The man has more power than the queen. Whoever did it will never get away with it. They'll be hunted the rest of their lives."

"You think so?" he asked.

"I am pretty damn sure of it."

"How can you be so sure?" he asked.

"Wim, this man has billions, he is almost sovereign, he knows world leaders, he's the queen's best friend. Trust me, whoever did this really put themselves out there. They'll have the whole world on their case."

"Smart-ass," he snapped.

As always, my opinion annoyed him—nothing new there. He changed the subject. "Get me a typewriter ribbon. You know where to get it, right?"

"Yeah," I said.

"I need it tomorrow. Here's the money. You always forget about everything, but you can't forget this—it's really important."

Wim was right, I was forgetful. But I understood from his voice and eyes that he meant business.

"Leave it at Mom's."

"Okay," I said.

The next day I cycled to the bookstore after school, bought the ribbon, and cycled back to my mother's home, where Wim was already waiting for me.

"Here you go," I said, and gave him the box with the ribbon, not knowing what he was going to use it for.

"Good job, Assie." He left right away.

That night, I slept at Sonja's again. Francis slept in the cot in the nursery. I lay with Sonja in the master bedroom.

Suddenly I was awoken by rapid, loud footsteps coming closer. I opened my eyes to see where the noise was coming from and saw six big men standing around the bed, their faces covered by ski masks. They all had large rifles pointed at us. Sonja and I had nowhere to go.

We held on to each other and screamed in terror. All I could think was, I'm going to die. The next moment, there was even more noise and a second bunch came barging in screaming loudly, pulling open all the doors and closets.

What was going on? Why would they want to kill us? I was pulled away from Sonja, dragged off the bed, and thrown to the floor.

"Get down! On your belly! Down!" they screamed. "Hands behind your head!"

I lay flat on my belly, hands behind my head. I tried to see what was going on behind me, and from the corner of my eye I could see one of the men standing over me with his gun pointed at my head. In front of me was Francis's room. I heard her cry and saw a large guy with a weapon go into the nursery.

I heard Sonja shriek, "My baby! My baby!"

She tried to get away from the large guy who was holding her down. Out of sheer desperation, I tried to crawl across the floor toward the nursery to get her, protect her, do anything, but the man who stood over me yelled, "Stay down!" and pulled me back by the legs. He put his foot on my neck and pushed my head down, grinding my cheek into the carpet.

I'd probably just made matters worse. I tried catching his eye, to see what he'd do. I saw the gun and was sure he was going to shoot and kill me. I couldn't get away from him, so I kept my eyes shut and just waited for the shot.

At the same second, I heard more screaming. Men in regular clothing barged in and shouted, "Police! Police!"

Police? I thought. Yes, it's the police! They're not robbers or murderers. It's the police, surely they won't shoot us, we'll survive this! I was still lying on the floor with the cop's shoe on my neck and could hear them searching the entire house. They were yelling at Sonja.

They pressed me for Cor's whereabouts. But I didn't know where he was. Cor would never tell Sonja or me where he was going. I was pulled up and brought into the living room. I asked them what was going on, but they wouldn't tell me anything. Sonja was being kept in another room. We weren't allowed to talk to each other. A detective walked me to the bedroom so I could get dressed.

Then the phone rang.

Sonja and I looked at each other and thought the same thing. It was Cor.

Sonja wouldn't answer, but the detective forced her to.

"Hey," she said, and she could hear Cor's voice. Before she could say a thing, the detective took over.

"This is Piet," he said.

Cor knew what this meant: a stranger in his house, taking over the phone. We were still clueless about what was going on.

After we'd both gotten dressed, we were taken to the police station in different cars. Francis went with Sonja.

At the police station, we were put in a room together.

"What do you think it's about?" Sonja asked, again.

"I don't have the faintest idea," I said. "You think Cor did something bad?"

"I don't know," Sonja said. "I can't think of anything, but it's a sure thing they're after Cor."

That much was clear. While Sonja and I were theorizing about why the police had taken us, the door opened and I was taken to a cell with a concrete bed and a toilet right next to it. The air was cold, and the walls were scratched with all kinds of texts.

Before long, I'd finished reading the walls. Hours went by. It was getting light outside, time for school. That morning I was supposed to take a German test from Mrs. Jansen, the strictest teacher of all. There was no way I could miss this test. I pressed the intercom button.

"Yes," said a stiff voice.

"Ma'am, I've got a German test to take. I'd like to leave." Silence.

I pressed the button again. "Yes."

"Ma'am, could you please let me out? I've got to be at school."

"No."

After that, I could press the button until I was blue in the face, but there was no reaction. I wouldn't make it for the test. How could I explain this to my teacher? Tell her I'd been in a police cell? She wouldn't believe it. I had always been serious and prudent, not a troublemaker. Why would I be in a police cell? I'd fail the test.

For hours my thoughts went in circles. Cor must have done something really bad, but I couldn't think what. He'd always been nice to me, and good to his mom, his sister, his half brother, everyone. He was funny and good company. What kind of crime would he be capable of? What was going to happen now? How long would I have to stay in here, and for what reason? If Cor was guilty of something, then why was it me they were after?

I thought about Sonja and Francis. Whether they were still together, or if Francis had been taken by Child Protective Services, something the police had threatened when we were still at Sonja's house. I wondered if Wim might be involved in all this. After all, he and Cor did spend all their time together...

A couple of hours later, the door swung open and a large guy came barging in. "Sign!" he yelled, holding up a document.

"Sign?" I asked in surprise.

"Yes, sign!" he yelled again, and I read the document. It said I'd been arrested in connection with the Heineken kidnapping.

Heineken kidnapping? What was this? The movie I'd seen the day before flashed through my mind, about the Franz Kafka trial. I'd wound up in a Kafkaesque story myself. I refused to sign, afraid that if I did, I'd never be released.

The large man didn't accept my refusal, though. He bellowed from within an inch of my face, "Sign it! You're signing right now!" I put my signature down with no idea what I was signing. Then I was taken to a room where I had to put out my hands and my nails were clipped. I was afraid. Knowing they were police was no longer reassuring to me. What else were they going to do to me? Why were they clipping my fingernails?

Twenty-five years later, I was given access to the file and found out. They were looking for traces of the chemicals that had been sprayed onto the ransom money by the Heineken company. The police wanted to find out if I'd touched any of that money.

After the clipping, they took me to another room. I was a minor, seventeen years old, and hadn't seen a lawyer yet. Back then I did not even know I had the right to one. Yet the police questioned me. They showed me pictures of Rob Grifhorst, Frans Meijer, Jan Boellaard, Cor, and his half brother Martin Erkamps. I have no recollection whatsoever of what I told them, but it can't have been much, as I didn't know anything.

Apparently, the investigators quickly drew the same conclusion. The following morning, my cell door was opened and I was escorted out onto the street without any explanation. I came home to an empty house. Where was everybody? Then came a knock on the door. It was our upstairs neighbor, holding Francis in her arms. At least I'd found her. That was the main thing—the others could look after themselves. She told me Sonja had asked the police to bring Francis back so the neighbor could take care of her for the time being. I asked her if she knew where the others were.

"The police took Gerard, too. I heard a huge noise in the staircase. The entire building was flooded with cops in combat gear. It was just like a movie. I could see him being driven away in a car from my window. Your mom went to Sonja's this morning, and she hasn't come back. I saw on the news she's at the police station as well."

"Sonja is there, too," I filled her in. "She was taken along with me."

"This is such a misery, isn't it, love?" my neighbor said.

The warmth in her voice was in such sharp contrast to the harshness I'd experienced just a short while ago that I broke down for a moment.

"What's happening? What's going on? I want my mom back, but I don't know what to do. What can I do?" I cried.

"Easy, easy. Everything will be fine," she said. "I've got a card upstairs from an investigator who asked me a lot of questions about you all. Maybe you should give him a call."

I was seventeen years old, naïve as can be, and had just experienced what can happen to a person who hasn't done anything wrong. Calling the police felt like reaching a hand out to the executioner who would then cut it off. The last thing I'd do was call the people who'd treated me so unjustly.

"No, they might come back for me. I'll just wait. I can look after Francis until Sonja gets back."

"All right, honey. If you need anything, I'll be upstairs." Ten minutes later the doorbell rang. I was still holding Francis as I answered. There was a gentleman standing at the bottom of the stairs. "Child Protective Services. I'm here to get Francis van Hout!"

Take Francis? "That won't be necessary," I shouted down, and I ran upstairs to the neighbor, holding Francis in my arms. The man from Child Protective Services ran after me.

"Open up!" I shouted to my neighbor. The creep grabbed my leg and I kicked him off, ran up the last few steps, jumped into my neighbor's house and slammed the door shut behind me. Just in time.

"Open the door," the man said.

"No," I said. "She's staying right here."

"Then I'll get the police," he said.

"You do that!" I yelled.

"Calm down," my neighbor whispered, "this won't work." She started to talk with the man. He told her I couldn't look after Francis because I belonged to this criminal family. Had the world gone mad? The neighbor convinced him that she would take care of the child. He agreed to this.

I felt relieved. Sonja would have gone mad with rage if I had given Francis to strangers. I couldn't get Francis to calm down, but our neighbor was a real motherly type and she knew how to soothe her.

Francis was asleep upstairs and I was sitting downstairs when I heard something at the door. I was paralyzed with fear. Wasn't it over yet? Were they coming to get me again? I hid behind the couch. Somebody was opening the door. Who was it? I heard them come in, curled up as much as I could, and held my breath.

"Anybody here?" It was Gerard!

I stood up from behind the couch and yelled, "Me!"

Gerard jumped in surprise. "What are you doing, idiot? You scared the shit out of me!"

Just this once, his scornful words were music to my ears. My little brother was back!

"What's going on, Ger?" I asked, hoping he'd have an answer.

"I don't know, but it's pretty serious," he said in a trembling voice.

He told me that he'd seen armed men going into our apartment and had tried to hide on the balcony. Before long, they'd found him and taken him to their car at gunpoint.

Only in the car had he been told they were police. He'd been terrified, and thought he was being kidnapped.

"So now what?" I asked. "Where is Mom? Where are Sonja, Cor, and Wim?"

"I don't know, As, I really don't." We were both in shock.

That night both of us stayed at home, waiting.

I wanted to see my mom so badly.

The neighbor invited us for dinner. The TV was on, continually covering news about the kidnappers. It was bizarre to hear the names of people I knew: Cor, Wim, and Martin, Cor's half brother. How could they have done this? It was inconceivable. "What are we gonna do?" I asked, and at that point we heard my mother call out, "Is anybody home?"

"Mom, we're up here!"

Finally, my mother! She told us she'd been arrested when she arrived at Sonja's house, only minutes after we'd been taken away.

The house was filled with SWAT team members, and one of them was guarding the door. My mom saw the door was open and started to go in. One of the SWAT guys pointed a gun at her head.

"Don't move," he said.

My mother wasn't impressed. "Will you back off?" she snapped. She pushed his gun aside and kept walking. "What are you doing here? Don't you have anything better to do? You should be going after the Heineken kidnappers!" she said in all sincerity, not knowing that was exactly what they were doing.

"That piece of shit Cor," Mom was saying now. "Why did he do it? Has he gone mad? And he's coming to our place? He's finished! Sonja can't see him anymore. What a filthy bum. Why didn't I see it sooner? That felon!"

"What are you saying, Mom?" I asked.

"Cor kidnapped Heineken!" she cried out.

"Wim was in on it, too, wasn't he?" I replied.

The moment I said it, she crumbled and sank down on the couch. "Wim?" she asked, perplexed. "Wim is involved as well?"

"Mom, didn't they tell you at the station?"

"No," she said. "Tell me what?"

"That Wim was part of it, too."

"No," she stammered, and stared in the distance. "No, they didn't tell me that. They only talked about Cor."

Her world had just collapsed. She started weeping.

"My boy, my boy—how could a child of mine do such a thing? How horrible, how horrible. Where is he? Is he at the station, too?"

"I don't know," I replied.

At that moment, the TV news announced that some of the Heineken kidnappers had been caught, but two of them were still on the run.

I watched my mom and saw the pain in her eyes. Her son was a fugitive.

"We may never see him again," she murmured. "They're getting away and leaving us with the mess."

Sonja was released the following day. As soon as she got home, she ran straight to Francis and held her tightly. The investigators had threatened to put her in foster care for good if Sonja didn't tell them everything she knew about the kidnapping.

Sonja didn't know anything, though, and only when they were fully convinced of this did they let her go. Sonja was a complete mess—mad at Cor, mad at Wim. How could they do this to everyone? We were all angry, but worried, too. Where could they be? What would happen if they were found? Could they be killed during their arrest? From the news, it was clear there was a huge hunt going on for them and that part of the ransom money hadn't been retrieved yet.

From then on, the police were on our backs, hoping we'd lead them to Cor, Wim, or the missing money. When we bought something in a store, they'd check whether we paid with ransom money.

We were free but not free. We were observed and wiretapped. We had no privacy left whatsoever. We were publicly depicted as a mob family, and everyone turned their backs on us, or made it clear that they would be justified in doing so. The president of my basketball association informed me that the board had decided that I should not be held accountable for my brother's crime, and that I'd be allowed to keep playing for the association.

Not accountable for my brother's crime? Allowed to keep playing? Why shouldn't I be allowed to keep playing?

As it turned out, my basketball association wasn't the only place where common sense went out the window; it happened everywhere.

Suddenly, just because I was "related to the Heineken kidnappers" I was complicit in what had happened. We'd spent all our lives under my father's dictatorship, so afraid of his wrath that we wouldn't have dared to run a red light, and suddenly in the court of public opinion we'd all become criminals—thanks to Wim.

The media eagerly agreed. Denial was futile. We were "evil," and there was no possibility of redemption. Everywhere we went, we were "relatives of," not independent individuals.

Our last name was all we had. The name Holleeder defined us.

I didn't want to lie about it and then have to invent more lies about where I came from. So I always gave my last name and replied in the affirmative when people asked me if I was "related to," at which point the person looked at me as if I was contaminated with some horrible disease.

This happened to all of us. Our shared experience strengthened our solidarity. Within this solidarity there was safety, so my mom, Sonja, Gerard, and I huddled even closer together.

My family, where I used to be treated as weird, became the only place where I wasn't the odd one out.

In My Heart

Three Positive Memories

OUR HOUSE ON EERSTE EGELANTIERSDWARSSTRAAT WAS PUT ON THE registry of protected buildings and had to be completely renovated by the Amsterdam city council. We moved to Egelantiersgracht temporarily. "Temporarily" turned into four years.

Sonja, Gerard, and I slept together in a room on the first floor. My bed was beneath the window. I had a view of the canal and Westertoren. By then, Wim had become a teenager and had a small room to himself. The living room was one floor up, and my parents slept in the attic.

"Assie, wake up. Look what I got you," Wim whispered softly so as not to wake anyone. I can't have been much older than ten. He often woke me up in the middle of the night and lay beside me on the bed. Often he'd brought me something, chocolate or other candy.

This time he'd brought me a thick chocolate bar and a doll, a puppet: a yellow bird with an orange beak and feathers. "It's for you," he whispered. "I won it at the fair."

"It's so pretty," I whispered back excitedly.

"Move over," he said and lay down next to me.

He'd always ask me to tickle his back, which I did as we lay munching chocolate.

"Do you like it?" he asked, proud to have made me happy.

"I love it!"

These secretive moments were incredibly exciting. If my father heard us, all hell would break loose, but Wim did it anyway. He didn't obey our father, and because he woke me up and lay next to me, I was disobeying, too. I'd never have had the guts otherwise, but I felt safe with Wim being so nice to me.

Once I reached puberty, I found it hard to accept my father's omnipotence. It caused the conflict after which I had to leave the house at thirteen and after which my mother, Sonja, Gerard, and I went to live on Lindengracht. When I was fourteen, my mother went back to my father, and I tried to be away from home as much as I could. I found an escape in basketball, and the gym became my home. I could be there every day of the week until eleven p.m. It was my salvation.

When I played basketball, I didn't think about anything. My aggression was interpreted as fanaticism, a positive twist to the emotion that used to bother me so much.

My gym teacher at grade school was amazed at my "golden hands," as he called them. I could throw most balls, no matter what kind or from what distance, through the net. He advised me in strong terms to develop this talent, but within my family this was not an option. To my father, every activity outside the house was a threat to his dictatorship. Every form of self-development was a personal attack against him.

It didn't even occur to me to bring this up at home. I knew without asking there wouldn't be any money or chance for a child to join a sports club and have to be taken to and from a gym.

Only when I started high school and learned to use public transportation did my world expand beyond the Jordaan quarter and I could start exploring without my father knowing. And he couldn't forbid what he didn't know about.

At school I happened to meet my cousin on my mother's side for the first time. He was at least four years my senior and looked after me a little bit, since "we're related." I was quite happy to have met this relative, for he was nice and gentle, just like my grandparents on my mother's side, whom I'd only met for the first time when I was eleven years old. He saw me playing basketball at school and asked why I didn't join his basketball club.

"You're good," he said. "You've inherited your mother's talent."

"My mother's talent?" I asked. I didn't even know my mother had any talents. I just knew her as my father's doormat.

"Yeah," he said. "She was an excellent korfball player [a Dutch sport similar to basketball]. Just like grandma." My jaw almost dropped to the ground in amazement. Both my mother and grandmother turned out to have played at the highest level. I had no clue, as I realized I pretty much didn't know a thing about my mom. But it was nice to know, and it explained my skills with a ball.

I told my mom I'd met someone at school who claimed to be my cousin. I told her the boy's name.

"That's right, he's your cousin. He's my brother's son. How nice the two of you are in the same school."

"He asked me to join his basketball club," I continued tentatively, aware it would burden her immensely to be asked something we both knew my father wouldn't approve of. "He says you used to play korfball and that I've inherited your skills," I added.

She smiled.

"Were you really that good, Mom?" I asked.

"Yes, and so was your grandmother. We won the national championship," she said with pride, and began telling me about the wonderful times she'd had. I'd never seen this side of my mom, and I listened in awe. It was a joy to see her glow while she relived her memories.

"So can I?" I asked when she was done telling, and I saw her smile fade into a pained grimace.

"You know your father will never allow it," she murmured softly. Then, suddenly, boldly, "But we'll do it anyway!" She was going to give her daughter the fun she'd known when she was young herself, and for the first time, she was daring to decide something on her own.

We left my father out of it. For a long time, he knew nothing about it.

I spent day and night training at the gym, constantly handling a ball. The practice quickly turned me into a major player on the team. I was appreciated, which stimulated me to get even better. I hungered for even more appreciation—I couldn't get enough of it.

Before long, every single day revolved around my sport. I wanted to reach the top, and I was asked to train with the Noord-Hollands Cadets' special team. One day, the association board showed up before training began, to break the news, and they handed me a letter with the invitation and where I should report. I knew it! If I just trained hard enough, one day I'd succeed. This might be my stepping-stone, my chance to get into the national selection.

The letter said I had to report for my first training session at the gym in Hoofddorp on Sunday at noon. Sunday was the one day my father didn't go to work, and I didn't know anybody else who could take me there, so my mom had gotten my father to agree to do it.

That Sunday morning my nerves woke me up early. Around eight a.m., I heard my mother shout upstairs, "We'll be right back!" I heard the door slam shut, and I went downstairs. My parents had left. At that point I was still thinking, They probably won't be long. I wanted to leave at eleven at the latest, for once I got there I'd have to change into my training clothes.

The clock struck nine and my parents weren't back yet. Nor at ten. Typical—surely they hadn't forgotten. They couldn't have. They'd be back any moment now. There was still plenty of time before we had to leave. But, at ten thirty, they still weren't there, and now I started to worry.

I decided to change into my training clothes so as soon as I got there I could go straight to the playing field. I was standing in the hallway, my bag packed and the invitation in my hand, staring at the door, hoping it would open and my father would be there to take me. But at eleven, there was still no one there.

Things weren't hopeless just yet—we could still make it. I just wouldn't be able to get accustomed to the court before the training session.

Quarter past eleven, and he still wasn't there. By now, time was getting very short and I was on the brink of tears. All the stress was making my body tense, which would really hinder my performance. Twenty past eleven: no Dad. Half past eleven. Forget it, I was missing out on the training. He'd ruined my chance.

One time in my life he was going to do me a favor, and he didn't show. I'd never asked him to take me anywhere or pick me up— I always got a ride with the other girls on my team. This time I couldn't, since I was the only one on my team going to the selection training. Just me!

I hated my father for standing me up, and I hated my mom for promising me she'd arranged it for me. How silly of me to put my trust in them, especially at the most important point in my life. I'd been training for years to reach this goal, and now it had all been for nothing.

I decided to call the Union to cancel, to tell them I wouldn't make it because I had no way to get there. I turned toward the kitchen where the telephone was, and I heard a car stop outside. Had he come after all? I ran to open the front door, and what I saw wasn't my father's Beetle but my big brother's brand-new Mercedes. He got out of the car, and I walked up to him, bawling my eyes out.

"What's bugging you?" he asked, annoyed. "What's with the crying?"

I explained how I had to get to Hoofddorp to train with the Noord-Holland Cadet team, how the Bald was supposed to take me there but hadn't shown up.

"That fucking dog," he said. "Get in the car. I'll take you."

I grabbed my bag and jumped into his car. Wim accelerated and drove to the Hoofddorp gym at a mind-boggling speed. I watched him as he handled the car like a Formula 1 driver. In that moment I felt immensely grateful.

At five minutes before noon we arrived at the gym. Thanks to Wim I'd made the training. I didn't need the Bald after all. I had Wim.

"Thanks so much, Wim," I said.

"Yeah, whatever, just get out of my car, handful, or I'll be late myself because of you," he said.

I got out of the car and he raced off again. There he went in his shiny, expensive car.

Two sports seasons later, I was struck by bad luck during training. I took a step sideways and sprained my ankle. The team's physiotherapist advised me to tighten my shoelaces and keep moving as much as I could to keep the muscles warm and avoid swelling. So I played on, but the pain was excruciating. When I got home, I took my shoe off, and in no time my ankle had swollen to the size of an egg. The pain kept me awake all night.

The next day my ankle looked even worse, and I couldn't walk at all. This was bad. Wim happened to drop by with his latest girl-friend. She introduced herself as Martine, and it was obvious she was some kind of model. She thought Wim should take me to the emergency room right away, and she came with us. We got there, and I was told to take a seat in one of the treatment rooms. Martine stayed with me while Wim parked the car.

After a while a doctor came to examine me. He looked at my foot and said, "This swelling isn't from today, is it? When did you sprain your ankle?"

"Last night," I answered.

"I can't help you, then. This is the emergency room. You should have come yesterday. You should see your GP."

"Excuse me?" Martine said, clearly not afraid to show her teeth. "You're sending her away in this condition?"

That very moment, Wim entered the room. "What's going on?" he asked firmly.

"He wants to send her away," Martine said. "She can't even walk! It's unheard of!"

Wim, six foot six and three feet wide, stood very close to the doctor and yelled in his face: "You're going to help her like you're supposed to, or I'll tear this place apart."

At decisive moments in my life, Wim stepped in for me the way a father should have. Admittedly, these moments were rare, but they made Wim stand out from my father.

Jaap Witzenhausen
1983

I met Jaap at a basketball game when I was fifteen and he was thirty-five. I'd just turned eighteen when we moved in together. Jaap was the exact opposite of my family: he was an intellectual. As an artist, he saw himself as a guardian and creator of culture. He was always criticizing mainstream opinion and lived a liberated lifestyle. He preferred spiritual values to tangible goods. As far as Jaap was concerned, wealth wasn't measured by expensive cars, but by one's knowledge.

Jaap didn't drink or hit people. As a matter of fact, he didn't have an ounce of aggression in him. People thought he was weak and feminine, but I knew I couldn't have done better. Jaap seemed to have been custom-made for me.

We were poor, but Jaap managed to put a feast on the table every night. He'd make something out of nothing. At the end of the day, we'd go to the market close to closing time and get the fish at a discount because the fishmonger would have to throw it out anyway. At first, I felt ashamed, because I thought it displayed poverty, but Jaap thought differently.

"The guy is glad to be selling it—we're doing him a favor. We're helping small enterprises survive like this."

We were serving a greater purpose!

Sometimes I'd stand next to him as he tore the outer leaves off the leeks before putting them on the scales. I felt deeply embarrassed: this was downright theft—what if we got caught? But again, Jaap didn't see it that way at all. "I'm paying for the leek, not for the foliage. They are swindlers, they should know the people won't be conned."

I was reassured. He was an activist, not a thief.

We lived on Kerkstraat, and every day we'd walk to the bookstore on the corner of Prinsengracht and Utrechtsestraat to browse through the books that were on sale: books on art, literature, philosophy, anything interesting we could afford. We barely had the money for food, but we were always spending it on books.

I was happy. We spent evening after evening with his—mainly younger—friends, discussing the effects of upbringing and to what extent parent-child relationships are determinant, but also all kinds of current events and what we should do about them. Jaap used to debate a lot, often on a level I couldn't quite comprehend, but had the rare talent of being able to convince everybody of his ideas.

I felt lucky to be with this great philosopher.

Shortly before Jaap and I moved in together, Cor and Wim were arrested in Paris. At La Santé Prison, my mom told my brother I was living with a man twenty years my senior, and my sister told Cor. They told them I'd left out of the blue and phoned a week later to tell them I had moved in with Jaap, and that was exactly what had happened. I was living my own life without sharing it with them.

When they returned from Paris, I was told their reactions. "That pervert could have been her father," Wim had said, and Cor had burst out laughing. "She's just like Wim. He's always after old spinsters, too."

"Don't worry, it'll be over soon enough," my mother had said. "Can you imagine Assie vacuum cleaning? Believe me, it won't last." But what everyone predicted didn't come true. Jaap and I stayed together.

During the day, I went school and he kept house, got groceries, did laundry, and every night put a great meal on the table for me and his eight-year-old son. This adorable little guy had lost his mom, and now suddenly had me as a new family member. I became attached to the boy and to the life that comes with raising a child.

Jaap told me he wanted to have children with me, and I thought, Why wait? We were already caring for one child, why not care for two? Unlike me, my baby would grow up in a warm and loving family with a truly affectionate father.

I was nineteen years old and seven months pregnant when I graduated from the athenaeum. My family was sitting in the auditorium: Jaap and my stepson, ten years old by then. Two months later, our daughter was born. We named her Miljuschka.

Two years after Miljuschka was born, our financial situation went from precarious to collapsed. Jaap couldn't support our family by selling his art, and he'd been benefitting from a program in which the government bought artists' works. When the arrangement was cut, we were left penniless. Jaap was forced to leave the seclusion of his workshop, and he began selling fantasies.

Over the next few years, he wandered from one self-made cultural project to the next; sometimes they earned money, but usually they didn't.

But he always gave himself an important title with an "assistant" at his disposal. He was busy all the time.

Meanwhile, I did the housekeeping because Jaap no longer had time. I took care of the children, and I worked as a cleaner to get us by.

Nevertheless, I was quite happy with our way of life; personal growth was still more important to us than material wealth. I wanted to study philosophy, and Jaap encouraged me. My family didn't like that at all. To them Jaap was a sissy because he allowed me to continue my education, and I was a bad mother for putting my daughter in daycare when she was three years old. I was enraged by their ridiculous traditional ideas. "No, what YOU did worked out so well!" I yelled at my mother. "Your entire life, you've been slapped all over your own home. You raised four emotionally disabled children, and now you want to tell me how to raise mine?"

I started studying philosophy, but a couple of years of financial misery and then a car accident made me choose another future for myself. I started studying law. Jaap was appalled. He was afraid I would change, but I managed to convince him I was only doing it to end our worries for the future.

In 1992, Cor and Wim got out of jail and started doing business right away with their friend Rob Grifhorst, a successful businessman who was for a long time suspected of involvement in the Heineken kidnapping. Grifhorst bought the sex and gambling venues that the late Joop de Vries had built up in Amsterdam's red-light district from de Vries's daughter Edith. She sold her Zandvoort beach club to Grifhorst, too. As many family members as possible—from our family and Robbie's—were involved in the company, because family doesn't steal from itself.

Cor van Hout in the Veenhuizen prison (1991)

Sonja, Cor, and Francis in Zandvoort (1992)

Robbie searched within his own circle for a suitable candidate to run the beach club. After deliberation with Cor and Wim, it was decided Jaap was most suitable.

I had serious doubts. I knew this would drag my family's influence into our new family, and that was exactly what I'd been trying to avoid all these years. We were penniless, though, and we couldn't go on like that. Wim was opposed to the idea of involving Jaap in the "family business," but Cor thought I should be given the opportunity for my partner to earn some money. My partner, not me, for I was a woman and women weren't supposed to work.

Jaap liked the idea of working by the sea, so we moved to Zandvoort and lived in a cabin next to the restaurant on the beach.

The beach club had a large terrace and so-called units where guests could sunbathe behind glass, shielded from the wind, and order food and drinks from the extensive menu. On sunny days, there were more than forty employees in the kitchen and waiting tables, and we worked twenty-hour shifts.

Jaap had never managed a hospitality business before, and even though it was a lot of work, he did well. Hiring personnel, managing sunbed rentals and supplies, keeping the books—he took care of everything.

Wim kept a close watch on Jaap, and every couple of days he stopped in to make him account for gross turnover, costs, and profits. Jaap had to monitor personnel closely, for Wim wouldn't have one penny stolen.

After one of his conversations with Jaap, Wim came to me. "Come with me for a second," he said, and we walked away from the pavilion. "What was yesterday's turnover?"

"Didn't Jaap already tell you?" I asked.

"Yes, Jaap already told me, but I want to hear it from you," he said firmly.

"I don't know. I guess it was fine; it was quite crowded," I replied, slightly taken aback.

"Crowded?" he repeated gruffly, and he started yelling. "That's nothing, Assie! I want to know numbers! Numbers! Is this Jaap guy stealing from me or something, since you won't tell me?"

That startled me. "No, of course he isn't stealing from you," I said.

"And how do you know, when you don't even know the numbers!" he screamed even louder, and poked his finger into my chest.

His logic was tight, but it was based completely on distrust. "How can you think Jaap is stealing from you? You don't really think he'd ever do such a thing, do you?" I said.

"Yeah, Assie? That's what you're thinking. The man is a poor sod, he's never had a penny in his life, and suddenly he sees all this money. That's what turns people into thieves, right?" he laid it out for me in the manner of a schoolteacher.

I tried to protest, but everything I said only fed Wim's anger. "You know, Assie, I do so much for you. I make sure your man can make a living, I do it for you, because you are my sis. And you are nothing but an ungrateful fucking punk! You listen to me now, for I'll say it just once. I won't be robbed by him. I'm not a retard! What is he thinking?"

Jaap was no thief, and I wasn't going to just take it in silence. "Jaap is *not* stealing from you!" I yelled. "How dare you say such a thing!"

I saw his eyes turn dark. He walked right up to me. "Say what?" he asked, standing really close to me. "Are you talking back to me? Well? I'm warning you, one more smart remark..." and he lifted his hand.

I was afraid he would hit me, and I cringed to avoid it.

"That's right," he grinned. "You've been warned. Mouth off at me again and you'll get it."

The same way Jaap had to monitor the crew, Wim made me monitor Jaap—without him being aware of it—thus driving a wedge between me and my partner.

From that point on, I felt tense whenever I saw Wim. His mood was unpredictable; one moment he could be sweet as honey, the next aggressive. I never knew what to expect from him.

I deeply regretted letting him into my life, but I couldn't blame myself, either. After all, what did I know about him? I was seventeen when he went behind bars for nine years, and mother of a family with two kids when he got out. During the years in between, I had painted a rosy picture of him based on the moments when he'd been there for me. But it was only now that we were actually getting to know one another.

That same year, the summer season had ended and we'd just returned to Amsterdam when the doorbell rang.

Oh, no, it's him again, I thought.

"Thought you'd gotten rid of me, sis?" he said cheerfully when I opened the door.

I was just glad he wasn't cranky.

"I need you to do something for me. Walk with me."

I got my keys and he stepped into the hallway with me. "You need to watch this lady for me," he said.

"What lady? What do you mean?" I asked.

"This lady is in trouble and should stay indoors for a couple of days."

"What kind of trouble?"

His mood changed. "You shouldn't be asking questions. You should just do it. Or is it too much to ask to help me out?"

"What do you want me to do?"

"Just stay with her for a couple of days and make sure she doesn't pull any stunts. Get your stuff and come along!"

"But, Wim, I can't just leave. I've got a family! What am I supposed to tell Jaap?"

"Jaap! Jaap! Always this fucking Jaap! Jaap is all you think about! Listen to me. If you don't do as I tell you, I'm in trouble. And if I'm in trouble, Jaap will be in trouble. I'll make sure he gets the shit beaten out of him!"

This scared me.

"Okay, I'll do it. Just give me some time to arrange for somebody to watch Miljuschka."

He'd gotten his way and calmed down. "I'll pick you up in an hour."

In the car, on our way to "this lady," Wim was cheerful again. Too cheerful.

"You're such a sweet sis," he said, a sneer on his face.

"Whatever," I said. "Just don't think I'm enjoying this."

"Oh well, I have to do things I don't like, too. There's nothing wrong with that. You should be glad you get to do your darling brother a favor!"

I wasn't glad. I felt stupid for letting him blackmail me like this, for letting him scare me into obeying him. I hated myself, because he had the power to overrule me. All those years he was in jail, I'd built up my own life and identity—then he got out and shattered both.

At the apartment door, Wim quickly added, "She's a heavy coke user and has to detox. Right now she wants to kill herself, so you should keep an eye on her. She can't go anywhere."

He unlocked the door. A woman was sitting in the living room. I recognized her right away. She was the redhead who was on the beach all the time, and whom I'd caught Wim kissing in the restroom while his wife and daughter, Beppie and Evie, were out on the beach sunbathing.

What the hell? I had to look after his girlfriends now? I had to leave my daughter behind for this? A small, chubby toddler with blond spiked hair appeared from a bedroom.

Wim pushed me forward. "In you go—why are you just standing there?" He gave the redhead a kiss and said, "This is my sis. She'll stay with you for a bit."

So I stayed with the redhead. She told me her husband had been shot to death recently. Fortunately, she'd met Wim. He was the love of her life, and he was going to leave his wife.

Wim came around regularly. They behaved like lovebirds one moment and the next, Wim was shouting at her and she was screaming about how she was going to kill herself. Every time, the little girl would cry along with her mother.

Wim came by again while I was playing with the toddler in her room. I heard screaming and a door slam. As usual, the redhead started crying hysterically, and the little girl ran toward her. I walked after her. The door swung open again, and Wim stormed toward the redhead. The toddler stood crying in the middle of the living room.

Wim stood towering right in front of the child and yelled, "Shut the fuck up, piece of shit! Won't stop crying. There she goes, yelping again, fucking retard! Whining all the time!"

I looked him in the eye at that moment and saw who he was.

I walked over to him and pulled him away from the sobbing girl.

"That's not okay, Wim. You're leaving right now," I said, and he let me push him out the door. That night, I prayed to God for the first time in years. "Dear Lord, I am grateful for my mom, sister, younger brother, Jaap, and my children, and now I ask You to get Wim locked up again. Amen."

At the end of the summer season, the guys sold the beach club and Jaap was out of a job again. But they had another one for him.

To test him, they took him to Spain and put him up with a couple of hookers, to see whether he would withstand the temptation.

He did. Jaap was faithful to me and declined the girls. He had passed the test. He was fit to run the guys' sex club.

Jaap had always been fond of the fringes of society. He said this whenever he tried to photograph prostitutes behind their windows. Now I was afraid this would be the end of our relationship, that he would be captured by this lifestyle.

And he did change. All of a sudden, Jaap had turned into the "man" my family always complained he wasn't.

Life in a sex club takes place mainly at night. Jaap worked long hours, and, "being a man," he wasn't accountable to me for his schedule.

I'd sensed for a while that the work was gobbling him up and he was no longer the Jaap I knew. He wasn't happy with the salary he was getting, and Wim suspected Jaap's bookkeeping had developed its own creative license. I found out when my brother came to our home and asked for clarification of the numbers. It ended in a huge fight, and my brother left the house in a rage. I had to come with him.

"He's stealing, that fucking asshole. He's actually stealing from me!"

"I don't think so. He'd never do that."

Wim had no way to prove it, but he sensed tens of thousands being pocketed every month. Jaap was discrediting me within my family.

"What are you doing?" I asked. "They're giving you a chance to earn money, and you're robbing them? Do you have any idea what might happen? Wim won't accept being stolen from."

Jaap responded with the usual quasi-cool that I'd always taken for intelligence. "I haven't stolen anything, and besides, there's no such thing as property."

Jaap had turned from an intellectual into a criminal. He couldn't keep doing this, though. I knew my brother.

"Stop it," I said. "This will end badly."

I traveled to see Sonja at her house in Spain for a two-week vacation. I was afraid to tell her anything, out of shame, and also out of fear of what would happen if Wim managed to prove his suspicions.

Jaap was to arrive a couple of days later, at which point Sonja was going to leave and I'd stay in her mansion with just him and Miljuschka. I was having doubts about the relationship. Jaap had changed. I felt alienated, and I wanted to use this vacation to get close again. Jaap arrived in the afternoon. He said he had to make a phone call.

"There's the phone," I said. But he couldn't call from the house—it had to be from a telephone booth. I pointed one in the neighborhood out to him. I thought it was weird, but I just said, "I've got a migraine, so I'm off to bed."

Jaap went to make his call. Miljuschka was already asleep, and I took the risk of leaving her alone for a few minutes. I snuck out after him, took a different route, and stood behind him unnoticed as he talked on the phone.

"I love you, buttercup," he said into the receiver.

Did I just hear him say "I love you"? I came forward, grabbed the phone from his hands, and asked, "Can I say something to her, too?"

Jaap was thrown completely off guard as I took the receiver. I said, "Hello, who is this?" and the call was disconnected.

Jaap looked at me like a schoolboy caught stealing from the cookie jar.

This was the last thing I'd expected. I ran back to the house and Jaap came after me. He pleaded, "Let me explain—it's not what you think."

His behavior disgusted me. I walked up to him and pushed him into the swimming pool. Every time he swam to the edge and put his hands on the rim to climb out, I stomped on his fingers. "You just keep on swimming!" I shouted.

Now Jaap was afraid of me. "Can I please come out?" he begged. "I'm getting cold!"

"You want to come out?" I said. "Just a second."

I went to the knife drawer in the kitchen and took out the largest and sharpest knife. "You still want to come out?" I asked, and waved the knife in his direction. I was out of my mind.

Jaap wouldn't take the risk and stayed in the swimming pool.

"You are such a *slut*," I said, and at that same moment, I heard a soft voice. "Mommy, what are you doing?"

I looked up and saw Miljuschka standing on the balcony overlooking the pool. She had woken up and heard the noises outside. I was startled and realized she had never seen me like this before; she was the only one I always managed to keep my calm with. She'd never seen what could happen when the abused child inside of me was awakened. And I didn't want her to.

"It's nothing, honey. Mommy is a little confused," I replied. "Come out now," I told Jaap. "I won't hurt you."

Jaap hoisted his fat ass out of the swimming pool and I went up to Miljuschka to reassure her.

"I'm sorry, honey. Mommy and Daddy are having a fight and Mommy lost it a little bit. But I've calmed down now."

"Okay, Mommy," she said. Her mother always did what she said, so she had no doubts. I never promised anything I couldn't live up to. Same thing this time: I didn't hurt Jaap, but our relationship was in pieces.

Jaap told me it was a one-off thing, the girl worked for him, and he had taken her home once when a client had hit her. They'd done a little kissing, nothing else. It was harmless and he couldn't live without me.

I didn't buy it, but I didn't want Miljuschka to grow up without a father, and I figured I shouldn't be so rigid. These things happen in relationships, and it could have happened to me just the same.

Once back in Amsterdam, he came home from an errand with scratch marks on his back.

"Did you go to her again?" I asked.

"Of course not. What makes you think that?" he said, with child-like surprise in his voice.

He had no idea how those marks had ended up on his back, but if I didn't trust him, we were finished.

From then on, he got offensive.

Every time I suspected him of cheating, he blamed me for being sickly jealous, just like my brother. I should see a psychiatrist. I was paranoid. I even started to believe he might be right; my brother was insanely jealous and it could be genetic, and recent events had actually made me paranoid.

A couple of months later, I hadn't shaken my sense of unease: I was convinced he was still seeing his "one-off." Shortly after our return from Spain, I discovered a Rotterdam telephone number in the memory of our telephone. I hadn't tried it, because I felt I should trust him. But I had written it down and kept it.

I decided to try the number to check whether he was still seeing her. I dialed, and a woman answered.

"Roxanna speaking."

Roxanna. So that was her name, and that was why Jaap had called me Xan that time when we were making love.

"Hello," I said, "this is Jaap's wife speaking. Can I ask you something?"

"Sure," she said with a heavy Polish accent. "Fire away."

"Are you still seeing Jaap?" I asked her bluntly.

"No, he see now some other girl," she replied. "Her husband is stabbed to death."

"All right." I played it as cool as I could, trying not to let on how this remark cut through my heart. "Can I ask you another thing?"

"Sure," she said.

"How long were you with Jaap?"

"We were together for eighteen months."

She began to tell me about their relationship as if she was having a regular chat with a girlfriend.

"He thinks I'm so special. He doesn't want I work in club. He says money not important, I must go to school, I am so smart. He try make baby with me. If I have baby, he leave you. But no luck, I'm happy. He all blah blah. He likes make babies everywhere. He sick," she concluded.

I was flabbergasted. Not because of what she told me, but by how clearly she saw him. I secretly admired the woman who had destroyed my relationship—she said what I'd never wanted to face but had always known.

I confronted Jaap with what Roxanna had told me about him having a new girlfriend. I begged him to be honest about it. Yes, he did, and I was crazy. I was sickly jealous.

Shortly afterward, it came out that Jaap had impregnated another woman, the one whose husband had been stabbed to death.

Because he always lied to me, I had surreptitiously recorded a conversation during which he asked her to keep her pregnancy secret from me. I wanted him to be honest for once and decided to force him into it. I met with him and played back the conversation. I figured he'd have to tell the truth now.

He looked at me with big innocent eyes and shouted, "You've really gone mad. You constructed this recording? You are really sick!" So ridiculous was his worthless defense that I burst out laughing. This confirmed without a doubt that I'd been living in a fantasy world all these years.

At the same time, I realized this relationship had also given me the freedom to become who I was. I'd been able to grow as a person, I was a law graduate, and I had a wonderful daughter.

Excellent foundations for starting a new life.

I've heard it said that the number of months it takes to get over a relationship equals the number of years it lasted: that would have to be thirteen months. But I didn't intend it to take that long. I gave myself three months to get over it and that was it. I had lost a lot, but gained a lot, too, and I should rejoice at that.

What goes around comes around. What I'd done to Jaap's girlfriend before me was done to me by the lady with the Polish accent, and what she did to me was done to both of us by the woman who'd popped up with her pregnancy.

Pregnant.

Meaning Miljuschka would have a half brother or half sister, and I figured I shouldn't look at this pregnancy through the lens of my pain, but from her point of view. I wanted Miljuschka to have as natural a relationship as possible with her father, and thus with his pregnant girlfriend, whom Miljuschka would probably encounter at some point. So I took the initiative to have a "nice" coffee date with Jaap's family-to-be.

The four of us sat in a café on Middenweg rather stiffly. Miljuschka didn't have a clue what to do with this strange lady who was cheerily telling her she was going to have a "little brother or sister."

"Mom, who's that lady?" she whispered into my ear.

"She's Daddy's new girlfriend, and she's going to have a baby, remember?" I said, embarrassed because she was whispering in front of the new girlfriend.

"Oh, yeah," she replied without seeming to remember anything. After half an hour we were all glad we could go our own ways. Miljuschka and I walked to my car, and I made an attempt to close the meeting on a light note. "Isn't it exciting? A baby brother or sister. You'll have so much fun!"

"I guess," she replied indifferently.

Before Miljuschka got to know her, this lady, too, was replaced by another. Jaap had left her so quickly, she never bothered to inform the child about her biological father.

Meanwhile, I'd moved to a house in Rivierenbuurt, a nice middle-class neighborhood, and Miljuschka and I were enjoying it there. She had a good routine with her father, which pleased me.

Every Wednesday, he'd pick her up from school, they'd spend the afternoon together, and he'd drop her off at home around dinnertime.

One night when he came in, I said, "We're having endive for dinner. Would you like to have some?"

"No, thanks, but we have to talk," he said gravely.

"Sure," I said, "what's up?"

"You know my job at the club will end soon, right?"

Yes, I knew, for Wim had come over to tell me. Jaap had created a financial mess and my brother was enraged. "He's been stealing, the pervert, so he's out. He completely ruined the business. All he cared about was what landed on his dick. That fucking asshole!"

"Yes, I know that," I told Jaap.

"This means I won't be able to give you money any longer," he said dryly.

"What do you mean?" I asked.

"Exactly what I just said. Soon I'll have no income."

"So what are Miljuschka and I supposed to live on? You know I don't earn enough to get by. I can't even pay the rent here." I started to panic.

"That's your problem. I've got to move on, too," he said, standing in the doorway, ready to walk away from his responsibilities.

Just before walking out he remembered something. "Oh, here's some mail for you." He took an envelope from his inside pocket and threw it on the doormat. Then he was gone.

I picked up the envelope and opened it. It was a payment reminder for a loan for seventeen thousand euros that we had lived off as a family and that had suddenly turned into "mail for me," since the loan had been taken out in my name.

Not only was I penniless, but now I was in debt as well.

I ran after Jaap. "Wait a minute!" I shouted down the stairwell. "You're not seriously leaving us behind without a penny, are you?"

"Yes, I am," he said without a hint of emotion. "And don't you dare request child support, or I'll tell the court you're a cocaine dealer. You can try denying it, but you know as well as I do it's not about the truth; it's about what people think. You don't think they'll believe a Holleeder, do you? And you'll lose your kid." He looked up at me triumphantly.

He was right. No one would believe me.

I didn't request child support. I couldn't take the risk.

Part II
Heineken's Curse

1990–2007

Amstelveen

1997

A FEW WEEKS AFTER THE FIRST ATTEMPT ON COR'S LIFE, WIM ARRANGED a temporary house on Anton Struikstraat for Sonja through Willem Endstra, a real estate mogul and Wim's friend, so she and the kids at least had a place for themselves while they figured out what to do next. She appreciated Wim's support. He and Cor might not agree on how to resolve the conflict with Mieremet and Klepper, the men Wim insisted were responsible for trying to kill Cor, but he hadn't entirely forsaken her—or Cor. She wanted to believe Wim was still on their side, that he was no Judas.

It was time to decide about their future. Sonja suggested moving abroad, but Cor wouldn't have it. "I won't be chased away," he said.

The house on Anton Struikstraat wouldn't do for the long term. "You can see the rats running through the garden," Sonja said. So she went looking for another house.

Francis was already going to grade school in Amstelveen, and Sonja had put Richie in the same school when he turned four years old, together with his cousins—Gerard's children—so he would see familiar faces. Moving to Amstelveen seemed pretty logical.

A house on Catharina van Renneslaan was available to her if she wanted it. Because Wim had helped her with the previous house, she asked him to come check it out. He climbed onto the shed to take a peek inside and concluded it looked fine. He told Sonja she should take it.

The only problem was that the previous tenant was asking for payment for some of the furnishings he had installed. Sonja asked Wim for some of the money she had nicked from Cor and given to Wim for safekeeping.

He'd reacted quite strongly, saying, "You're whining about money now? I've got nothing now, so don't pester me, Boxer. I'm trying to sell the red building—after that I'll have some cash. That man of yours gives me nothing but trouble, so don't start putting me under pressure!"

Taken aback by his eruption, Sonja was afraid to ask further.

"So, did you like the house?" I asked her when I stopped by that evening.

"The house is fine, but Wim is being crazy again. He told me he can't give me my money because he doesn't have any."

"What do you mean by 'doesn't have any'?"

"He says he's broke. He's selling something. A red building or something. After that, he'll give me some of it."

Sonja didn't get anything, though. From the moment she'd asked for her money, Wim started dropping by. He explained it was too bad Cor hadn't paid the million-guilder fine that Klepper and Mieremet had demanded, because that left the issue unresolved. The message was still that he'd better just pay up.

Sonja told Wim to say this to Cor, but Wim wouldn't. He and Cor weren't on speaking terms. She should tell him; he was her husband, her problem.

But Sonja was afraid to. The last time she'd suggested it might be better if Cor just paid up, he'd gotten extremely angry. She knew for sure that Cor would never pay.

Later on, Wim showed up at Sonja's door with a solution to the problem. If Cor wouldn't pay, Sonja should pay his part of the fine. He'd settle it with the money she'd given to him for safekeeping. He delivered his message as if he were doing Sonja a huge favor.

Sonja had lost her hoard of cash. For a second she thought, No way, I don't want to do this, but immediately afterward, she was just glad she could safeguard the lives of her husband and children.

It was just money.

In the meantime, the conflict with Mieremet and Klepper had turned into an argument between Cor and Wim. Wim wanted to have Cor cut off, financially and otherwise. Their interests had to be divided. He was fed up with the trouble Cor caused him because of his excessive drinking, and he wanted to move on alone.

"He's just dropping me, Assie. That piece of filth," Cor said. "We went through everything together, and now he cuts me off, just like that. I made him—I took him along for the ride. He owes everything he's got to me, and when things get a little rocky, he bolts. He must be fucking kidding me, right?"

But Wim wasn't kidding, and he kept pushing for splitting up and dividing the capital he and Cor had built up with a little help from Robbie Grifhorst, thanks to the six million guilders missing from the Heineken ransom. In the end, Cor agreed. "Take whatever you want," he'd told Wim. Wim took the gambling halls and the sex club on Roompotstraat. He used Willem Endstra to cover up his illegal possessions. Cor "got" Achterdam, a red-light district street in the nearby city of Alkmaar.

By October of 1996, the split was official.

From that moment on, Wim's dealings with the Mieremet group became more and more open. Wim claimed that he was forced to join Mieremet and Klepper to survive the conflict with Cor.

Cor said, "He's a traitor, a Judas. He's sucking up to Mieremet and Klepper now."

Back then, I couldn't believe Wim would join the group that had tried to kill my brother-in-law, sister, and nephew.

"Listen, As, no one can be forced into siding with people who want to kill your family," Cor said, and he was right.

Wim wasn't forced to be around Mieremet.

It was his choice.

I felt ashamed at Wim's betrayal and thought he was weak, but I still wanted to believe he only did it to save us from a bloodbath.

That belief was eroding under the pressure of facts.

Sometime in early 1997, Wim and Mieremet stepped into my law office on Tijl Uilenspiegelstraat in the Bos en Lommer neighborhood. It was Sunday morning, and I was alone there.

"There." Wim pointed to one of the office phones. Without showing the decency of introducing himself, Mieremet walked over and started to make a call.

"What are you doing, Wim?" I asked. "Can't you ask?"

He didn't answer me. He and Mieremet laughed and talked to each other like I wasn't even there, then walked out again. They seemed to be on very familiar terms.

I was seething with anger, knowing I'd been used; my brother had abused my duty of confidentiality. He'd clearly wanted to impress Mieremet. Not out of fear, but to flatter his way in. Like the time after that, when he said he had a job for me and took me to a café around the corner, where Mieremet was already waiting.

Mieremet needed a lawyer to fix things for him, and Wim had told him he could get him one. His sister was a lawyer! Mieremet was interested and had summoned me.

He started to explain what he expected his lawyers to do for him, like taking things he needed to get to the prison, delivering messages, handing over information on other clients, and showing him files—and he told me I could work for him.

My brother had put me in a tricky situation. He was forcing me to choose between the criminal world and the normal one. Did I even have a choice, though?

I wanted to refuse, but I was afraid to. I knew that complying would mean my life was over. I'd be their property, prone to blackmail. And they'd include me in their practices, and I'd have nowhere to turn. Say goodbye to the independence I'd been striving toward all these years.

It was the last thing I wanted.

No matter how scared I was, I had to find the courage to refuse. On the way to the café, Wim had been telling me to make the right impression—I realized that was exactly what I shouldn't do. I had to come across as weak enough for Mieremet to reject me. I stared at him cross-eyed and made up some story about exclusively handling assistance cases, and never having seen the inside of prison except to visit my brother. I pointed out a long list of regulations for lawyers that couldn't be broken, and I made it very clear I never broke the rules, how the Justice Department was already watching me like a hawk, and that I would be a risk rather than a deliverer of results.

Mieremet threw a disappointed glance at Wim. This whiny bitch was nothing like the kind of lawyer he was looking for.

I'd dodged the bullet.

Wim walked me back to the office. He was cross with me; if I had just played along he could have gotten insight into Mieremet's business. I played dumb and avoided challenging him as I knew it would only feed his anger. I was angry that he'd wanted to hand me over to this madman, but what really enraged me was that he'd obviously chosen to associate with the criminal who'd had bullets fired at his brother-in-law, sister, and nephew. I was amazed at his impudent assumption that I'd get involved with such a person.

He just kept pretending it was completely normal.

Sometime after, he rang my doorbell. "Walk to my car with me." He'd just gotten back from abroad, he said, and he'd bought a couple of watches. He opened the trunk and took out a beautiful box. "Have this one," he said, and handed me a white gold Chopard watch. I was surprised. Apart from a puppet and the hundred guilders when he'd kidnapped Heineken, he'd never given me anything but misery.

He hadn't bought the watch especially for me but for a girlfriend who didn't like it, and because it was purchased abroad, he couldn't take it back to the store. There were two other boxes in the trunk. I could see from the boxes that they contained watches, too. He saw me looking at them.

"For Klepper and Mieremet," he said. Klepper and Mieremet, the men he supposedly had no connection with.

My stomach turned over from disgust. This proved that he'd crossed over to Mieremet's gang. Did he really expect me to be fine with that?

I was deeply ashamed of my brother. Wim didn't mind at all, though. No more excessive dinner parties with Cor for him; he dined at Le Garage with Endstra and Mieremet now. He skipped Francis's birthday party but went to Mieremet's daughter Kelly's and even took his girlfriend Maike. Instead of Richie, he now played with Mieremet's son Barry, who was Richie's age. He didn't come to Sonja's birthday party but celebrated with Ria, Mieremet's wife. A boat outing was planned for her thirty-fifth birthday, and Wim took Endstra as his guest.

Wim had found himself a new family. We saw him only when he could use us.

Life After the Attack
1996/1997

COR CAME BACK TO THE NETHERLANDS FROM BELGIUM AND MOVED into a villa in Vijfhuizen with a tennis court, outdoor Jacuzzi, and a shed that had been converted into a clubhouse, which Cor called the Speakeasy. There was a pool table, a huge screen displaying the horse races and every other sport he could bet on, and several fridges filled with booze.

Family, friends, and business partners would come over to hang out with Cor every day. The party was on again. Cor was playing tennis in the morning, playing pool in the afternoon, doing some business in between. He spent the rest of the day gambling and boozing. No need to go out; he had his own private club.

Ever since the attack, he'd avoided going to Amsterdam or any other location he had been known to visit regularly. He tried to pick up his life from where it had come to a grinding halt that horrible day on Deurloostraat.

Life wasn't the same, though.

The previous attack had failed, but at any moment someone could be coming to finish the job.

He constantly calculated where, when, and how a shooter might appear, and he took some extraordinary measures: using an armored car with a chauffeur to drop him off at a certain place and pick him back up so he wouldn't be on the street any longer than necessary, avoiding fixed patterns, never remaining in one place for too long, not making any appointments up front, traveling separately from the children as much as possible, having the bottom of the car checked for bombs. All of it became a part of life after the attack.

Being with Sonja and the children could no longer be taken for granted. Cor's presence had become risky for them. Sonja thought it was too dangerous to be living in a house with him. So she lived in Amstelveen and Cor spent most of his time in Vijfhuizen with his entourage—a group of trusted friends. One was his chauffeur, another got groceries and cooked, yet another took care of the garden while Cor stayed in the Speakeasy, drinking, gambling, and doing business.

Sonja and the children would often spend the day with him, and he'd spend the night with them regularly, but they were careful never to follow a pattern.

On the night of October 6, 1997, Sonja and Cor were asleep at the Amstelveen house, four-year-old Richie in between them as always. At five a.m., they were awoken by a huge bang: the front door was being kicked in.

"Police! Police!" Within moments, a SWAT team pulled Cor out of bed and put a sack over his head.

Sonja had recently taught little Richie never to put a sack over his own head, even in play. "No, no, no, he'll choke! Mommy, Daddy is choking!" he screamed.

"You—go downstairs, sit on the couch, and stay there," Sonja was ordered.

She took Francis and Richie downstairs and sat down on the couch. She couldn't touch anything or make any calls.

"Do you have any money or weapons in the house?" one of the investigators asked.

"No," Sonja said.

"Yes, we do!" Richie exclaimed. He jumped off the couch, went to the closet, and pulled a stack of money out from underneath the clothing. "That's Daddy's!" he said when the investigator took the money away.

Around the same time Sonja had her front door kicked in, my telephone rang.

"This is supervisory judge J. M. speaking. We are with your brother Willem at the moment, and we can't get ahold of his lawyer, Bram Moszkowicz, to represent him. He requested we call you for assistance."

"What? Now?" I asked in surprise.

"Yes, as soon as you can, please. We can't wait very long," he replied.

"All right, I'm on my way," I said, angry. Great. I was trying to avoid being linked to him. Now everyone at the courthouse would see me as his *consigliere*.

Such disgrace.

To make matters worse, I happened to know supervisory judge J. M.; I'd been in his court for an arraignment shortly before. My reputation as a lawyer would be ruined, but I couldn't refuse Wim, either. Couldn't he show a little respect for my life, my world, just this once?

I drove to Wim's apartment on Van Leijenberghlaan. When I got there, I identified myself and was let in. The supervisory judge was at work in the living room and looked up when I came in. There I was, Holleeder's little sister, who came running the moment her big brother called.

Wim was standing in the middle of the room. Maike was there with him. It was an awkward situation. I'd always wanted to keep my professional life separate from my private life, and here I was practicing my profession in a private setting. Nevertheless, the supervisory judge played dumb and behaved like a professional. "Your brother is under suspicion of money laundering and participating in a criminal organization dealing in hash—"

"He's talking about Cor!" Wim interrupted, and I thought, How can he say that with the Justice Department right there in front of him? Splitting up doesn't mean being more loyal to the Justice Department than to Cor, does it?

"You may observe, but you may not interfere in any way," the supervisory judge said to me, as though he hadn't registered Wim's remark.

"Of course," I said. I thought, Cor is a suspect, too, so they'll be at Sonja's house. How would she be holding up? The children? Cor?

The supervisory judge asked Wim, "Do you own a car?"

"Yes, it's downstairs," Wim replied.

"May we have the keys? We want to search the car."

Wim handed over the keys and told me, "Go downstairs with them. Keep an eye on them."

I walked to the car that was parked on the street. The officers opened the trunk and took out a bound pile of documents. It was a city council report on plans for the red-light district.

I was startled. Having this found with him was extremely inconvenient, considering the rumors that already surrounded his activities in the red-light district. This might be the confirmation. Back upstairs, the search was finishing up. When everyone left, I stayed behind with Wim and Maike.

"It's all because of that big fat dog—he had to get into hash," Wim said, irritated. "All I got from that guy is misery. I thought I got rid of him, but he still gets me in trouble."

I was really annoyed with the way he put Cor down in Maike's presence—he was no saint, either. His association with real estate brokers hadn't turned him into a law-abiding citizen. He still hung out with the major Dutch drug lords—what difference did it make if they were called Cor van Hout or Mieremet and Klepper?

I left him and drove straight to Sonja's. There was no need to ring the doorbell. The front door was gone.

Inside was havoc, and she was busy cleaning up the mess. Richie came running to me.

"Assie, Assie, the cops took Daddy away!"

"Did they now, son?" I asked.

I told Sonja, "I've just come from Wim's. They were there as well."

"Where is Wim now?" Sonja asked.

"At home. He didn't have to go with them."

Francis came into the room and we hugged. "How are you, honey?" I asked. She looked pale. Her cheeks were tearstained.

"Oh, Assie, I was so scared. I heard a bang and noise downstairs. At the same time, I heard people on the roof. I thought they were attacking us from everywhere and were coming to kill us. I tried to hide in my closet, but there were already two masked men pointing their guns at me. I only found out they were cops then. I was ordered to stay on my bed, but all I could do was cry. I yelled that I wanted to go to Mom and Dad. That's when I ran to their bedroom. They'd put a sack over Dad's head, and Mom was screaming. Richie stood next to the bed, crying—he was shaking all over."

I held her tight to calm her down. She's the second generation to be traumatized by a police raid. From then on, she'd always remain on alert at night.

"Are you mad at your dad because this happened?"

"No," Francis said. "I felt bad for him having the sack over his head. He could only wear a T-shirt, and they took him away in his underwear. They jerked him around, yelled at him. He just said, 'Take it easy, I'm cooperating!' It was horrible."

"I was really lucky, though," she went on optimistically. "My girlfriend was supposed to stay over, but she canceled at the last minute. Imagine the fright she'd have gotten if she'd been here?"

"That is lucky for sure," I replied. "She'd have been traumatized for life."

"I might have gotten expelled," Francis said.

Poor Francis. As a fourteen-year-old she didn't want to stand out at school and was trying to lead as normal a life as possible while her father brought all kinds of madness home, and she couldn't really blame him for it.

"Did you call Bram Moszkowicz yet?" I asked Sonja.

"Yeah, he'll go to the police station as soon as he can."

Cor was taken into custody during an investigation named City Peak, which had started out as a search for the vanished Heineken ransom but was changed into possession of drugs and firearms. Sonja and the children entered another era of prison visits.

Again, Cor made the best of a bad situation. Before every visit, Sonja would buy two tiny bottles of baby shampoo, rinse them out, fill them with Bacardi, stick these into her armpits, and smuggle the booze inside. She'd done the same thing during his previous jailtime; only then she'd used milk cartons, which she'd hand over to the guards.

Cor got through his sentence just fine.

During the investigation, it became public that the first attack on his life had been recorded on video. The Justice Department had filmed it themselves but had held the video back.

"It's fucking unbelievable. They keep getting me back in for a composite drawing, and the whole time they've had images of the culprit," Sonja said.

According to the Justice Department, release of the video would have compromised the investigation into Cor van Hout. The investigation into his involvement with hash trafficking turned out to be more important than solving the murder attempt on Cor and his family. Cor and Sonja filed a preliminary injunction for the release of the tape, and Cor publicly offered a reward for any tips on the culprit.

The court wouldn't go there, though: showing the images would compromise the privacy of those who'd agreed to have police cameras put up in their homes.

"I don't care where the camera was. I just want to see his face. Even a tiny picture would do, just so I can see who it was," Cor protested.

No, he and Sonja couldn't see who had shot at them. "That's how it is, Assie. They'd rather have us gunning each other down," Cor said when he called me to thank me for being at the preliminary injunction to show moral support.

In the end, Cor was sentenced to four and a half years in jail, but he was to be released at the end of 1999. He'd cut a deal with the prosecutor, Fred Teeven.

"Cor wants you to come visit," Sonja said.

"Sure, I'll come with you next time," I said.

"No," she said, "he wants you to come as his lawyer. There's something he wants to discuss with you."

I'd never visited Cor as a lawyer before. When Wim made me turn up for the search and seizure, I failed at my attempt to keep my work and private life separate. I'd let go of the illusion I'd ever be regarded as separate from my family. I strictly kept to advocacy regulations, and otherwise, people could think what they pleased. Cor had never asked me for anything, so it had to be important. That's why I went.

At the time, he was imprisoned in the town of Zwaag. I met Cor in the lawyers' room. We sat facing each other, whispering.

"I've made a deal," he said. "I was set up, Assie, in multiple ways, and I know how it went down. I want you to know about it. But you can't tell anyone—as a lawyer, you're bound by a duty of confidentiality."

"Don't be silly. I've never told anybody anything."

"I know, but that's not what it's about," Cor said. "It's about you being able to invoke your duty of confidentiality toward the Justice Department at all times."

"Got it," I answered, and Cor started talking. After our conversation, I kissed him goodbye. "I'll be home soon, Assie. See you soon."

"Well?" Sonja asked. "What did he want to see you about?"

"I can't tell you, Son. I'm bound by a duty of confidentiality," I said.

"Whatever—you can still tell *me*, right?"

"No," I answered.

"Oh, come on, As. We're talking about my husband here."

"I know, but I have to honor my duty of confidentiality no matter what."

After Cor went to prison, Wim, who'd stayed out, started showing up at Sonja's door again.

After the failed attack, it was to be expected that Cor wanted revenge. He'd been buying guns and had stocked up a considerable armory, and he'd had a soundproof basement constructed in which he'd been practicing shooting with a select club.

When Wim found out, this danger had to be averted at all costs, and he and his cronies ensured that the cops knew about the guns.

Through someone in Cor's entourage, they'd also discovered he was dealing drugs, and this information was leaked as well.

Wim had killed two birds with one stone: he'd drawn attention away from his investments with the Heineken ransom, and disarmed his opponent.

It was typical of Wim—if he couldn't get rid of you with bullets, he'd do it through the Justice Department.

Sonja didn't want to see Wim anymore. For a long time, she'd hoped Cor was wrong in claiming Wim had switched sides. There was no denying it now. She'd often hear from others how he was partying with Klepper and Mieremet. Wim kept denying he was close to the enemy, but at the same time he was friendly enough with them to keep asking Sonja for videotapes for Mieremet's son Barry. Cor told her to let Wim come over and to hear him out.

Cor had been inside for some time when Sonja went to visit him. Afterward, she came to me.

"Guess what?" she said the second she saw me.

"What?"

"Cor was planning to sell the Achterdam, but the buyer was warned off. He got a visit from Mieremet, Klepper, and...who else do you think?"

"I have no idea," I replied.

"Wim!" she exclaimed. "He made Klepper tell the buyer that the Achterdam was theirs and he should keep his hands off. While showing Klepper out, this guy saw Wim quickly moving to hide behind a tree. Too late, he'd been spotted. Well, what do you say about that?"

"That's bizarre," I said. "Now what?"

"Now the buyer has backed out. But Cor says that's not the point. It's about Wim, showing what he's all about. He wants to take whatever Cor has."

"Cor would never allow that to happen, right?"

"I wouldn't think so. For now, I'm glad he's still inside. This can't end well."

That wasn't the only reason to await Cor's release in suspense, though...

The Second Attempt

2000

THE FIRST ATTEMPT ON COR'S LIFE HAD FAILED. AND BECAUSE IT HAD failed, it was certain there would be a second try. Cor knew Mieremet had tried to liquidate—or assassinate—him, and Mieremet must have expected revenge from Cor's side, especially because his wife and child had been with him. It was only logical that Mieremet would now try to beat Cor to it.

The question was who'd be the first to go.

Still, time went by and nothing happened. Cor was released at the end of 1999.

By then, Wim had joined forces with Endstra, Mieremet, and Klepper full on. I hardly ever saw him.

Until he suddenly reappeared at my door.

In the middle of the night, I was startled awake by the doorbell. I was afraid to open up until I recognized our family ring: two short, one long. I opened the door and saw Wim standing there.

"Put on your shoes. We're going outside."

"What? It's the middle of the night. I have a fever. I shouldn't even be outside. I'm ill."

"Come outside, it's urgent. Or do you want me to wake the neighbors?"

"I'm coming already, for God's sake."

"Listen up. Do you know where Cor is living?" he asked in a friendly tone.

I was on my guard right away. "I wouldn't know," I said.

"Listen," he whispered, "I need to know where he's staying. It's extremely important, because Mieremet won't back off. I can only protect Sonja if you tell me. Otherwise they'll just launch a rocket into her house and they'll all be dead. The children, too."

"But I told you I don't know."

"You're with Sonja all the time, right," he insisted. "Now do as I say. I'm not kidding. The Mieremet crew is deadly as fuck. They've iced dozens. They'll do it just for kicks. And he's really pissed them off."

"Listen up: I don't want anything to do with that stuff."

"Listen up?" he hissed into my ear. "You don't tell me to 'listen up.' Who the fuck do you think you are? You think you can tell me what to do? You'll do as I say, or every fucking person dies. A rocket is going in there and you can put the pieces of your sister back to-gether. Take your choice. If you don't, then you've killed them! You hear me? You've killed them. It's on you!"

He had me cornered.

I knew full well Mieremet was mad, and I also knew Mieremet wouldn't leave it at this. I'd heard about the violent methods Mieremet and Klepper used and how easily they applied them.

When we were in Cannes, Mieremet's sister-in-law was there as well, and Cor told me Mieremet had done her husband, too, just for hitting her.

There were others around Cor who'd had dealings with Mieremet.

One of them said his son was beaten for no reason, and it had caused him to flee the country.

And of course I'd gotten to know their violent side through the Deurloostraat attack, which proved they wouldn't even spare wives and children. Because we all knew it wouldn't end with this first attack, I took the threat very seriously.

So, I had expected another attempt, but not that *he* of all people would inform me of it. Betraying his friend by going over to Mieremet's side was one thing, but lending a hand in icing his own best friend was unbelievable to me.

And now he wanted to get me involved! Not because he thought I'd be loyal to him (he knew I spent a lot of time with Cor and Sonja) but because he knew I loved those children to death.

If I said, "Fuck off, I want nothing to do with it," and something happened to Cor, Sonja, and the kids, I'd regret it for the rest of my life, and I would indeed feel responsible for what had happened to them.

That's exactly what he'd intended.

By uttering the words "it's on you," he'd literally put it on me. Of course, I told myself, that makes no sense, but what good would knowing that do if they ended up dead?

Doing nothing wasn't an option.

I had no idea what I should do next. Stalling until a resolution presented itself was the only thing I could come up with. "I'll see what I can do," I said.

"Good."

The following morning, I went over to Sonja's early. I'd tossed and turned all night, searching for a way out of this.

For one thing, I had to tell Sonja they were all in danger, and from what corner to actually expect the danger.

Different from before, the relationships were clear now: Wim was in the Mieremet camp and had turned against Cor, his blood brother.

Sonja began hyperventilating as soon as I told her about the previous night. "What? He's threatening my children? First they nearly shoot Richie to death, and now they're threatening my children again? I'm not giving him the address. Is he out of his mind? What should I do, As?"

"I don't know. Keep Cor away from here. I'll say you don't know the address, and even if you knew, you wouldn't tell him. I'll tell him that Mieremet shouldn't threaten your children. You should be glad you know what his plans are now. At least you'll be able to see it coming this time."

That same evening, he was back on my doorstep. "Well?"

I told him Sonja didn't know and she wouldn't tell him even if she did.

"Ah, so she's taking Corry's side? That's not so smart. Tell her that."

"You can tell her yourself."

"Oh, no, I'm not going near there anymore. If anything happens, I want to be far away."

In the meantime, Sonja had told Cor that Klepper and Mieremet were at it again and had used Wim as a messenger. He told me and Sonja to keep in touch with Wim and hear what he had to say, wanting to keep his enemy close. I agreed with that and could see the advantages, but I had doubts as well. What if Cor blabbed to someone when he was drunk, and Mieremet, Klepper, or Wim heard about it?

Cor had sworn that wouldn't happen. But I wasn't reassured. Cor often couldn't even recall what he'd done the day before. If Wim and Mieremet discovered I'd informed Cor, they might have me killed, too. So I had to take into account that Cor would blab at some point. I hedged by telling Wim I only passed on his messages to Sonja at his request. I couldn't help it if Sonja had passed things on to Cor.

After that last visit, he didn't stay away long.

"Listen, As, I can't hold this off much longer, you know? What she's doing is very annoying."

He kept delivering the same message. He needed information on the places Cor visited. Me not knowing anything started to bug him. He began to increase pressure on me.

One day Wim and I were at my mother's house when she was looking after Richie for Sonja. My mother was in the kitchen. Wim was standing in the living room, and Richie sat on a chair. I sat on the couch, facing Richie.

Suddenly he stepped behind Richie's chair, put his arm around his neck, took a gun from his pocket, and pointed it at Richie's head. "Hey, Richie boy!" he shouted. He looked at me and hissed, "Tell me where he is!"

Then he let go of Richie, gave me a piercing look with his dark eyes, and shouted cheerfully in the direction of the kitchen, "Bye, Stien, it was nice to see you. I'm going now!"

He walked out.

I ran over to Richie and took him in my arms.

I was astounded. Threatening Richie, his own nephew, *my* nephew, a seven-year-old child. Why would he do this if he wanted to prevent Sonja, Richie, and Francis from becoming collateral damage for Klepper and Mieremet? For that's what he'd been claiming: "I'm acting in their best interest, and so should you so I can make sure they won't get hurt."

And suddenly I understood: his intent wasn't to protect them from Mieremet and Klepper at all. If he had really wanted to protect them and make sure they weren't murdered along with Cor, he'd never treat Richie like that. He wasn't worried about Sonja, Francis, or Richie; he was just using them to try to get closer to Cor.

He was the one who wanted to murder Cor, and he was going this far because he was growing impatient. Things weren't moving fast enough for him. Cor had to die, and he didn't mind using Richie to get to him.

It was him!

I knew Sonja was on her way over to pick up Richie. After what had just happened, I had to see her immediately. I dialed her number. "Are you almost here?" I asked when she answered the phone. For us, this is code for "Hurry, something's up."

"I'll be right there," she said right away.

"Will you stop pacing up and down and sit down for a second?" my mother said.

My mother hadn't seen what Wim had done to Richie, and I couldn't tell her. It would be too much for her.

Sonja walked in and looked at me questioningly. I went into the bathroom so Mom and Richie couldn't hear us, and she followed. I switched on the light and she locked the door. She stood in front of me.

"Tell me," she spoke softly.

I told her what had happened. Sonja's eyes grew large, and she stiffened and then began to shiver all over. She didn't speak.

"Son, what do you think?" No reply. "Hey! Did you even hear what I just said?" I spoke up, hoping to startle her into responding.

She didn't speak, just kept staring into the distance. I grabbed her shoulders and shook her. "Son! Stop it!"

"What's going on?" my mother yelled from the living room. "What are you doing?"

"It's nothing!" I yelled back.

"Son," I said, "cut it out."

She was still silent but walked out of the bathroom to Richie, pulled him into her lap, and started to cry.

"What's wrong, Mommy?" he asked. My mom gave me a puzzled look.

"Nothing," I said. "It's nothing. Mom, please stay out of it."

"Sonja?" I said, still wondering what she was thinking.

"I'm done thinking, As," she said, as she always did when things started to overwhelm her.

Sonja was as scared as she had been since the first attack. She wouldn't let Richie out of her sight even for a second. Now that he had revealed himself as the perpetrator by threatening Richie, Wim increased the pressure even more and stopped hiding behind Klepper and Mieremet. He said Yugoslavs had already been flown in. There were people ready for action. By now, they were all aware of Cor's whereabouts. There was no stopping it now.

Wim threatened Sonja in increasingly explicit ways, sending his messages through me.

If she wanted to stay alive, Sonja had "to do this little thing." She had to leave the blinds open when Cor was there.

"If she doesn't, you know what will happen." He made a gun gesture with his hand. "Go tell her."

It became harder and harder to get anything through to Sonja. "Son, are you on medication again?" I asked.

"Yes," she said. She'd increased her dose of Oxazepam.

"Why are you doing that? You look like a zombie again! Stop it."

"No, As, I won't, or my head will explode. I can't handle this without meds. The pills help make it all go away."

I told her what Wim wanted her to do.

"I won't do it," she answered blankly. "We'll all just go."

The pills were doing their work. Wim had met his match: Sonja had turned as cold as he was, and had become fearless, too.

★ ★ ★

I was at home with Richie and Francis when he rang the doorbell. "Come down!" he yelled.

"Rich, you stay with Fran," I said.

"I don't want to!" Richie shouted in a panic, grabbing hold of me.

Since the attack on Deurloostraat, he couldn't be left alone without freaking out. I didn't want to take him downstairs or anywhere near Wim, though.

"Fran, keep him here," I told Francis, and got him off me.

"Come on, Rich," Francis said, and pulled him away. Richie tore himself loose and followed me anyway.

"What's that kid doing here?" Wim grunted.

"I can't get him to leave me. He's scared, you know."

"Hmm," he said, dismissing the comment.

The three of us stood in the hallway at the bottom of the stairs, Wim and I facing each other, Richie in between us. Wim leaned forward and pulled me toward him. "Well?" he whispered.

"She won't do it," I replied.

"She won't do it?" he repeated. I could see him begin to swell with anger, his eyes almost popping out of his head.

Richie was still standing between us. With his right hand, Wim got a gun out of his pocket, pulled me closer with his left hand, and held the gun over Richie's head. "She's still siding with Corry? She doesn't know what she's getting into. That's her choice. You know what will happen."

He let go of me. I pushed Richie up the stairs to get him away from Wim as quickly as possible. Wim turned away in a rage, stormed downstairs, and slammed the door behind him.

Richie hadn't been aware of what had happened because he'd

been standing in between us, but at the top of the stairs stood a child who'd seen it all.

I told Sonja what had happened because she had refused to help Wim.

From that moment on, she left the blinds half open, scared of giving the wrong signal by shutting them or leaving them open entirely.

Sonja had let Cor know it had started again, but Cor did nothing. We didn't tell him everything, especially about the increased threats, for fear of a war in which we and the children would get killed, too. But Cor knew Wim and Mieremet couldn't be stopped.

I couldn't understand why Cor didn't take action himself.

In the meantime, Wim was aware that Sonja wasn't getting him any closer to Cor. He'd applied maximum pressure by using Richie, but he'd achieved the opposite with Sonja: she froze and didn't move or respond to anything. At the time, he seemed to let it go.

He hadn't dropped by for quite a while when shots were fired at Cor as he was getting out of his car outside his and Sonja's house on December 21, 2000. He was able to dodge the bullets and get to a safe place because Sonja quickly opened the door for him.

The next morning she noticed that a bullet had penetrated the wall less than twenty inches from the door.

Cor immediately said that Wim was behind it.

In public, Wim always denied any involvement. He claimed it was Mieremet's doing, as he'd done after the first attack. Back then, I believed him.

But everything became clear after September 22, 2002.

On February 26, 2002, John Mieremet was shot on Keizersgracht after meeting with his lawyer, Evert Hingst. It didn't take him long to realize that Wim and associates were behind the attack; they didn't want to return the money he had invested with Willem Endstra.

If Mieremet hadn't survived the attempt on his life, the truth about the attack on Cor might never have come to light. Mieremet decided his only chance of survival was the publication of an interview with the crime reporter John van den Heuvel in *De Telegraaf* on September 22, 2002. In it, Mieremet spoke of Endstra's role as banker to the criminal world, and my brother's role as the guard of that bank.

Shortly after the interview was published, van den Heuvel was robbed and his computer was taken. Endstra and Wim had hired a gang of Yugoslavians to break into his house. Wim brought me a printout of van den Heuvel's notes from conversations he'd had with Mieremet.

He wanted me to read the notes and give him my impression. What I read shocked me. The notes said that Wim was the one who'd pointed out Cor and Sonja's house on Deurloostraat to Mieremet and Klepper, *before* the first attack.

Everything fell into place: Wim's behavior after the first attack, his so-called forced switch to Camp Mieremet, introducing me to them, the watches he'd bought them, the fine Sonja had paid him.

He'd been associated with them all along.

The Third Attempt

2003

ON JANUARY 24, 2003, I WAS IN COURT AND ABOUT TO GO INTO A HEARING. I had a friend with me who had been eager to attend a court session. I remember exactly where I was standing when I got the call: right in front of the Van Oven Hall.

I answered the phone and heard a hysterical scream. I heard my sister's voice. She didn't say anything, she just screamed.

"What is it! What is going on? What is happening?" I asked. An unknown male voice took over the call.

He said, "Sonja is here."

"Who are you?" I asked. "Where is my sister, what did you do to her?" I was under the impression that this strange man on the phone had abducted my sister. "Let me speak to my sister," I shouted.

"As," said Sonja, and she started screaming again. She scared me.

"What is it, Son? Tell me what's wrong!"

"Cor is dead! Cor is dead!" she yelled.

The male voice took over the call again and said that Cor had been shot. He'd been standing outside a Chinese restaurant with his friend Robert ter Haak when two men drove up on a motorcycle and fired at Cor with a machine gun.

"No, no, no! Sonja, where are you?" I shouted.

"I will go to him," said the unknown male voice.

I asked my friend to drive me to Sonja's house. I was totally beside myself and incapable of driving.

Sonja called me in the car. "They were wrong, As!" I heard hope in her voice.

Robert, the man who had been standing next to Cor, had been killed, but Cor was alive and had been taken to the hospital, the police had told her.

He was still alive!

I wanted to go to the hospital, too, but I didn't know which one, and I couldn't reach Sonja to ask her. Eventually I had my friend drop me off at her house in Amstelveen. Soon after, two policemen came and searched the house.

I called my mother to come to Sonja's house, because I didn't want to leave the two officers alone there and I needed a car to go to the hospital. My mother came to Sonja's house, and Gerard picked me up to go with me.

Meanwhile, I kept trying to reach Sonja to find out how Cor was. The male voice picked up again and said coarsely, "Here's your sister. She has to tell you something."

From the way he said it, I knew something was wrong. Sonja came on and said nothing. I just heard her crying softly but uncontrollably.

"Son, are you there?" I asked.

"Yes," she sighed.

"Is it bad?" I asked, afraid of her answer.

"Yes, As." Sonja sounded as if she had no strength left to speak.

"Is he—?" I couldn't say the word, afraid she would confirm it. There was silence.

"Son," I asked again.

"Yes, he is—"

He's dead, I repeated to myself. He can't be, he can't be dead. He had survived two attempts. Twice he had defeated the end death brings, and I was sure that he could do it again.

We arrived at the hospital. As fast as I could, I climbed the steps to the entrance and ran to the ward where they were keeping him. I was talking to him, afraid I might be too late and his soul wouldn't hear me. "Cor, you can't go yet. It's impossible; you must stay with us. Don't leave."

At the end of the hallway I saw Sonja. I ran toward her and threw myself at her.

"Son, say it's not true. Tell me he's still alive."

She shook her head. "He's dead, As."

A doctor came to see us. Talking to him, we saw Francis come in. She had also driven to the hospital thinking that Cor was badly wounded but still alive. At the hospital entrance, a friend of Cor's had been waiting for her, and she knew enough.

"He's dead, isn't he?" she said, and the friend nodded.

"How is this possible?" she asked the doctor. "You told me he was still alive."

"I'm sorry," the doctor said, "there has been a miscommunication. The man who was standing next to him is fighting for his life, but your father passed away."

It was a mistake that took away any hope of ever seeing her father again.

"Can we see him?" asked Francis.

"No," the doctor said, "he's not here. He is still in Amstelveen."

"In Amstelveen?" Sonja said. "Then we'll go there. Will you pick up Richie from school before a stranger tells him what has happened to his dad?" Sonja asked Gerard and me.

"Of course," I answered. "Should I tell him, or would you rather do that yourself?"

"Please do it for me, As. I can't handle that right now."

"I will, we'll go there now."

Richie was surprised to see us, but apparently had no idea what had happened. Without saying anything about it, we headed to Gerard's house, where my mother was waiting. Richie was joyfully talking about what he had been doing at school.

My head was spinning. How should I do this? How should I tell him his father had just died?

"We're going to see Grandma," I said.

Richie loved her, and I was happy she would be there when he heard the news.

My mother was already upstairs in the bedroom, and Richie ran toward her: "Grandma!"

I followed him.

"Hello, darlings," my mom said.

She looked at Richie and started crying.

"What is it, Grandma?" he asked, and took her hand. "Are you in pain?"

"No, love," she said, "I'm not in pain."

I started crying, too, and I saw Richie was confused. He felt something bad was going on. I had to tell him. I gathered all my courage and said, "Come sit with me. I have to tell you something, sweetheart."

"Is Mom dead?" he asked fearfully, as if he suddenly realized why we were crying.

"No, darling, not your mom. Daddy is dead," I heard myself saying.

After I uttered the words, a heart-wrenching, dark growl escaped his little body. He started shouting. "Mama," he cried out. "I want to see Mama, where is Mama?"

"Mama will be here soon, honey. Granny and I are with you now. You can hold me tight."

Richie put his little arms around me and cried until he was so worn out that he felt weak in my arms.

"Here, Mom, please take him. So I can ask Son what else I can do." Sonja and Francis had driven to the place where Cor had been shot. Sonja wanted to be with him, hold him right there on the sidewalk, but she wasn't allowed to. They were doing forensic research, and she was not to disturb the crime scene. Cor had become a crime scene. He was there on the cold ground, unreachable to everybody who loved him.

It was useless hanging around there any longer. Francis came to us, to stay with her uncle and aunt, her grandmother, and Richie. Sonja drove to her own house, and I followed her.

We sat there, overcome with grief. The doorbell rang. It was Wim.

I opened the door and sat back down on the sofa with Sonja. We cried. Wim sat down between us, put his arms around us, and cried with us.

After a while he got up and left. After all we had been through together, it didn't feel right.

We still hadn't seen Cor, and Francis did everything she could to get in to see him. The police were being difficult, but as young and as sad as she was, she managed to pressure them enough that we were allowed to see him that night.

Sonja, Francis, and I went there. We left Richie at home. Sonja didn't want him to go.

We arrived at the hospital and had to use a back entrance. A couple of cops were waiting for us.

Before we went in to see Cor, they warned us that we might be shocked, that he did not look like himself, that he had been brutalized.

Sonja and I went in first, to see if it was safe for Francis to see her father like that.

There he was, in a white gown on a table. Two burning candles stood at both ends of the table. I looked at Cor's face and his hands.

They had literally shot him to pieces.

Sonja ran toward Cor, screaming. "No, no, no!" She took his head in her hands and kissed his lips. "Wake up, Cor, please, wake up!" she cried and shook his head, as if trying to rouse him.

It was best Francis didn't see him like this, but against our advice, she'd followed us into the room.

"I have to see him," she said, "or I won't believe that he is dead."

"Go on, then," I said.

Francis walked toward him hesitantly, took his battered hand and put it to her face. "Daddy, Daddy!" she cried. "No, Daddy, you can't be dead!"

Through her tears she kissed his broken fingers.

I put my hand on his arm and tried to look for a sign of life in his face. "Look at me, Cor," I whispered, hoping he'd open his eyes. "Look at me," I said louder, but nothing happened.

Cor didn't open his eyes. He never would again.

After a while, we were asked to leave the room. We had to leave him again. One by one, we kissed him goodbye.

"See you tomorrow, love," Sonja said.

Francis and I looked at each other. Sonja still could not believe he was gone.

We drove home.

It was later in the evening when the doorbell rang, startling me.

"Who is it?" I asked.

"Me."

It was Wim.

"Son, come outside for a bit," he called over my head to Sonja. Sonja, still in shock, followed him like a zombie.

After half an hour, she was back.

"What did he want?" I asked when Sonja came back. She gestured me to follow her to the bathroom, like we used to do when we talked about Wim. She switched on the dryer to drown out our conversation. The police had searched the whole house today and we didn't know if they had installed bugs.

"He asked for the shares of Achterdam. Do you think what I think?"

"I think so," I answered.

The shares of Achterdam: the person who owned them was the owner of a couple of whorehouses in the city of Alkmaar's red-light district. It had been a joint project by Cor, Wim, and Robbie following the investment of the Heineken ransom in Amsterdam's red-light district. After they went their separate ways in 1996, Cor got the Achterdam shares.

"Box, I need the shares for those whorehouses," he had said to Sonja, and Sonja could now only think that he was behind Cor's death.

She told him she didn't have the shares. He'd gone ballistic, had ordered her to go find them, gotten into his car angrily, and driven away.

The next day he was back. He took Sonja outside again and "comforted" her. Cor had been a filthy dog anyway, she would mourn him for just three months and then her grief would be over. Cor was a serious alcoholic and for the kids his death was a blessing. Had she found his shares yet? Oh, and didn't Cor have gold? She should hand that over to him now.

She couldn't refuse, but Sonja, determined that Wim should not profit from Cor's death, improvised: Cor had sold all his gold. She had one bar left, and she wanted to keep that for the children, if he was okay with that.

Wim was beside himself. "One bar left?!"

With Cor out of the way, Wim thought Sonja would be easy prey, but she stood firm.

Days later, Wim called and told me to come see him.

"Listen, As, I need Sonja. You have to get her and take her to the Amsterdam Forest Park. She will have to give her house in Spain to Stanley Hillis, because the hit men have to be paid. So go get her now. I'll see you in the forest in one hour."

I was stunned. Had I heard him correctly? The gunmen had to be paid? Was he talking to me about Cor's hit men? Sonja had to pay for the murder of her husband, the father of her children, by donating her house to his posse? The house Cor had named after his daughter, Villa Francis?

I hurried to Sonja's and told her what he had told me. She turned white as a sheet.

"You see he is behind all this, As?"

"Yes."

"What now?"

"You have to come with me to Forest Park. He'll be waiting for us."

"No!"

We were scared of what might happen to us there in the forest. We parked the car and walked toward him.

"Hey, Son." He told Sonja what he'd told me. "You have to give your house in Spain to Stanley Hillis because the hit men have to be paid."

Sonja had told him twice before that she had nothing to give him, but Wim wasn't having it. He grew impatient. And we had seen firsthand how fast his impatience could turn to violence.

Sonja's Grief

IT WAS THE DAY WE BURIED COR. SONJA AND I WERE VERY TIRED, AND we were lying on her bed discussing the burial.

"It went exactly as Cor would have wanted it," said Sonja.

"Yes, I think so, too. I think he would have liked it very much." I switched off the light. "Let's go to sleep."

Less than five minutes later I heard Sonja's voice in the darkness. "Did you do that, As?"

"What, Son?"

"No, I thought not, but I wanted to be sure."

"What do you mean?" I asked.

"Cor came and kissed me. I felt his lips on mine."

"Are you okay, Son? Are you not losing it a bit?" I was worried.

"Not at all. Really, he is still here. He won't leave us alone. You know I don't believe in miracles, but it's really true. He came to give me a kiss."

I understood what she was saying. I felt Cor's presence in the room, too. Being a rational person, I didn't want to acknowledge it, but after Sonja told me, I was sure. He was still here.

"Sweet dreams, Cor," Son said. I was quiet for a minute and then echoed, "Sweet dreams, Cor."

★ ★ ★

Immediately after Cor was assassinated, I moved in with Sonja. Living with her, I saw firsthand how Wim dictated Sonja's life now that Cor was gone. Her house was his house. He walked in and out and brought with him a holdover from his Klepper and Mieremet posse—Sandra.

Sonja had to look after her so he could occupy himself unhindered with his other women. And if Sonja was unable to do it, Francis had to step in.

Sandra wasn't the only woman she had to entertain, though she was the one Sonja loathed most passionately.

And entertaining his various women was not Sonja's only task. Wim's life was in danger, and Sonja had to drive him around in his bulletproof car whenever he felt like it. Sonja would have to get the car, which was parked in a garage in Amstelveen, off the street, so that they couldn't place any bugs or bombs underneath it.

"It's extremely ironic, isn't it, Son? You of all people helping him to survive," I said when Sonja suddenly had to skip dinner because Wim wanted to be driven somewhere.

"It drives me crazy sometimes," she replied.

"How do you cope with it?"

"I do it for the kids. They keep me going. I would have killed myself a long time ago if it wasn't for them. I would have crawled up next to Cor."

She left the table. "I need to go before he starts asking where I am."

Shortly after the funeral, Wim said to me, "You know, As, it's for the best. They cry for two months, and then they forget about it. That fat one was a fucking asshole anyway."

He had told Sonja the same thing, and later I read the same sentence in Endstra's back seat conversations.

Meanwhile, on the day of the funeral he had been crying with us on the sofa, displaying his so-called grief for everyone. A great actor.

He also wanted to "contribute." He overheard a discussion between Sonja and the undertaker about a small bill she still had to pay but which she could not cover at that point. Wim immediately saw an opportunity to strengthen his alibi and had me transfer the amount from his account, and he subsequently told everybody he had paid for the funeral.

Soon afterward, he had me come to Stadhouderskade to meet him.

"Walk with me," he said. "Any news?"

"No, no news."

"Okay, fine. Hey, As, that money I paid for the funeral, I really think it's a waste of my money. It's clean money, so I have to get it back into my account, you see."

I felt a knot in my stomach. Did he say *waste*? Yes, of course it was a "waste" now. He had already accomplished his goal. He had broadcast everywhere that he had contributed, and in criminal circles he had claimed, for convenience's sake, that he had paid for everything.

"I actually loaned it to her, didn't I, because she was short of money."

All of sudden it was a loan. Well, okay. She didn't want him to contribute anyway.

I had only been able to convince her to accept the money because otherwise I feared he would catch on that we saw him as the perpetrator.

That same day the money was in his account. Sonja was glad she could transfer it back to him.

* * *

The attacks on Cor had made it impossible for him and Sonja and the kids to function as a normal family. After the first one in 1996, being together was no longer easy or normal.

For a long time, Sonja and the kids would see Cor only briefly, at various secret locations. Cor started drinking more after each attempt. Despite all the lows, they stayed together, connected for twenty-five years by their love and trust, the children, and all they had been through together.

Cor's death ended that period. Sonja thought she could know no greater loss.

But she was wrong.

A few days after the funeral, Peter R. de Vries, one of Holland's most famous investigative journalists and a friend of Cor's, came to see Sonja. We were sitting at her dining table when he said he'd like to share something about Cor, but he didn't know if he'd be doing the right thing. He wanted to keep nothing from her, but maybe she didn't want to know.

"Of course I want to know," Sonja said.

"Okay, well. Cor had an affair with someone at my office."

I saw Sonja's face turn red, but she remained calm. She asked how it happened, and after Peter answered, she said, "I'm glad you've been honest with me. I now understand why some people at the funeral were acting so mysteriously."

Sonja saw Peter out, and as soon as the door was shut, she started to cry uncontrollably. "The bastard! How could he do that to me? And carry on the affair for two years!"

Cor was no saint, she had known that; she had dragged him out of brothels more than once. But this was different. This was a relationship, and he'd never done that to her before. He had taken this woman to his house in Nigtevecht and to Sonja's house in Spain, where they had spent time in Sonja's bed.

After finding out about this relationship, she wanted to see what the woman looked like.

Sonja's grief about Cor's affair was clear to Francis. She too wanted to know what this other woman looked like.

We went to see Peter de Vries, to ask if he had a picture of her.

"Yes, I think so," Peter replied.

"Can I see it?" Sonja asked.

He looked for a photo and handed it to Sonja.

Sonja was silent on the way back. "How are you, sis?" I asked.

"It hurts a lot. I've been played for a fool. For two years. Everybody knew except me. It feels like a knife in my back."

"Yes," I said, "I understand."

"No, As, you don't. You could confront Jaap when he had an affair. You could shout at him, hit him. I can't do anything. Cor is gone, and I'm left behind with so much anger and incomprehension. I hold that against him the most. You have no idea how that feels."

When we got home, she went to bed. We heard her crying all night.

The next morning, she brought me toast and jam and sat down on my bed.

"As, I have been thinking carefully. I'm not going to have twenty-five years' worth of memories destroyed by what happened. It's the way it is, and I don't love him any less."

Part III
Hidden Agenda

2011–2013

A Plan Forms

2011

THE KIDNAPPING OF BEER TYCOON FREDDY HEINEKEN AND HIS DRIVER Ab Doderer in 1983 had established Wim's reputation as a ruthless criminal. The details of their brutal treatment shocked the world.

After his release in 1992, he became the menace of real estate tycoons. In the years that followed, a wave of contract killings hit the Amsterdam world of real estate and the criminal world. And every time, his name was mentioned as the contractor. Everybody was terrified of him. And we were more terrified than all of them, because we knew him best.

Cor's life had ended on January 24, 2003, on the cold cobbles of a street in Amstelveen. He had just had a meeting with his friend Robert ter Haak in a Chinese restaurant and was standing around talking when two men on a motorbike sprayed him with bullets.

Sonja and I didn't know who had fired those bullets at Cor, but we knew who his murderer was. There was no reason to assume that we wouldn't suffer the same fate, a fate Wim reminded us of constantly.

"You know what I'll do, right?" he would threaten us, whenever we tried to determine the course of our own lives.

Yes, we knew what he would do if we didn't obey him unconditionally. Everything in our relationship with Wim was determined by fear of his violence, so we lived by his rules. We walked on eggshells, did everything to prevent becoming his next victims, tried to survive our life with him, and above all, kept quiet.

But every day we felt like we were betraying Cor. We felt dirty for passing time with his killer. We desperately hoped that Wim would pay for what he had done to Cor and to us, but we didn't dare take action against him. We became more afraid as the killings continued. Murders of people who, like Cor, thought they were his friends.

Going to the police was not an option. If Wim were to find out that we had talked to the police, he would "immediately take care of this." And the risk that he would find out was enormous. He had often told me about his rats, corrupt contacts inside the police organization who informed him about investigations in which his name came up. No, he wouldn't hesitate one second to have us killed.

No one talked to the police about him and survived.

Wim's friend Willem Endstra, a real estate mogul, made as many as fourteen statements—in secret—in the back seat of a police car. They led to nothing, but Wim still found out.

Endstra was murdered.

The criminal Kees Houtman made confidential statements to the police. He was killed on the doorstep of his house.

No matter how we looked at the situation, we kept arriving at the same conclusion—if we took action against Wim, it would mean the end of our lives. All we could hope for was that the Justice Department would prosecute him one day. But Wim remained a free man, and even worse, he kept riding his Vespa, the "Holleeder scooter" as the media started calling it. He seemed untouchable.

It took until 2006 for him to be arrested. Not for the liquidations but "only" for extorting, assaulting, and threatening Willem

Endstra, Kees Houtman, and Thomas van der Bijl, another old friend of Wim's.

Wim had known Thomas for as long as he had known Cor. Thomas was more than a friend to Cor. He was like a brother, and because of that, he was part of the family. He was always there, at all the important family gatherings, and after every pivotal event— from the moment he gave his car to Cor and Wim to use as an escape vehicle after the Heineken kidnapping, up to carrying Cor's coffin at his funeral.

Thomas had been witness to all of Wim and Cor's crimes. He was always around during Cor's entire career in the underworld, and he helped him out on many occasions. He and one of Cor's family members dug up the Heineken ransom in Paris and exchanged the registered and marked money so it could be invested. He ran the affairs at the Achterdam and took care of cleaning the companies in Amsterdam's red-light district.

You could trust Thomas totally; he was as silent as the grave.

The last couple of years before Cor's death, their relationship suffered under increasing pressure. Cor had always been a heavy drinker, and two attempts on his life, and Wim's treason, he had become a serious alcoholic. His sunny character gave way to a grim side.

His old friends, Thomas, for instance, had known Cor from the time he didn't have a dime. His new friends knew only the Cor who always picked up the bill when he was drunk and threw money at people. Cor gave you money or he could make you some money, and certain people were drawn to that. And Cor let it happen, because paid friends don't walk away when you're drunk and obnoxious. It turned Cor into an intolerable person. He had his "friends" kiss his feet for a thousand guilders; they would stand in line.

Thomas couldn't tolerate that behavior, but Cor was not going to improve. He wanted to, but he couldn't, and shortly before Cor's death, Thomas had enough. Their twenty-year friendship cooled.

Throughout that friendship, Thomas had been there not only for Cor but also for Sonja. When Cor and Wim were arrested, Sonja didn't have a dime to spare. She had to scrape together the money for her visits to see Cor at Le Santé prison in Paris, and Thomas pitched in. She had barely enough money for gas, so Thomas would line her car up next to another one and siphon gas from that car into hers.

When Cor's life was in danger and his family needed to be extra careful, Thomas took Sonja to where Cor wanted to meet her and kept on doing it faithfully even after he fell out with Cor. Sonja hardly ever had a man in the house, because Cor was mostly out or in prison, or in hiding. And when Cor was there, his two left hands prevented him from even changing a light bulb. Thomas helped her out with household chores. He was always there for her.

Thomas didn't like Wim. And not because—as Wim always says—Cor went out with Thomas's sister Anneke when he was sixteen and left her for Sonja, Wim's sister. It was true that Cor betrayed Anneke with Sonja and Sonja with Anneke, until Sonja put an end to that by getting pregnant.

But all these shenanigans were going on when all three of them were still young. Sonja and Anneke would later spend time together as mothers at the school playground. Anneke would make pancakes when Francis played with her daughter Melanie during a lunch break at school. The women had long since normalized their relationship. There were no old wounds left, and it never was the reason Thomas didn't like Wim. Thomas didn't like Wim because of his character.

Wim, in turn, had never liked Thomas, either. Why? Maybe because Thomas had once driven Wim's then-girlfriend Beppie from

Amsterdam to Hotel Beauvais to visit Wim. Because Beppie had been in a car with Thomas for hours, Wim would later suggest that his daughter Evie wasn't his but Thomas's. I suspect that he didn't like Thomas because he doesn't like anyone.

But Thomas was sincere in his friendship for Cor right up until the very end. Even though he wasn't interested in shallow Cor, who drank, partied, and allowed people to live off him, he honored their friendship. So after Cor's murder, Thomas stood up for him and turned against the people he held responsible for his death. He directly accused Wim of murdering Cor.

Determined to get justice for his friend, Thomas, who never talked, started talking. Thomas understood the risk involved, but he thought he'd be safe, because at this point Wim was locked up, convicted for extortion. What he didn't know was that Wim had made arrangements for the liquidation before he went in. That's why Thomas was murdered on April 20, 2006. A man named Fred Ros was prosecuted and found guilty of Thomas's assassination.

No fewer than two of Wim's victims—Thomas van der Bijl and Willem Endstra—had predicted their own assassinations to the police. Both had pointed to the perpetrator while alive.

Nevertheless, the police were unable to gather enough evidence for the prosecution of one single liquidation.

Wim got off lightly: he was sentenced only for extortion and got a measly nine years.

For us, his detention didn't change a thing.

Wim was behind bars, but he still had an impressive network of connections of whom we were just as scared. We knew that the prison walls were no obstacle to him; Thomas van der Bijl's death had proved that.

To us, it was the ultimate demonstration of power, having somebody killed while being incarcerated in the most secure prison in the country. So we did what he wanted us to do: We lived by his rules. We were there for him twenty-four hours a day. We kept quiet. And every day we felt like we were betraying Cor.

From 2006 to 2011, we desperately hoped that the Justice Department would come up with enough evidence to prosecute Wim for Cor's death and for other liquidations. Some of the hit men were being prosecuted by this time, but not Wim. Nobody dared testify against him.

One of the contractors, Peter La Serpe, admitted to having killed Kees Houtman, together with Jessy Remmers. In return for the confession, the Justice Department agreed to give him a new identity and all necessary protection, but even he didn't dare make statements about Willem Holleeder in public. La Serpe had privately pointed to Willem as the commissioning party for the killing of Kees Houtman, but he demanded that this part of his statement be excluded from official testimony—for fear of his life and the lives of his family. Once again Wim got away with murder.

Then, in February 2011, Stanley Hillis was assassinated. He was Wim's partner in crime before he was locked up in 2006. Wim always spoke respectfully of the Old Guy, as he called him. He was only in awe of people who were even more ruthless than he was. Hillis was a powerful criminal with international connections, Wim was proud to tell others. He was big in Yugoslavia: he could arrange for a whole army of Yugoslavs and even owned a couple of tanks.

Wim talked to us about Hillis's involvement in extorting Endstra and his liquidation. Hillis was, according to Wim, the one who decided in a final meeting with Endstra that "he [Endstra] couldn't pay anymore." It meant that paying up wouldn't extend Endstra's life any longer: he would be assassinated. With Hillis free and doing Wim's dirty work, I resigned myself to the fact that testifying against Wim and surviving was out of the question.

But with Hillis's death, Wim had lost a powerful ally, someone that he could rely on while inside.

It was the first time Sonja and I seriously considered testifying against Willem.

If we wanted to act, I thought, we needed to do it before Wim's release in January 2012. At least now he was still in prison, and through information from criminal circles and my visits to him, I knew that his position in the criminal world had weakened considerably. As soon as he got out, though, he would be back at the top in no time and testifying would become impossible.

Sonja was receptive to my argument.

We decided to ask Peter de Vries for advice.

Sonja and I agreed that Peter—like nobody else—could assess the step we had in mind. As a crime journalist, he had solved several cases for which the Justice Department could not gather the evidence. He knew our whole family, he knew Wim's character, and he had been very good friends with Cor until Cor died.

After Cor's death in 2003, Peter was, unlike Cor's other so-called friends, the only one to take a permanent and unconditional interest in Cor's children. Peter was not interested in a friendship with Wim. So we would not have to be afraid of him telling Wim about our conversation.

Sonja and I had discussed all the risks we'd run if we shared what we knew with Peter. My only doubt was that he was, after all, a journalist. Had he not, despite his friendship with Cor, tracked down the co-kidnapper Frans Meijer? Maybe he would let the journalistic value of our story prevail over our friendship. That could jeopardize our lives. But Sonja didn't doubt Peter for one second.

"He would never do that, As. He would never betray us. He knows what Wim is like, and he knows what is at stake for us. Believe me, he won't."

"But what if he accidentally lets something slip? He won't mean any harm, but you know what Wim is like. Whether it's the neighbor, the baker, your best friend, or his worst enemy, he wins people over and extracts information from them, even their deepest secrets, without them realizing it. We can't take that risk."

"As, Peter is no fool. He's known Wim for more than twenty-five years, he knows what he's made of. It is time to start trusting someone," she said, "and I trust Peter fully."

"All right," I said, "I'm convinced. If you say it's okay, we'll do it." Still, I dreaded confiding in someone who was not a family member. Sonja and I had never spoken to an outsider about what we knew.

Sonja asked Peter to come to her house. We asked him to take a walk with us, because we didn't want to be recorded by wiretap.

"Peter," Sonja said, "can we tell you something without you repeating it? You cannot publish it, either, because you will put us in danger."

"Of course. If you don't want that, it stays between us," Peter said.

Sonja looked at me and said, "You tell him."

"Peter," I started, "we want to tell you that we've known for quite some time that Wim ordered Cor's assassination and that we can no longer live with that knowledge. We want Wim to pay for what he has done. We are planning to go to the Justice Department, before his release, hoping for him to get arrested for giving the order. We think he should be locked up for good. Cor is not his only victim. This man is a menace to society, and I'm afraid he'll start killing again after his release. That's why we want to make statements about everything we know, but we'd like your opinion first."

Peter was not surprised; rather, he seemed sad. He asked about details as if he hoped our stories were untrue, that we hadn't lived through all this. But when our answers and explanations made clear to him that this was our reality, he fell silent.

Peter thought our plan to go to the Justice Department was very dangerous. He was worried for us, and for Francis and Richie.

"Just look at Endstra, and Thomas," Peter said, "they didn't survive their talks with the Justice Department."

"But," I said to Peter, "that was when he was at the top of his game and he and Stanley were still out there. Now he's in jail and his network has all but disappeared. If we want to take action, it has to be now."

Peter had his doubts. "You don't know what he's still capable of," he said. "It's an enormous gamble, and you can't assess the risk."

I was disappointed, but I knew it was true. Telling our story would be suicide. The relief it would bring, finally telling the truth, would soon be outweighed by the fear and danger we'd have to live with.

I figured the subject was closed, but then Peter asked a question: "How can you prove he has shared this information with you?"

How could I prove it? What kind of question was that? Would I just make it up? Why would anyone not believe me? As if I would risk my life for nothing.

But Peter was right. Suppose I *did* tell everything I knew; it didn't guarantee that Wim would actually be convicted. Wim, a master performer, would simply deny what he had told me, and I wouldn't have a leg to stand on. If I was that afraid of him, why did I spend so much time with him? Why would he confide his criminal activity to his little sister, a woman, no less? He would do anything to distort the facts and make it seem as if I would benefit from him being wrongly sent to prison.

Peter was right again—I couldn't prove that Wim had confided in me about his crimes or that he told me that he ordered the various liquidations. Without that evidence, and with Wim's irresistible charm, no one would believe me. If, in the best case, they did believe me, the question of whether my declarations were seen as solid proof still remained.

Sonja accepted Peter's arguments immediately. "If Peter says so, we shouldn't do it. Peter is an expert. He knows Wim well and often cooperates with the police. I am glad we asked for his advice. We won't do it."

"Let the Justice Department handle it," Peter said.

But they couldn't "handle it" alone, not without more evidence. I decided to take matters into my own hands.

Wim had used me as his sounding board for years. I knew the ropes in criminal circles, and when I became a criminal lawyer, he started seeing my value to him. I was the ideal combination: someone with judicial knowledge who could think like a criminal. Plus, our family ties guaranteed him my unconditional loyalty and silence.

Over the years, I had developed from his annoying little sister into a full-fledged discussion partner. He had started sharing more and more with me.

I wasn't happy about this myself, but it was not up to me. I didn't decide on our relationship. Wim comes as he pleases and that's only if he can use you. Your needs don't count, and his do. That's why you can't get him out of your life. He decides when to meet, and you have to be available. If not, he comes looking for you and torpedoes your social life or job, so that you know you'd better be available next time. If you resist, he will turn on you: "If you're not with me, you're against me."

And then things will end badly for you.

So I couldn't avoid contact with him. To stay on his good side for as long as possible, and not become his adversary, I had accepted the position of confidante. He could rely on me; at least, it was imperative that he thought he could.

Wim would soon be let out of prison. With his release in sight, I decided to try to expand that position, hoping I would end up with enough evidence to put him behind bars. And, almost as if Cor was helping me, I soon got an opportunity to set my plan in motion.

At the end of 2011, during the lead-up to his release, an incident occurred between Wim and Dino Soerel, who was also being prosecuted for extorting Willem Endstra. Soerel claimed that Willem had misused him while extorting Endstra by falsely naming Soerel to Endstra, though he had had nothing to do with it. He wanted to call Willem as a witness, and he asked him, through his lawyer, if he was willing to do it.

Wim refused because he had not admitted to extorting Endstra and never would. In order to make Soerel's statements—that Wim had wrongly implicated him—seem untrustworthy, Wim put his own spin on the narrative: Soerel had forced Wim into making "false statements" under threat. He deliberately shouted this story over the prison phone to both his lawyer and to me. So the Justice Department knew his story, a story that would also be his alibi should Soerel testify against Wim. He knew that doing this wouldn't be looked upon favorably by the underworld, and, indeed, some of his criminal colleagues thought he was a back-stabber.

Wim could no longer trust his old friends, and I grabbed the opportunity to strengthen my role as a confidante. Friends come and go; family is forever. He needed me. And just as he had with Cor and his best friends, this time I also had my own hidden agenda.

The Release

2012

On Friday, January 27, 2012, I wait for Wim at the park and ride at the Arnhem exit, a place we agreed upon before his release from prison. Apart from Stijn Franken, his lawyer who would drive him here, nobody knew about this meeting. Stijn had arranged with the district attorney's office for Wim to leave the penitentiary a day early to keep him from being mobbed by the press, or worse. During his time in prison and his trial, he'd gotten so much publicity—books, articles, TV shows—that he'd become a celebrity, and he needed the extra security.

I've been waiting here for an hour when they drive up. Wim gets out and approaches me, brimming with energy. Happy as a child.

"Hi, sweet sister of mine," he shouts excitedly. We say goodbye to Stijn and I tell him to get in. "Is the car clean?" he asks.

"Of course it is." I've done as he taught me, arranging for a car that I know has no wiretap or tracking device.

I drive him to the location I've arranged for him, a chalet at a holiday resort some fifty miles from Amsterdam, rented in my mother's name.

During his second detention, which began in 2006, my brother developed a serious heart condition; he suffered from leaking heart valves. He barely survived heart failure, but as my mother used to say, a weed doesn't perish. Frankly, I was surprised he had a heart at all.

He claimed the doctors had given him no more than two years to live. The end of his life was near, and he threw himself into the role of feeble coronary patient until the last day of his detention. He denied himself everything, with a hardened discipline: he didn't use salt and stuck to his maximum intake of fluids, six cans of Diet Coke per day.

He should have gotten an award for his performance.

Within an hour of his release, he had ditched his diet. It was no longer relevant to his story or his privileges in prison.

On our way, we pass a McDonald's. I stop to let him enjoy a hamburger.

"Oh, this is great, Assie. I've really missed this," he says with a chuckle.

After we put his stuff away and he checks the location—and approves of it—we make an appointment with Peter R. de Vries, the crime reporter. Wim knows he would be hunted for comment and a first picture after being released. He wants to avoid this by giving a statement and a photo to the media now. Peter is the chosen one. This way, others will stop chasing after him and he can control the message. I wonder what he's planning.

We're supposed to meet Peter at the entrance of the forest, somewhere in Gooi. While we wait for him, Wim wants to be briefed on what has happened over the last couple of years. In the forest we can speak freely for the first time, without a guard behind a mirror recording everything. We're still alert to directional microphones, though, so we whisper. We discuss Wim's current position in the criminal world, every investigation he was involved in, his women, and the need to make money.

With each minute that passes, Wim gets crankier; it doesn't take long for his true personality to surface.

"Call Peter! Where is that son of a bitch? Who does he think he is to leave me waiting here? I gave him a scoop!" he rages.

I call Peter, who says he is on his way. He arrives within minutes, and Peter and I exchange greetings. I feel uncomfortable. Not long ago, I told Peter that I never wanted Wim to be released. Now here I am, Wim's confidante. Peter doesn't let on. He knows the danger I would be in if Wim knew how I really felt about him.

In his conversation with Peter, Wim focuses on his poor health. His heart will be functioning at only twenty-five percent, he says; he has a short life expectancy, and the doctors gave him two years to live five years ago. His heart will give out any day now. He shows Peter his collection of pills and tells him about his strict diet, explaining that he only eats what he cooks himself.

I have to hand it to him: it's a smart play. He wants his enemies to underestimate him. A sick old man, not worth spending money for a judicial inquiry or a liquidation.

Wim successfully pulls the wool over Peter's eyes—his specialty—and Peter leaves with the message that Wim wants published all over the media: he is not dangerous but terminally ill.

After the meeting with Peter, we go shopping in Naarden to supply the chalet. We deliberately choose an out-of-the-way town so as not to reveal his whereabouts.

His image has become iconic; he is recognized and spoken to wherever we go. He relishes the attention, and everybody seems to have forgotten why exactly he is so famous.

But I haven't.

Heading back to the chalet, I start talking indirectly—in case of wires in the car—about the liquidation, or assassination, of Stanley

Hillis. Wim turns to me and puts his finger to his lips. I stop talking. We're driving on a back road, and he says, "Pull over here."

I park the car in the emergency lane. "Get out," he says.

We walk a ways down the road before he stops me at a safe distance from the car. I know because he taught me: wires in a car can pick up sound from as far away as a hundred yards.

He stands in front of me, a savage look on his face. "We killed them all, all of them."

Then he turns around and walks back to the car.

Back at the chalet, we watch a couple of TV shows. He is particularly interested in *De Wereld Draait Door,* where Peter R. de Vries is talking about Wim's health. Wim's mission has succeeded: he has signaled that he is harmless.

"Now I'm free to speed things up again," he says.

It's late and Wim asks, "Are you sleeping over?"

"Thanks, but no," I say. "I'm going home."

"Nah, you're staying, aren't you? You're not leaving me here all alone," he asks in his familiar, coercive style that leaves you no choice. "You don't enjoy being here with me, do you? "Well, too bad, because I do like it. You can't leave."

That first night I stay over, reluctantly. I sleep on the couch, next to the sliding glass doors. Despite all the security measures I've taken, I'm still afraid we have been followed and that Wim's former criminal friends will riddle the chalet with bullets. In these peaceful, leafy surroundings, I see danger everywhere. I'm not scared of dying, but I refuse to die because of him.

That used to be different.

There was a time when I would have given my life for him.

After the Heineken kidnapping, when we were all treated as

pariahs, I totally believed in the us-against-the-rest-of-the-world myth of family loyalty he had taught us.

But once I found out that Wim was capable of killing his own family, I knew. The outside world wasn't our enemy. He was.

That night in the chalet I lie awake all night long. I am consumed by the thought that nobody knows where we were. That Wim is already asleep and unguarded, that I could get rid of all traces of DNA by torching the house.

That I have the chance to kill him now.

After that sleepless night, I drive home. Sonja is waiting for me.

I tell her that I almost killed our brother, but was too cowardly to do it.

"I'm glad you didn't do it, As," she says. "I don't want him to get off so lightly. That punishment would not be painful enough." Sonja wants him to spend the rest of his life in prison. That way, he would know how it felt to be betrayed, every day, the way he had betrayed her husband, his friend, Cor van Hout.

She is right, and I wish the same fate for Wim. "But that's only possible if we stand up against him and testify," I say.

"Right," she agrees.

"Then you know what will happen."

"Yes, I know," Sonja answers. "But maybe we should take that risk."

Dying I

2013

"THEY WANT TO TALK TO YOU. YOU CAN REACH THEM AT THIS NUMBER," Peter said, and he handed me the card of the Criminal Intelligence Unit (CIU).

I had known this was coming. I had asked Peter to contact the Justice Department on Sonja's and my behalf, to say we might be willing to speak with them. But when I looked at the number, I panicked. Only now did the reality sink in of what a meeting with representatives of the Justice Department would mean. I was gasping for air and tried to look relaxed in front of Peter.

"Thanks. I'll be in touch," I told him, and put the card in my pocket.

Once in the car, I entered the number in my phone under a different name and ate the card. I couldn't take any risks at all.

On my way home, my stomach was gripped by fear at the thought of calling this number. A deeply rooted, all-encompassing fear of Him—of Wim, of Willem Frederik Holleeder, alias the Nose. My brother.

One day after Wim's release, he and I were walking from the Scheldestraat to the Ferdinand Bolstraat. A man approached us, and while he looked at us, he put his hand in a small shoulder bag.

Instinctively and without speaking, we split up. Wim took one side of the street, I the other. Better not stay together when there is going to be a shooting. Better one get shot than both.

Our eyes were focused on that bag. We both scanned the carrier. Was he a hit man or not? Judging from his looks and movements, he could be; he fit the profile.

Over the years, you develop a sixth sense for this kind of thing. You learn how to judge not only how a person looks, but also the direction of a glance and the resoluteness of a walk.

The guy took his hand out of the bag. It was nothing. I started walking alongside Wim again.

"Nothing going on," he said.

"But better safe than sorry," I said.

We had discussed Wim's death before, when he developed his coronary problems. I had agreed with him that Sonja and I together with Sandra, Wim's girlfriend, would make the decision to pull the plug if he were reduced to a vegetable.

"Did you take care of it?" he asked from behind the glass when I visited him in the Scheveningen prison. "The three of you, right? Because I know what you're like, Assie. You'd pull a plug on me when you see one. Sonja can't decide anything, so Sandra will be decisive. She loves me the most."

He had talked with us repeatedly about not wanting to become a vegetable, but had never mentioned the possibility of death by assassination. His whole life, plus ours, was geared to that, but it was never discussed. After Endstra's extortion and before he was arrested, I finally brought it up.

"Are you after my money? Is that it? Are you having me whacked?"

He had that familiar black gleam in his eyes, and I saw that he meant what he said. I ended the discussion because I didn't want to risk him really thinking that.

On that day when we were walking on the Scheldestraat, I tried again. I wanted to know how somebody who decides so easily about the lives of others thinks about death himself.

"Are you not afraid to die?" I asked.

"No," said Wim. "I've been there, when my heart stopped. I got a little dizzy and suddenly I was walking down the street toward a white light. It was pretty relaxed, kind of nice, really. I felt okay and then I heard Sonja crying out, 'Wim, come back, come back, Wim, come here!' She winked at me, beckoning me over. I walked up to Sonja and I stayed alive.

"So, no," he continued. "I'm not afraid to die. You don't realize when it happens, and you don't really feel anything."

What he told me was in contrast to the psychological and psychiatric reports in which he admitted being afraid of dying in prison. That he wanted to be with his family so badly, to be able to cope with his brief life expectancy.

When I confronted him about this, he said, "I just did that to be a bit more comfortable inside. Those reports came in really handy in that respect."

So, he didn't fear the prospect of death. "Being locked up is worse," he said.

Well, this would have to be it, then, I thought. I couldn't be weak. I had to "strike first in the dark," for Francis, for Richie, for Cor.

To really punish Wim, we had to put him behind bars. Permanently. The solution of the criminal world—liquidation—was out of the question. Sonja didn't see that as punishment, didn't think he should get off that easy, and I took her point.

"Let him suffer, too, the way we've been suffering for years," she said.

It was torture to think that he might get away with everything, throw his arms in the air, pull a sorry face, and cry out, "But I always get the blame! Whenever there is an execution it's always me who did it!"

"He's good at that," Sonja said. "Acting pitiful. You know what is a pity? That Cor spent his last seconds on the cold cobbles. *That* is pitiful. That my kids don't have a father, *that's* pitiful. He shouldn't get away with acting all pitiful about Cor. Let everybody know what he is really like. I want to tell the truth, finally."

For years he had pulled the wool over everyone's eyes with his sanctimonious behavior. All for the benefit of his ego.

Dying like a godfather would just add to the Wim myth. I agreed with her, but I had a hard time thinking of Wim spending every day in a cell. If he ended up bleeding on the cold cobbles like Cor, we would never have to look over our shoulders again.

"He has always said that if he gets a life sentence, he will kill himself," said Sonja. "Let him do his thing, just as long as he dies knowing that we got our revenge for Cor's death."

It was simple. To fight Wim the way Sonja wanted to, we needed the Justice Department. I had to put aside my feelings and look at it more practically.

This was why I had turned to Peter R. de Vries, who had initially advised us against talking to the CIU, and asked him to pave the way for a talk.

I stared at the number Peter had given me.

Calling for an appointment meant that I would be confirming what he had told the CIU about Sonja and me during his pre-interview. Calling meant that I might be willing to testify against Wim. Calling meant that at least one detective would know and could tell my brother.

I couldn't prevent him from finding out that I had talked to the Justice Department. It was best to assume it would happen and to give him a plausible reason for my contacting them. That's why I had told him beforehand that I had a good relationship with one CIU officer. It was an alibi I had created soon after his release, when I told him that I would talk to this officer for his benefit.

"Comes in handy, doesn't it?" I said, exactly what he wanted to hear.

"Always, Assie," he said.

My work as a lawyer in criminal cases made it plausible for me to have such a contact, and he swallowed my story. Should the Justice Department leak that I had contacted them, this would be my alibi: "You knew I was talking to the CIU. But I do it just for you."

It was the best I could do to protect myself against corrupt detectives, but it was still a risk.

The next day I made an appointment.

The Meeting

On January 21, 2013, I nervously called the number. A female voice said, "Michelle speaking."

"Hello, Peter R. de Vries gave me your number, and I would like to make an appointment," I said.

She immediately knew who I was and asked if I could meet tomorrow.

"Yes, I can," I said.

She said they would call me back about the exact time.

I said, "Could you please text me? I'd rather not speak over the phone."

They sent me a time and location around midday: six p.m., Newport Hotel, Amstelveen.

The meeting was set.

That same afternoon, I drove to Sonja's to tell her. "You really made an appointment?"

"Yes," I said, "I no longer see any other option. I'll just go and see what happens."

"Shall I come with you?"

"No, let's wait and see. They are cops, after all. It's best if they haven't seen you yet. That way they can never say you were involved in this. Also, you can't account for where you are. If he calls and you can't be reached, he will start thinking all that crazy stuff again. He's used to that with me, but he will mistrust you. So I'll just go on my own."

On my way to meet the CIU, I checked my mirrors constantly to see that I wasn't followed. I had taken a different car because if Wim saw my car, he'd wonder why I was at that hotel.

I was nervous. He used hotels as meeting places. He could just as likely be there, too, and I'd run into him. Or he would just sidle up to me suddenly, as he often did. I never knew how he tracked me down, and it always gave me the shivers.

I got a message on my phone. "Hi, please let us know when you're there. We'll pick you up in the lobby."

I arrived at a big, majestic hotel not far from the place Cor was killed. I entered the garage and parked my car. I had to collect all my courage to climb the steps to the entrance, but I gained strength from the knowledge that we were doing this for Cor.

I went in and was startled. It was a terribly complex space with niches everywhere, many entrances and exits. If he was here, or if he came in, I would never be able to notice. What a crap location and a bad start: I immediately regretted accepting this meeting. If this was the way they handled my anonymity, I couldn't expect much good to come of it.

I sat down in the lobby. Every second there, my feeling of unrest grew. I had taken a big enough risk just showing up—I couldn't wait around for them. I was just getting up to leave when a blond woman approached me.

"Astrid?" I nodded. "I'm Michelle, we spoke on the phone."

She was clearly with the police; she looked sprightly and had a clear gaze. Not a rat, from the look of it. I instantly decided to go with her. Silently we walked to the elevator and got in. The doors closed. The walls started closing in on me. I was short of breath and sweating.

We stood there uncomfortably.

"So good of you to come," Michelle said, trying to break the ice.

I nodded politely, but it certainly didn't feel good. In our family, it's seen as a disgrace to talk to the Justice Department. It goes against all our principles. We are not "traitors."

This was bred into us by my mother. The Germans had taken her father during the war. My father's father had been "a dirty collaborator," my mother used to whisper so my father couldn't hear her.

At the same time, I knew I wouldn't be here if Wim hadn't forced me into this situation, and I held on to my motives.

"You are hard to reach, aren't you?" Michelle tried, to keep the conversation going. "We've been trying privately and at work, but we just couldn't get through."

"That's possible. I am not keen on people I don't know," I replied curtly.

It was true. With a family like mine, I can't afford to have strangers contacting me. I never know their motives. It could be the press looking for a juicy story, a police informant who wants to infiltrate the family, my brother's colleagues who are looking for him, or even enemies who want to get at him through me. I do everything not to be available to these people, because it's never about me.

"My secretary submits every request for contact to me. I never meet with strangers, and my private life is restricted to my family," I added, in an attempt to be a bit more accessible. I realized that since her first question, I'd been avoiding real contact.

But I didn't come to play games. I was in this elevator for a reason, I reminded myself. Don't choke now. I needed to break the silence, for Cor.

The elevator stopped on the second floor and the doors opened. I walked with her, and Michelle knocked on a hotel room door. Again, I was afraid I might see a familiar face. What if I were to meet the rat Wim got his information from? What if this person was tempted to mention at the dinner table or in a bar that he or she had met with "his sister"?

All these thoughts raced through my head just before the door opened.

A tall, redheaded young woman asked me to come in. Thank God she didn't look familiar, and her accent betrayed she was from out of town. She wasn't someone who'd be in contact with Wim. She was too ordinary.

She extended her hand. "I'm Manon. Good of you to come," she said, but she didn't reassure me. My God, what was I doing here? I totally froze, and the thought that I was breaking Wim's rule to never speak with the police grabbed me by the throat. I felt I would suffocate.

"Would you like a drink?" the woman asked.

"Some water, please," I replied.

I could feel that my mouth was dry from the tension, and I was breathing irregularly and superficially. I wanted to let go of my thoughts, but I was flooded by negative experiences with the Justice Department that had fed my suspicions against them. My family's potential reactions to my decision to even talk with them ran through my mind.

"You think the department will believe what our family relations are really like? They have a whole different outlook. They see us as a secluded mobster family. They might think that Wim sent you, to play a game. And if they do want to believe you, you will only be used by them. Look at how they set up Thomas van der Bijl. He testified against Wim, they offered him no protection whatsoever, and he was killed not long afterward. Or say you succeed, and he goes to prison for good? Then what? You know he will have you assassinated if you talk, no matter what. And will they protect you? The Justice Department is just as bad as Wim. Why would you do it? We are scum to them. They'll do nothing for you. They'll think of you in the same way they think of Thomas's wife, Caroline van der Bijl. Her husband risked his life and died for testifying against Wim, but when they speak of her, the DA calls her 'that whore from Gelderse Kade.' Do you think they see you differently because you are a lawyer? You are a Holleeder!"

They were right. Since the Heineken kidnapping, the surname Holleeder automatically reminded everybody of Wim, and, worse, people thought I was just like him.

The Justice Department had included me, along with the rest of my family, in his posse and in the criminal world. I was included in every investigation into Wim or Cor. They bugged my phone, raided my house, and confiscated my stuff.

"Good of you to come," Manon said once more, interrupting my train of thought. "We heard there is a threat, is that correct?"

"Yes, it is—there is a threat." I pulled myself together. "But that's not why I'm here. The problem is not the threat; it's the cause."

I was laughing internally. These people really had no idea what our lives were like. We had been living with threat for so long, we didn't know any better. We were not about to whine about that.

"The cause?" asked Michelle.

"Yes, the cause. My brother."

"Your brother? Which one? You have two, right?"

"I mean Wim," I said. "You know who I'm talking about, right?" Yes, they sure did, and so we arrived at the subject we were all there for. I was about to put right the distorted image of our family. "If my brother didn't always cause so much misery, we wouldn't have a problem. But he keeps on going. And it's only natural that there will be retribution."

"It must be really hard on you," said Michelle, but I could read on her face what she really thought: You have always backed your brother and now that he's bothering you, you come here complaining?

But she was wrong about that. Wim had been a problem ever since I could remember, but we could handle it. We always solved our problems our own way, and didn't need the Justice Department to do it for us. In fact, interference by them would only make things worse. I didn't want anything from them; on the contrary, I came to give the Justice Department something. All they had to do was their job as an investigation service.

"We are used to it, but it's about time it stopped. This man is a permanent menace to the public order."

Before I continued, I brought up their responsibility to me. "I'm taking a huge risk by talking to you. You should know that if my brother finds out, it could only have come from you. If this conversation is leaked in some way, I won't survive that. My brother knows what I know of him and about him, and he will not hesitate to have me assassinated."

I noticed they didn't take my words very seriously. I was his sister, right? The only image they had of life in the underworld was apparently based on what they saw in mobster films like *The Godfather*. Films where the paterfamilias could never muster any love or compassion for anybody except his own family.

But our life was no Godfather movie, no romantic portrait of a criminal family; it was a harsh reality in which one person made life miserable for the rest. If they couldn't see that, I would not continue talking. The conversation would end.

"No," they hurriedly said, "we fully understand. You really don't have to worry. Apart from the district attorney Betty Wind, nobody knows about this meeting, and no one will ever know."

"I certainly hope so," I said, "because my life would be at risk. Everything is different from what you think. To us, but also to everybody else, not being in his good graces means that you are against him. And if you are against him, you know what will happen. Wim makes no exceptions because we happen to be family. On the contrary, because we are, he expects more than unconditional loyalty. But our supposed loyalty is not based on love; it is forced by pure fear. That loyalty is always focused on him, it's never mutual—he betrays us whenever he sees fit."

I explained that people always thought of us as one big happy family with Wim at its center and assumed that we shared the same values and principles, but that the reality was totally different and that all the other family members thought the same thing: namely, that Wim was a monster.

The women were surprised. They hadn't pictured our "close family" this way. But they wanted to move on. They had understood that I was also able to testify about the crimes he had committed, and they asked if I could tell them about those. I could, but I wouldn't—not at this point. I first wanted to see what kind of people I was dealing with.

I had planned, in this first meeting, to give them insight into my family relations but not give them anything substantial about any criminal activities. Should there be a leak, they could only leak that

I thought he was a psychopath and an asshole to the family. I could always say they were lies meant to pit us against each other. But if I gave information about one of the liquidations, he'd know that came straight from me.

But maybe I could give them some idea about what subjects I could discuss, they suggested.

"I can say that we're talking about very serious matters," I answered.

Maybe I could talk about those matters next time?

"Maybe," I said. "First I have to talk with my sister. If she won't testify, I won't either."

They said they would like to meet me again, and that in the meantime they would talk to their superior.

As the meeting came to an end, I felt relieved. I had finally shared the truth about my family, that we weren't Wim's extensions and that we could think and judge for ourselves, albeit not openly. But that sense of relief disappeared almost immediately once I set one foot outside that room and reality closed in on me again. My reality, ruled by him. Ruled by fear about what I had just done—I had broken his iron law. My stomach turned. I ran down the stairs and threw up in the ladies' room.

I was never going to do this again. I was never going to snitch again.

I got in my car and drove directly to Sonja's to tell her about my conversation. She was waiting for me at the door.

"Jeez, look at you! You're as white as a sheet! What happened? Was it that bad? Any rats there?"

"No, nothing bad, it's all right. I'm just so nauseous. I threw up. I don't feel well. It'll pass," I said.

"It's because you talked."

"Yes," I said, "*that* was hard."

"You think they were rats?"

"I don't think so. You never know, of course. But I didn't tell them anything important, anything that would indicate to Wim that I'd talked about him."

"Good," Sonja said. "What did you tell them?"

"That we no longer want to pay for the suffering he causes. And a bit about what he's made of and that we are not one big happy family."

"What was their reaction?"

"I got the impression that they were surprised."

"What now?"

"Now I'm scared to death that he's going to find out," I answered.

"That's not what I mean."

"They want another meeting. Obviously they want to hear what I have to say in order to see if they can use it. But I'm only up for it if you are. If not, it's no use."

"I understand. I really want to, As. But the kids..."

"But they are already in danger. I don't know, I have to let it sink in a bit."

"Why don't you go lie down," Sonja suggested.

"No, I have to get back in case he comes over. If I'm not there, he'll start looking for me. It's best if I'm available."

"Okay. I love you."

"I love you too, sis."

I got in my car, drove home, and got into bed.

That night, the bell rang. It was Wim. And if he was down there, it meant that I had to go down, because we didn't talk inside. Oh, no, I thought. Was he here because he already knew? He must be!

"Hurry up!" he said. Once again, things weren't going fast enough for him. Things never do.

"I'll be right down," I cried out.

I felt caught, insecure, convinced he had found out. And if he hadn't yet, I was still afraid I would betray what I had done. I felt weak. But I knew I had to pretend nothing was going on so as not to arouse his suspicion. There was no room for weakness.

Before I went down, I quickly checked the mirror to see if he could read from my face what I had done. I had to control my nerves, because otherwise he would see that something was going on and would make sure to find out what had led to my strange behavior. He knew me inside out. Okay, the last step: straight face, and go!

"Hey, sweet brother of mine," I said as naturally as possible.

We walked the steps toward Deurlostraat until he judged it safe to talk.

"Any news?" he asked.

Any news? It was the line practically all of our conversations started with; he was always looking for information about him or others that he could use. Possessing information about his associates, the Justice Department, and his victims is his strength. He makes it his business to know all there is to know, preferably about one of his enemies.

I was used to the question.

But this time it sounded different to my ears. It was as if he had asked, Shouldn't you tell me that you spoke to the cops?

In the second that followed, I felt as if all my blood was draining from my body. I got dizzy and thought I was falling over. I had to keep thinking, this is anxiety, anxiety because of the realization of what I have done. But, I told myself, he knows nothing. He can't know. Come on, As, get a grip.

"No, no news," I answered. "All quiet on your end?"

"Yeah, but always sharp, you know?"

He told me he had spent the whole evening with a former enemy, which meant that that enemy had started to confide in him again, so he had nothing to fear.

He still trusted me with his position. Thank God—that meant he wasn't onto me. As long as he shared his life with me, I knew I was on his good side. We discussed his night a bit longer, he had to go somewhere else, and we said goodbye.

When I got home, a huge feeling of guilt overwhelmed me. I was betraying my own brother. My brother who confided in me and who had no idea he was walking with me toward his downfall.

In the mirror, I saw tears running down my cheeks. "I hate you!" I screamed at my own image. "You're just as bad as him!"

I didn't know what was worse: hating him for what he had done, or hating myself for handing him over to the Justice Department.

I felt the veins in my brain compress and a huge migraine kick in, which put an end to my thoughts.

Until the next morning. When it started again.

The bell rang. Wim again.

"Assie, are you coming out to play?" he shouted up. Oh, no—now he was trying to be funny. What was happening here? He's never funny. He was onto me. He had to be.

"Shhh," I hissed. "Think of the neighbors. It's seven a.m.!"

I didn't have time to dress properly, so I grabbed yesterday's clothes and went down. I didn't want to keep him waiting, and I wanted to know why he was so jolly.

It was a terrible idea of mine, that meeting. I felt a deep regret. From now on, I would have to live with the fear that someday he would find out.

Why in God's name did I want them to know what he was really like? What did I gain from it? As if these people could help us. I had given them a show, and they had briefly enjoyed our misery.

I felt awful.

"You should see Sonja," he said.

"Okay," I said.

"Tell her to come to Gelderlandplein, at eleven a.m. I need her there for a moment."

"All right, I'll see to it," I said. And I thought, Thank God, he still needs me; he knows nothing.

"I have to get out of town now. Take care of it. She has to be there. And don't call."

"Okay, no problem," I said.

I got in my car and drove to Sonja's. I let myself in and called her by the nickname Cor had given her, because of her kickboxing. "Boxer, where are you?"

"I'm still in bed," she called.

I went to her. "You have to do something for him."

"No," she said. "I'm not doing anything for him anymore. Nothing good comes of it."

"Are you going to tell him that yourself, Boxer? Because I won't. Here, call him."

I threw my cell phone on her bed. It was seven thirty in the morning, I had just had a giant migraine attack, and Boxer knew as well as I did that if she wasn't at Gelderlandplein by eleven, all hell would break loose. She would break a pattern and he'd get suspicious. Because I told him I'd take care of it, his anger would be directed at me, too, and I didn't need that right now.

"Boxer, I just spoke to the cops. Now is not the time to act all smart against him. Let's not deviate from the regular pattern. We've done enough of that—I can't take any more. So do what you normally would."

She saw I was very tense. "Okay, I'll go. Tell me about yesterday. How was it?"

"Well," I said, "very scary. He's been at my door twice since. I'm afraid he knows."

"Knows, silly, how?"

"You never know with him, do you? The cops were two young and pretty women—for all I know they could have been rats, some women he met in a bar. I don't know, I'm just rambling. I'm scared. I immediately got a migraine yesterday. I feel like I'm seeing ghosts."

Sonja tried to calm me down. "He can't know, at least not yet. Do you honestly believe he could have slept with one of them already?"

"Well, it's possible, right?" I said. "He fucks everybody he can use, doesn't he?"

"No," she said, "he really can't know yet."

"That's what you say. But the appointment was made one day in advance, and what if these girls put it in their agendas for everyone to see? Box, I swear to you, I have regrets, you don't want to know. What have I done? He's going to kill me!"

"Take it easy, As. There's nothing going on. He still has you do things, so don't worry."

"If he finds out, I'll be dead. I'm never doing this again. I won't talk to them anymore."

Lawyer

1995

MY RELATIONSHIP WITH THE JUSTICE DEPARTMENT WENT BACK DECADES and was extremely troubled. I had good reason to distrust these people and to fear putting my life in their hands.

In 1988, I went back to university. I studied philosophy at first, but that didn't work. I didn't understand the university system, and I didn't know anyone who had experience with it. I couldn't even find the lecture hall, and when I finally did, I didn't understand my classes. What were these people talking about? I felt I lacked the kind of intellect necessary for keeping up with this level of thought. I quit and started studying law.

I was convinced this had nothing to do with my family and the events surrounding the Heineken kidnapping but rather with the subjects I had studied in high school. I convinced myself that I would have gotten my degree in a language or in history if that could have paid the bills. Since Jaap hadn't proved to be a steady breadwinner, being able to make money myself was essential to me.

I graduated in 1995; by then, my background was proving to be somewhat problematic. It occurred to me that the positions I'd aspired to originally—public prosecutor or judge—were beyond my reach because of my family background, so I decided to become a lawyer.

Through Wim's intercession, Bram Moszkowicz wanted to give me a chance by acting as my patron, and the wonderful Bob Meijer fortunately was unprejudiced and offered me office space. With this I'd met the final conditions that enabled me to be sworn in as a lawyer.

I invited Sonja, Gerard, and my mother to the swearing-in ceremony. My mother was proud of her daughter: I seemed to prove to her that it hadn't been her fault that her son had committed a serious crime. She had another child on the right side of the law. I guess I restored the balance between good and evil within her family, and I was happy I could make her feel that way.

Rather naively, I also invited Cor and Wim to attend the ceremony. They'd served their time, and I didn't want to cut them off because of their past. After the ceremony, we'd celebrate with drinks and snacks at my new office.

The day before the swearing-in, I still hadn't received any information on the location and time. I felt uneasy and started calling to find out what was going on.

I was put through to a woman at the Amsterdam Prosecution Office. "You won't be sworn in tomorrow, ma'am. The Justice Department has objected to your joining the legal profession."

"What for?" I asked.

"Because you were a suspect in the kidnapping of Mr. Heineken." I was flabbergasted. I asked if they might be mistaken and were confusing me with my brother. "I am A. A. Holleeder. I think you got me mixed up with W. F. Holleeder," I said.

"No, ma'am, you were a suspect in this case, and the public

prosecutor Mr. Teeven wants to go through the entire file before you can be sworn in. So tomorrow is off."

She hung up. I felt dizzy. What was this? Never in my life had I ever been so much as fined. I was the mother of two children, I worked my ass off, I got an education to advance in life, and now the Justice Department was preventing me from working as a lawyer because I was related to one of the Heineken kidnappers?

This was the same judiciary that had barged into my bedroom twelve years ago, pointed machine guns at my head, dragged me from my bed, thrown me to the floor, put a foot on my neck, and locked me up in a prison cell. The same judiciary that had taken away my privacy, that had followed and monitored me. Was it all starting again, all because of a crime I had had nothing to do with? Was this their revenge for my not ditching Wim and Cor? Never had I imagined I could be condemned this way by the very top of this same judiciary, led by people with university educations, so-called enlightened people.

I didn't feel like associating with them any longer, but I'd invested all my money into setting up my office. I had made financial commitments, such as renting my office space, and I'd just found out that Jaap had another woman on the side.

I had to move on.

I called Bram, and he advised me to get in touch with the dean, Mr. Hamming. He turned out to be out of the office, and his substitute didn't want to be involved in a matter concerning this specific last name. The substitute told me to wait for Mr. Hamming's return.

The day went by and nothing happened. I assumed I wasn't going to be sworn in, and I was glad I had at least found out in time so

I didn't have to make a fool of myself as the only one out of twenty candidates who couldn't take the oath.

I'd already resigned myself to that when the phone rang. "Miss Holleeder?" a voice said.

"Yes," I said.

"This is Mr. Hamming. Your swearing-in will proceed." Then he hung up.

At the swearing-in ceremony, he shook my hand and said, "All the best!" with a rather obvious wink.

This gave me just that bit of hope that there were people who could look past the stigma, people who judged me for who I was, not for what my brother and brother-in-law had done. But it was also clear to me that there were those at the Justice Department who'd never be prepared to do so.

In the summer of 1996, I was at work when my babysitter called to tell me ten detectives, a prosecutor, and a supervisory judge had searched my entire home and taken Miljuschka's collection of Disney videotapes. The babysitter was just a sixteen-year-old girl, and at that moment she was with my eleven-year-old daughter—they had forbidden her to call me.

Two children, exposed to powerful people who forced their way in uninvited and turned the entire house upside down in their presence, and they hadn't even had the decency to inform me so I could have come home to reassure the frightened kids. I inquired, but I was never given any explanation for this search and what investigation it was associated with.

I found out later that they were looking for videotapes featuring a prosecutor, presumably recorded at Cor, Robbie, and Wim's sex club, the same one Jaap ran.

The prosecutor who came to my house, Mr. Teeven, the same person who had obstructed my swearing-in, had bought this story about the videotapes from a prostitute called Emma, in exchange for a generous amount of money as well as immunity from prosecution for a number of ram raids committed by her and her boyfriend. The tapes had supposedly been recorded by Cor and stored inside my house.

Teeven was so keen to clear up this oversexed prosecutor's actions that he'd bought some cock-and-bull story from the prostitute and was now hitting a wall. It all turned out to be a lie, but in the meantime, my privacy had been invaded unjustly, and my babysitter and child had been terrorized in the name of justice.

I didn't get so much as an apology.

This was the third time I'd been pestered by the Justice Department.

And it didn't end there.

Starting from that same year, 2005, several people told me they'd been approached by the Justice Department requesting information about me. The department was determined to expel me from the lawyers' register, because "such a person surely shouldn't be a lawyer." *Such a person?* As a lawyer, I took on assigned cases exclusively; I never took on any case with the slightest connection to my brother. I was completely transparent.

Who was behind this witch hunt?

There was yet more to come. On July 3, 2007, my secretary called. "Supervisory judge P. M. is on the phone. He needs you to come over."

Come over? I didn't understand. I hadn't overlooked a witness hearing today, had I?

"Put me through," I said.

"Good morning, Miss Holleeder. We are at your house," I heard P. M. say.

"My house?"

"Could you please come by? We want to search your house," he continued.

What was going on now? Wim was locked up, so it couldn't be about him. I settled some things at work and drove home, where about six men stood waiting outside, the supervisory judge included.

"Could you please let us in?" he asked.

"What is this about?"

"You've been designated as a suspect in the laundering of the Heineken ransom."

Was this some kind of joke? The Heineken kidnapping, again! I was seventeen years old when that took place, I didn't have any involvement in it, and yet twelve years later they refused to swear me in, and now *twenty-five* years later they're on my doorstep, blaming me for laundering the ransom?

"Are you dealing with the rest of my family as well?" I asked. Whenever they bothered one of us, they usually did the same to the others. I felt bad for my mother; she'd been through these judge-approved burglaries so often.

"No, not with your mother or sister."

"So, this is about my brother again?" I asked.

"No, your brother is not a suspect," the supervisory judge answered.

Now I was really confused.

"Is there something you'd like to tell me?" P. M. asked.

"I'm claiming my right to remain silent," I replied. Forget it, I thought. As if I'd want to tell you anything. About what? About six men going through my underwear, touching my things, violating my privacy? No, I had nothing to say.

★ ★ ★

All the Justice Department had ever done was get me into trouble
and cause misery. Why would I let them into my personal life, a
personal life they'd tried to destroy? How could I know they weren't
plotting against me? So far, they hadn't given me a single reason to
trust them. On the contrary, I trusted them as little as I trusted my
brother.

Francis and Wim

2013

W IM HAD ALREADY CALLED ME EARLY IN THE MORNING, BUT I'D BEEN busy at work. When I got home that night, he was standing at my door. "Come down for a minute," he commanded.

What was it this time? I walked down. He stood waiting beside his scooter. He had a gloomy look on his face, and as soon as I got to him, he fired away.

"I was with Sonja and I asked her, 'How is Franny?' because I already knew Franny's baby had been born, and I wanted to see what she'd say. She says, 'She's had a baby girl' and that I can drop by next week when she's rested. Assie, that's disrespectful, saying, 'You can drop by next week.' Ya know, As, there's just no respect. Who the hell do they think they are!'"

He was mad. Mad at Sonja and at Francis, the niece he thought he had once been so close with. Now Francis was an adult, having children of her own, and Wim felt like he barely knew her.

After Wim's arrest, when Francis was still a baby, she would kiss his photo every day, and every week she went with her mother and grandmother to visit him in La Santé Prison in Paris. They'd leave at two thirty in the morning to get to La Santé in time to step into the visitors' line that formed along one of the prison walls at eight. Outside. There was no shelter from rain, wind, snow, heat, or cold.

The guards opened the gate at noon and the first in line were let inside. The gate closed at one p.m., and if you hadn't gotten in by that time, you couldn't visit and had to leave. Being at the front of the line was essential. Inside the gate, a medieval staircase led up to the visitors' area: chilly, tiny spaces of hardly four square feet, with a glass pane keeping visitors and prisoners apart. Touching was not allowed.

Sonja and Francis visited Cor; my mother, Wim. Swapping during the visit was forbidden. But sometimes when Wim and Cor's visiting cells were next to each other and the guard wasn't paying attention for a second, Sonja and Francis would quickly swap places with my mom and see Wim.

Later on, when Cor and Wim were put up in a hotel pending their extradition process, their wives could stay with them and Francis came along, too. In the Netherlands she also went to visit her uncly—as she used to call Wim. From when she was ten months old until she was nine, she always came along to visit him, and after his release, she'd meet her uncle at her dad's house.

But as the years went on, Wim stopped coming over.

Children are of interest to Wim as long as he can use them to make other adults vulnerable. If he wants something from an adult, he'll be great with their kids. Once he was in, he would use the child as leverage to get his way. One moment, people would be moved by the way he was playing with the kids, and the next he threatened to kill them if Daddy or Mommy wouldn't live up to his demands.

We tried to keep our children as far away from him as possible, which generally worked pretty well, because personally he didn't give a rat's ass about them. As soon as he began taking an interest in one of them, we knew it meant trouble.

Wim told me someone outside the family had told him Francis

had given birth, and he wanted to know why we hadn't told him and why he hadn't been invited to come see the baby. He himself knew the answer to this question—Francis was terrified of him.

Sonja and I never actually told Francis and Richie what Wim had done to their father. It would have been life-threatening knowledge, as Wim thinks that children who know about "it" can't be allowed to grow up, "for they might take revenge."

Francis did know, though. She was nineteen when Cor died, and had witnessed countless traumatic incidents both before and after his death.

When she was at the swimming pool with her dad and she counted the scars from the bullet wounds, marks of the first attempts on his life, he'd always tell her, "Your uncly did that. Your uncly is a Judas."

After the second attack, she'd heard Cor shouting that Wim was behind it.

Immediately after her father's death, we warned her never to trust Wim, to watch out for him, never to go with him for anything, and to keep Richie away from him. We didn't tell her why, but she understood full well what we meant.

For a while Wim had seen Francis as a way to Cor's money. When that failed, he soon dropped her.

Now all of a sudden he showed interest in her again.

According to Wim, Francis had told one of his girlfriends that he'd "iced her dad."

I tried to get him to change his mind. Surely he knew we were too scared to say anything about him. That's why I couldn't believe Francis had actually said this.

But he knew for sure.

"Assie, you listen to me. You gotta talk to her. One million percent: the person who told me about it doesn't lie."

"Wim, she had a few drinks that night, she got emotional." That didn't make any difference to him.

"So she said it drunk. And I get to deal with the shit? I can't have that, Assie."

How could Francis have been this stupid? We've always warned our children: Don't drink alcohol. People who drink loosen up and don't know what they're saying. Don't talk to people who know Wim; they will pass everything on. She'd been brought up on this doctrine, and now the worst had happened anyway.

To Wim, Francis's statements had changed her into a threat he'd have to control. If the authorities got wind of it, they might use her to testify against him.

I was told to pass on to Francis that if she "snitched on him," he would "snitch on her mom." If Francis's blabbing led to his conviction for Cor's murder, he'd tell them Sonja had ordered him to do it and Francis would lose her mom. "Go tell her! She'd better know what she's doing!"

He wasn't done yet, though, for, naturally, Sonja too was accountable for what Francis had said and she'd have to pay for it.

"I don't care about seeing the baby, but see, you don't talk to me that way, I'm not a fucking retard. And you know what happens, As: I'll get angry. And if I get angry, I can't be nice no more, and you'll have to pay up."

The mealymouthed way he threatened them made me sick to my stomach: *I'll get angry. And if I get angry, I can't be nice.*

It all sounds so childish, as if he's a harmless four-year-old, acting from his primary emotions. A four-year-old will get angry and doesn't think you're nice anymore. Wim makes himself seem small and harmless by imitating the emotional development of a preschooler. But he is far from harmless.

He knows it, we know it, and our background knowledge of

what he has done adds a deadly edge to his words, so we know what the consequences will be if we do not comply without him even having to tell us.

The threat is followed by the extortion, which he presents as well-intentioned advice from an experienced mature man to his younger sister.

"You know what it is, As—it's all about goodwill. But if there's no goodwill, she's got nothing left, and she'll just be a victim and she'll have no right to anything. It's just a matter of goodwill, and she should respect it. She doesn't, so you get the right to nothing."

I must admit, he's a magician with words. He says everything without saying a thing. You're able to understand and interpret his words only when you know his history. What he's saying here is that he determines whether Sonja will get anything—Cor's estate, the proceeds from the movie based on the book *The Kidnapping of Alfred Heineken*, written by Peter de Vries (based on interviews with Cor).

She can have what was her husband's as long as Wim grants it to her. As long as she does everything he wants, the way he wants it. He is goodwill personified.

"But see, As, they shouldn't think they're smart, they shouldn't think they can offend me. I'll take measures, they'll end up like the others, and I'll show them."

I'll take measures. They'll end up like the others. Words that cut through my soul like a knife. Words that pointed to his previous deeds, to the history we shared: to Cor.

It really meant, I won't leave them alone, I don't care if they're family; to me, they're just like the others, and just like my other victims, just like Cor, they'll get liquidated.

That was the message I was supposed to deliver to Francis, a message containing a confession to her dad's murder and, at the same time, a death threat to herself and her mother. As if this didn't have enough impact in itself, he chose to send this message to her at the most vulnerable point in a young woman's life—the birth of her child.

All the moves in Wim's chess game are well planned.

To prevent him from asking for Francis's address and going there himself, I said, "I'll go tell her right away, don't worry."

We'd never told him where Francis lived and intended he should never know. Once he knows where you live, he'll drop his terror at your doorstep at any moment.

I called Francis from the car to say I'd "drop by."

These words were enough for her to meet me in the hallway with fearful eyes. She knew I'd drop by only if something was up. And if something was up, it was always about Wim.

"What's up?" she asked, face pale. Sonja, who was visiting her, came outside, too.

"He's being a pain about something you supposedly said about Cor." She immediately knew what I meant, as we'd discussed it before. "I'm supposed to tell you not to mention it ever again."

Francis started to panic.

"But, As, I won't say a word, not to anyone, really. Can you tell him I'm not talking about him at all? What's he up to now? Is he coming after me, As, after Nora?"

She was scared to death, scared for her child. Sonja just stood there, overcome.

"Don't worry about it. It'll blow over," I told Francis as casually as I could.

She looked me straight in the eye, and I could tell she knew I was lying. "You know it won't, As. You don't fool me. I know him. You know it won't blow over."

"Fran, you're right. I can only promise you it will be okay. I promised to take care of you. I promised your dad I'd look after you. Haven't I always?"

"Yes," she sobbed.

"Don't I always keep my promises?"

"Yes," she whispered.

"Well then, when I say I'll make sure you'll be all right, it means I will. You believe me?"

"I do," she said, softly.

I looked at Sonja. "I can't allow this to happen," I told her, and she knew right away I was alluding to my interview with the Justice Department.

"It'll be fine," I told Francis again, but I could see the fear in her eyes when I left her at the door.

I drove back to Wim to reassure him that Francis wouldn't talk.

"I sure hope so, for her and her mother," he said, still enjoying the terror he could impose on them.

For that moment, it was resolved.

But he always circles back. He really is a dog, a bad dog that should be kept away from children because it'll bite.

A bad dog has to be put down or kept in a cage for the rest of its life. Legally Wim couldn't be put down, but locking him up in a cage was a possibility. I'd need the help of the Justice Department in getting it done, though. One day earlier, cooperating with them had still seemed like a repulsive idea, but after today's events, I knew there were no other options. I had to do it for Francis, for ourselves, for all of us.

The next day I texted my contact at the CIU. "Wednesday, same time, same place, same interviewers?"

They replied, "Fine. Same time, same people. Have a nice evening."

The interview took place in the same location as before, and I had to go through the same nerve-racking ordeal to get there without being spotted by Wim.

When I got there, I saw Michelle waiting for me and I walked straight through. We joined Manon, who was waiting for us in an upstairs hotel room.

"I'm glad you're here," she said.

This time around, I was almost happy to start the interview. The anxious look in Francis's eyes was vivid in my mind.

I was asked if I was willing to talk to the CIU officer about the ins and outs of an extraordinary witness trajectory. I would have to specify what subjects I could testify about.

Up until then, I hadn't told them what I knew about certain events. I had given some cryptic clues about Wim's role in several liquidations, but I wouldn't say which ones—or exactly what I knew. I preferred discussing this with their boss, the CIU prosecutor. I was extremely cautious about sharing my information.

The women would let the officer know what I'd said and make an appointment.

"I guess you'll let me know when," I said, and we parted.

That evening, I expected Wim to appear on my doorstep, but it remained quiet.

The next morning at six thirty, I sat waiting for him all dressed and ready to go, as I did every morning. Because of the constant risk of a raid, Wim always gets up at five a.m. and hits the road. He doesn't like being surprised in his sleep, so he likes to set off extremely early. There are not many people he can go to at that time of day.

I'm one of the few.

I always made sure he wouldn't find me still in my nightgown, because it takes me at least an hour to get dressed and I didn't want to leave him by himself, as he'd use the time to go through my personal things. He does this with everyone he knows well. "It's okay, right?" he'll ask, seemingly surprised. "You've got nothing to hide, do you?"

But that morning he didn't come. Nor did he show up the following day, and the day after that I still hadn't heard from him. Now I really began to worry.

Paradoxically, not seeing him was even scarier than seeing him. I'd rather have him on my doorstep every morning at six thirty than not hear from him at all. If I saw him, at least I could gauge his reactions, see whether he knew anything and whether he still trusted me. If I didn't see him, I lost that control and I had no idea what he was thinking or planning. Maybe he wasn't around because he already knew I was talking to the Justice Department. Maybe he didn't want to be around "in case something happens," as he'd told me before.

Then, the next morning at six thirty, the doorbell rang. Yes, he was back! I hurried downstairs.

"Good morning, bro!" I said cheerily, because for a moment I was genuinely happy to see him after the days of tense waiting. I looked him straight in the eye so as to discern any distrust. I got the impression there was none.

"Morning, sis, wanna take a stroll?" he asked.

"Okay," I said. "Long time no see."

"No," he said. "I had things to do."

During our walk I observed him closely. I analyzed the tone of his voice, his expressions, his gestures, his reactions, and the things we talked about, trying to figure out whether he was onto me. He seemed to be relaxed and unsuspecting.

Which meant that the women I'd talked to hadn't leaked anything yet. I'd survived a second interview with the Justice

Department. I didn't want to jump to conclusions, but they seemed to be keeping their word.

When I got home, I got out the prepaid cell phone I'd bought for all communication with the CIU people. I didn't make calls using my personal cell phone account, as the number was linked to my name. I wanted to leave a minimal trail. They were still the police, so I remained cautious.

I saw they'd sent me a date and time.

The appointment with their officer had been made.

Rats

MY APPOINTMENT WITH THE DISTRICT ATTORNEY MS. WIND WAS TO TAKE place this week, and ever since I'd set the date, all I could think of was something Wim had said to me when we were walking through the Amsterdamse Bos after his release: his rats were his trump card, the secret weapon he reserved until he really needed it.

It sounded like he had someone in a high position, and I immediately wondered if this was the reason he'd been ruled out of every single liquidation trial.

I'd already made a number of subtle attempts to find out who it could be. But it is impossible to bluntly ask; for Wim, asking a direct question proves you're working with the cops. In my whole life, I'd only ever dared ask him one question. He would never tell me about his rats.

I kept worrying about their identities, and as the appointment drew nearer, the uneasy feeling intensified. Who knows—it might be the district attorney I was about to meet!

Wim texted me to come to the Gelderlandplein shopping center, which gave me an opportunity to make a last attempt at finding out who his rats were.

The more useful I could prove myself to be to him, the better the chance that he might tell me. "On my way," I texted back, and got the tiny device I'd found in my search for new possibilities to record him. It was small enough not to stand out. Because Wim is always going through my things, I'd hidden it inside the ceiling and I couldn't get it back out easily.

I was really hoping this new device would enable me to make a recording. I'd practiced in order to figure out where it could best be placed. Now it was stuck on the back of my bra strap, the safest spot I could come up with, presuming my brother wouldn't suddenly grab at his sister's bra. I put on an undershirt, a sweater, and a jacket to make it invisible. To be certain, I wore a large scarf, too.

I had to hurry, because I couldn't keep him waiting. He'd get angry, and I'd start our conversation at a disadvantage.

Wim was sitting inside a coffee shop where we'd meet regularly. I went inside and sat at the table with him. Two guys entered the place. Wim and I looked at each other and, without saying a word, got up and walked out: undercover agents. We walked up to the corner and stood opposite each other.

W: "Well, they sure enjoyed listening in."
A: "Yeah. Yet they also have some who don't look like cops at all, all tattooed and pierced."
W: "Sure, but you know how you can tell? When they pay the bill. They need the receipt or they can't account for their expenses to their boss. Ha!"

His eyes wandered to the height of my bosom.

W: "Take that scarf off, you look like an idiot. It's bloody hot."

He started tugging it and grasped at my bra strap. I was petrified and felt the device slip away. Where did it go? He might discover it!

He kept going:

W: "You look like an idiot, it's fucking hot. Take that thing off!"

It was true, it was the warmest day of the year so far, and I looked like an Inuit down in the tropics. I didn't want to remove the scarf, though, for fear he'd notice the device under my sweater.

I couldn't believe how stupid I'd been not to check the forecast beforehand. Next time I really had to keep that in mind, because this was the behavior that would raise his suspicions—the last thing I needed.

I broke into a sweat, not because of the temperature, but from pure stress. How could I get out of this in a credible way?

A: "No, leave it, I don't feel warm at all. I feel sick and chilled to the bone. I think I'm coming down with the flu."

I chose to go on the offense; the best defense where he's concerned. I went on:

A: "If I'm embarrassing you, I can just go home. You should be glad I came at all."
W: "No, never mind. You'll just have to make me look stupid. Let's take a walk."
A: "Wait a minute. I need to pee first. I'll be right back."

Without waiting for a reply, I walked toward the coffee joint's restroom to look for the device. With shaking hands I groped across my upper body. Thank God, there it was! It had gotten loose and stuck between my trousers' waistband and my undershirt. Thank goodness I'd tucked my undershirt inside my waistband; otherwise it would have fallen to the ground.

I tightened my bra strap and put the device back. It was the best solution for now because I wanted to continue recording. Next time I'd have to glue the device to my skin. I hurried back out and we started walking.

W: "Any news?"

I started talking about the CIU connection I'd brought up with him, the man we referred to as This Guy. It was a subject that always interested him because it might be of use later on.

A: "I attended this training session, and I met the man I sometimes
     talk to."

I lied to steer the conversation in the direction of playing the cops. I was hoping it'd get him started on his rats.

A: "He said to me, 'Call me sometime, maybe we could discuss a
     deal.' I just said, 'I'll see.' But I was kind of feeling like he
     wanted to tell me something. You know?"
W: "If he wants to talk, you gotta go hear him out. You know that,
     right?"

As intended, I'd aroused his interest.

A: "Sure thing."
W: "You gotta go hear what he's got to say."

That's what he taught me: Always listen, never tell anything.

A: "Yeah, I think it's more about seeing if you have something to
    say."

I made it about him. I knew the only one he's ever interested in is
himself.

W: "Either way, you gotta go hear him out. Say, 'How are you?' Be
    nice: 'How are you? Yada yada, you wanted to see me? What
    can I do for you?' That's how it's done. What I always say too
    is 'What can I do for you?'"

He instructed me on how to move forward with This Guy, "pulling
information," as we called it.

W: "They'll feel like they owe you something then, too."

It's a manipulation tactic that has proved very lucrative for him.
He's always "helping the other person out"; that's how he ties people to him, and once they're tied down, he'll take advantage.

   We continued our conversation, and what I'd hoped for happened: he started talking about the rats.

W: "So you don't say anything, just listen. I know for sure he'll ask
    about the rats."
A: "Yeah."
W: "Know what I mean? He'll ask about it, for sure."
A: "Sure, that'll be it. Of course, it is still a big mystery."
W: "But, see, if he starts on that, tell him, 'My brother is scared of
    them, because you can never be sure about these types.'"

Damn, he didn't tell me who they are. He just provided me with a reason why he "couldn't" say who they are, which I should pass on. Then he explained his so-called fear.

W: "See, because if they can give information, they can create information, too."

A: "Yeah."

W: "You get it? It's like a game."

A: "Yeah, that's it. You never know the truth, do you?"

W: "Look, Assie, instead of paying to give out information, you can also pay to create information."

A: "Sure thing."

W: "You see?"

A: "In other words, the rats can't be trusted, either, even if they pretend to collaborate with you?"

W: "Dirty rats, they can sell information or have it created for cash, either way. You could say 'Just write down he's the one and this and that.'"

A: "Ah, that's what you mean. From this side."

W: "Yeah, everybody can do that, you know."

He was saying every criminal could steer information in the direction he wanted suspicion to go. Apparently, though, not every rat was equally flexible, and Wim distinguished between them.

W: "The rats who are dirty can take it really far. You know what I mean?"

A: "Yeah."

I realized I didn't want to be sent to This Guy, because I wasn't even in touch with him anymore, and I backed off.

A: "I'll see if I hear anything. Should I be calling him?"

Now that I'd been in for a penny, I had to be in for a pound.

W: "Yeah, you should call him for sure. You should say, 'How's it going, what can I do for you?'"

This got too hot for me, and I came up with an excuse.

A: "You know, I get the feeling I'm caught up in some sort of game where you can never tell what the truth is."

He felt the same.

W: "Don't do it then, leave it. It's not so smart if they find you out. You know what I mean. Then don't, love—let them sort it out themselves. If he's got something to say, he'll come to you anyway."

The lesson was, Don't go to them, they'll come to you. The cops come to you only when it's in their interest.

W: "He won't come to warn me. He won't come to say, 'Your brother should watch out for this and that.' You see? He just won't."

I understood he was talking about a liquidation.

A: "Why not? That would be something, wouldn't it? If something is up, shouldn't they warn you no matter what?"
W: "No, they'll do it through the CIU. He won't do it himself."

A: "Right."

Wim didn't think he was useful after all.

W: "He won't talk about an investigation, either. He just wants to hear stuff. It won't work. So far, they've given me shit. They wanna have it all, and I already know what they'll say: 'Won't he talk?'"

I agreed with him, and we changed the subject.

We'd talked about rats, but I hadn't managed to get him to say who they were.

That night, I couldn't get to sleep. The dark evoked one ghost after another. Talking to the police—what had I gotten myself into, and where would it get me? Luckily, in the morning, most of the ghosts had vanished. Everything looks different in daylight. I decided I should just let it go and take things as they came. I'd rely on my intuition and end things with the CIU as soon as I got a weird feeling about it.

The time had come.

Michelle picked me up at the elevator again. Her presence had a quieting effect on me; she seemed sincere. Manon was waiting in the room, greeting me as soberly as she'd done previously. A female district attorney got up and shook my hand. "Hello, my name is Betty Wind. We've seen each other around, haven't we?"

Indeed, I'd seen her before but had never spoken to her; I'd always kept my distance from public prosecutors because I couldn't be sure they weren't "sent" by the Justice Department to infiltrate my family through me.

"That's right, we've seen each other in court," I said.

With Wim's remarks from yesterday still in my mind, I immediately thought of his "trump" and who it might be. It hit me she was kind of his type: pretty, thin, well-dressed. At the same time, I knew this didn't have to mean anything; Wim would shag a troll if it was to his advantage. Betty Wind asked me what I had to say.

"I can tell you the truth," I said, "but after spending an hour with him, you'll be convinced the reality he's holding out to you is the actual truth. You'll be thinking, These two sisters are out of their minds, the poor man hasn't done a thing."

Betty said calmly, "I do know him. He acts extremely charming in court, as well. I've noticed all of that."

She appeared to see through Wim's naughty-boy act in court and knew it didn't match his reputation. It seemed like I'd found a prosecutor who might finally see right through him. This was a must. Anyone else would get lost in his maze of conspiracies and never get to the truth.

Michelle and Manon had told Betty about the picture I'd painted of Wim's personality, and this, too, sounded familiar to her, though she'd never expected him to treat his own family the same way he treated his victims.

"I get that," I said, "but that's because you couldn't know our family has been victimized by him for such a long time. We can't say anything negative about him, for he won't accept it."

"I'd like to know what precisely you can share with us," she said.

Out of suspicion, I hadn't let on much about that in my earlier interviews, and I'd only spoken cryptically about what I knew about the liquidations. "Enough," I said.

"Such as?" she asked.

Without mentioning his name, I said, "Who he has iced." Fear crept up on me while I spoke the words. "If it gets out that I'm talking to you, it'll be my death sentence. Before I tell you anything, I need to know what you'll do with the information and who'll be involved."

"Don't worry, your talking to us will be kept between the three of us for now, and you really can trust us," Betty said, trying to reassure me.

"With all due respect, I don't trust him, and I don't trust you, either. I can only trust my sister and myself. It's my experience that everyone can be bought, and those who won't be bought will yield out of fear for their well-being or that of their loved ones. Paying a visit to someone's kids' school is easy to do—he's done it. That's why I need to know what will happen with my information before I tell you anything."

"That's why I'm here, to explain it to you," Betty said.

The bottom line was that I'd have to tell them what I knew first. They'd put it down in a written statement, and based on this statement, it would be decided if it qualified as "highly confidential." If it did, my statements would be used in a prosecution against Wim only with my explicit consent. Should I back down at any point, the statements would never be revealed. But even if I did go through with it, the Justice Department wouldn't automatically use them. That depended on whether the State's duty of care allowed the use of my statements. Put differently: When the Justice Department deemed it too dangerous for me, they could still decide not to use my statements.

I didn't like what I heard. I'd have to unfold my entire life for them to put down in writing and only then decide if it was of any use to them?

To me, sharing the information verbally with the Justice Department was dangerous enough, but the existence of written statements made it even riskier. What if Wim got his hands on them? Besides that, I would never know if giving my statements had made any difference, whether they'd actually use my information against him.

In the scenario they laid out for me, I'd be left with no control over my personal safety whatsoever. Why was it so important to write down what I said? Telling your story within a confined room still enables you to deny it ever took place, to deny what people may claim. It's a completely different thing to have your story written down and taken away, out of the reach of your power and influence.

Who would be reading it?

I could already picture one of these women walking into the prosecution office, waving my statements above her head and saying, "Guys, look what I've got here! It's a statement from Holleeder's sister. You won't believe how fucked up this family is! These gals are washing their dirty laundry in public. You really should read this!" I imagined the whole department having a ball with these statements and the rat meanwhile managing to make a quick copy and taking it with him as fun reading material for my darling brother.

"Yeah, right," I said, "I'd rather bite my tongue off and bleed to death than put a statement in writing."

I'd have preferred to use my brother's method: whispering all the damning information into their ears, leaving no evidence of having spoken with them. Betty wouldn't have it, though; a written statement was mandatory or they wouldn't be able to do anything.

"Suppose you've got my statement on paper, though," I said, "you won't even know if you'll use it. Why not hear me out now? As a prosecutor, can't you decide right now how a statement could help you?"

"No," she said, "it has to be done in peace and quiet. We need to consider if these statements support other evidence and if all together it will be sufficient for prosecution, conviction, and possibly a sentencing."

This sounded reasonable enough, but their strategy didn't alleviate my anxiety.

"Where will you be keeping this statement?" I asked.

"Inside a safe," Betty said.

"Inside a safe..." I echoed.

A safe didn't impress me at all. A safe offers zero protection if you don't know who has access to the key. And that's something I can never be sure of.

"Who is able to access this safe?"

"Just me and my superior."

"Okay," I said, "your superior will have a key as well. But I don't know your boss. And I have no way of knowing what he'll do with this key, so that doesn't reassure me. For example, as a CIU officer, could you be shoved aside by a case officer, or, for all I know, by an undersecretary or a minister dropping by to raid your safe? How will I know your superiors don't have their own keys without your knowledge? That they'll take a peek and leak it so I don't have a way out? I want to trust you, but I can't tell what others will do. Suppose you conclude it lacks relevance, or I decide to refrain after all? Then what?"

"We'll sign an agreement in advance, confirming this statement may be used exclusively with your consent," Betty said, "and without your consent, it will be destroyed immediately."

"Destroyed how?"

"Through the shredder," she said.

"What about the audio recordings?"

"Destroyed too."

"How does that work? Can I be there to see it's actually done? I'd want to see it with my own eyes."

"No, you've got to take our word for it." Another minus point for her.

"But how many people would get to know my identity? How many will be involved without my knowledge?"

The thought of losing control scared me to death. The more people know, the bigger the chance of leaking.

"For the time being, it will just be the three of us," Betty said. "We'll get other people involved only later in the procedure."

I didn't have the faintest idea about all the formalities my testimony would involve, or all the departments it would have to pass through. I wouldn't have dreamed this many conditions would apply. I painted pictures for Betty of all kinds of situations that might occur, which she tried to counter as best she could.

Eventually she just looked at me a bit pityingly, as if she were thinking, How sad to have to go through life that suspicious. "You're going to have to put a tiny bit of trust in us to handle your case responsibly," she said.

Trust? Reality will prove your trustworthiness, I thought. You'll only stop being trustworthy if things end badly. By then it will be too late for me.

It was a tough conversation for both parties.

After what she'd told me, I was still too unsettled, and I left.

"How did it go?" Sonja, who'd been waiting for me at home, asked. "Was it a rat?"

"No, she wasn't a rat. She's onto him," I said.

"Now what?" Sonja asked.

"I don't know if this will work for us."

"Why not?"

"It's all about phases. First they want to talk, then they want a written statement. After that, they'll decide if it will be useful to them and if they want to continue with us."

"Oh, I won't do that. Not when he's still walking around free. It's way too dangerous, As."

"They say we can trust them."

"Like hell we can. And what about his rats? I won't do it. I'm not writing anything down. It's just too risky. Do you trust 'em?"

"I don't trust anyone, but I think these three women are okay. I don't think they'll screw us on purpose. I'm just worried about the top. That scares me more. What if he's got his rat in there? Then these three have no authority, they'll just have to do as the boss tells them. I really don't know yet. But if I go through with it, I won't do it by myself, Box. So what are you going to do?"

She was quiet for a minute, then spoke.

"It's tough, but I can't say if it's the right thing to do. Right now, we're all still alive. It's not much of a life, but at least we are alive. If we testify, we probably won't be, and is it fair to do that to our children? How are these kids supposed to make it without us? Who'll protect them from him? That's what's bugging me. I really don't understand why he hasn't been shot yet. Everyone around him drops like flies except him. And he's got so many enemies."

"Then you're just sitting around waiting for someone else to do something. That's easy, leaving it to others. So far it hasn't gotten us anywhere. We're dependent on fate. I'd like to take my fate into my own hands, and I don't care what happens."

I was so fed up. All those decades, we had to be silent about everything we knew. All those years, he'd burdened us with his horrible information, stuff he had done. All those years, he used everything we held dear to put pressure on us. He destroyed the things we loved. Used us to serve his own best interests while undermining ours in every possible way.

We'd become his security system, his place to safeguard his secrets. He owned us. He had crowned himself king of the family, and we were his subjects. He had us living in constant fear of saying something wrong, continuously threatened against talking to the police.

I couldn't keep on living under this regime. It was eating away at me. I needed to break free.

I knew for certain that if I told what I knew, it would be clear instantly that my statements should be highly confidential. I had to gamble, had to believe that they wouldn't be shared with others or Wim himself—at least not by the three women.

"I'm going to take the first step," I said finally. "I'll testify. I am certain it will be deemed a highly confidential statement and after that we'll see. If something happens to us in the meantime, the Justice Department will at least have something to go on. I'll take the risk."

"Fine, if you do it, I'll do it too. I'll take the plunge with you. It's about justice for my husband, and for my children's lives."

Even after I was fully committed to my mission, I still wavered sometimes.

"We're the same, Assie," Wim would tell me at least once a week. And it was true. Of the four children my mother had, the middle two, Sonja and Gerard, and the oldest and youngest, Wim and me, were very much alike in character and behavior.

Our characters prevented us from being victimized. As small and powerless as we were, we wanted to take our fate into our own hands by trying to defuse my father's unpredictable behavior.

As a child, I'd developed a tic of repeating my every movement. Opening and closing the door twice, putting my shoes on twice, touching the doorknob twice. It kept me quite busy. I'd figured out that by touching everything twice, I could control my father's willful behavior, so he wouldn't beat us.

One night—I was seven and Wim was fourteen—I saw him shutting the fridge twice.

"You're doing it too," I said.

"What?"

"You do everything twice too."

He looked at me, understanding, and in that moment I felt a strong connection.

Had I been a boy, I might have turned out just like him. Maybe it was being a girl that prevented me from compensating with violence and bravado. Maybe I had used my intellect instead, safeguarding me from a similar path in life.

Who am I to condemn him for the coincidence of being born male? Should I, of all people, be the one to do this to him, while we might well be "the same," as he claims?

"So you'd be the same as him just because you both repeat some stuff?" Sonja asked, dryly. "Nonsense, As. How can you even think that way? You're nothing like him. Would you shut up about it? He's an evil person, and you're not!"

"No, but if I'd been in his shoes, I might have acted the same way. I might have murdered someone close to me if they were threatening my life."

"But he did it himself—he's only got himself to blame for these situations! Because he's been selling everyone out his entire life, he ends up in situations that make him decide to get rid of people. But he doesn't have to! He chooses it consciously. You'd never act that way. So stop saying you are just like him. That's what he wants you to believe, so he can manipulate you. And it's working. He's making you believe you are an exception to the rule, but you're not."

Sonja was right, and I knew it. I am no exception to him; he sees me only in terms of how he can use me. But he sure knows how to make you believe it, that you're the life ring just barely keeping him afloat in his ocean of misery. Maybe I wanted to be just that, on the lookout for that moment of connection from long ago, even though I know that Wim is long gone, even though I know what he's turned into.

Once again, I'd made the mistake of hoping he harbored real emotions. I'd let myself be disarmed by his feigned affection in the middle of my battle against him. I really couldn't afford this. I had to keep my guard up and couldn't be tempted into a situation that would prevent me from seeing the attack coming.

Meetings with Betty

LEADING UP TO MY NEXT MEETING WITH BETTY, I WAS CONSUMED BY thoughts of what I should tell her. I cried a lot, slept poorly, and got edgier by the hour. I drove everyone around me crazy, but besides Sonja, no one knew what was wrong with me. Nobody could know what I intended to do, because what they didn't know, they couldn't pass on.

Then the day finally arrived. Michelle texted, "Hi, 4:30 p.m., second elevator. See you later."

At four fifteen I was on my way to the agreed location when I got another text: "Betty just got sick and can't make it. We're here, though—is that all right with you? She'll try to be back later this week."

I was suspicious right away. First they had me come all the way over, and not even fifteen minutes before our meeting, the CIU officer cancels? I'd prepared mentally for this interview, and now she wasn't going to be there. Was she really sick? Or was she thinking I would share my statement with Michelle and Manon so easily? I'd explicitly said I only wanted to speak with her, only with an officer.

Michelle was waiting for me.

"Am I being played here?" I asked, perhaps a bit too aggressively.

She was taken aback but recovered quickly. "Of course not, Betty just got sick."

She sounded so sincere that I felt ashamed. This moment was so heavy for me, it was messing with my common sense. I had to relax. "Betty hoped she could be here until the very last minute—this meeting is important to her as well. But she couldn't hold anything down and simply couldn't come. We're not playing you, honestly." Michelle spoke calmly, and I could tell by her tone that she was telling the truth.

"Okay," I said, feeling reassured. "Sorry about my behavior, but I've been feeling really apprehensive about this."

"I understand," Michelle said. "Would you like to set up the next meeting anyway?"

"Okay," I said.

"Back already?" Sonja asked. "That was fast."

"She wasn't there, she's sick," I said.

"Ah well, shit happens."

She didn't suffer from paranoia. Then again, she hadn't gone through the hell of interviewing yet. She hadn't had to rake everything up again.

"I think I'm starting to lose it," I said.

"Then you have to stop it, As. If you can't deal with it, you should get out."

"No, I'll be fine. It's just so heavy. Recalling everything, going through these emotions again." I started crying.

Sonja hugged me. "Cut it out, Astrid, you're making me cry too," she said through her tears. "Listen, regardless of whether we go through with it, Cor is proud of us."

A week later, I had another meeting with Betty.

She started by saying, "Sorry about canceling last week, but I was really sick."

"I know," I said. I couldn't say "I don't mind," as it had been pretty clear to the other two that I most certainly had. I still felt a bit ashamed about it. The past week I'd tried to get more sleep, and I had been able to get used to all the horrible memories. It made me slightly more pleasant to be around.

Betty got started. "What can you tell us?"

Oh, no. I'd resolved not to cry, and I was tearing up at the very first question. The hurt was so intense that even after ten years I couldn't speak about it without shedding tears.

"He did Cor," I said, and automatically made Wim's customary gun gesture.

"Did" can mean anything, but the gesture makes the meaning absolutely clear.

"He had Cor murdered, his own brother-in-law," I said. I'd said it. After a decade of silence, I'd finally said it aloud!

I was startled by how good it felt to utter those words at last.

I no longer felt torn, and, most important, I no longer felt like I was betraying Cor. Suddenly I found myself talking about the other liquidations Wim was responsible for. I was engulfed by an enormous sense of peace. At last, I could do what *I* wanted, what *I* considered just and righteous, what matched *my* norms and values. At last I could tell the truth about him. I no longer had to lie for him.

What a marvelous feeling.

Whether I was ready to make this statement to the whole world, him included, was a different question, though. I would only do it if Sonja did.

The fear of leaks and retribution remained. But now that I'd made the very first statement, it was irreversible. As of now, I knew my life was in the hands of these people. If they betrayed me, or were careless enough to let someone else do it, I was dead.

To take the edge off this idea, I told myself I might just as well walk under a bus tomorrow and not take life and death so seriously from now on. Besides, it felt so good to actually be able to tell the truth that I took the anxiety in stride.

When I got home, I told Sonja everything.

"I told them I'd testify if you would. Will you testify?"

"Yes, I'll do it too," Sonja said.

"I'll go first then. No sweat. We'll take turns. See how things unfold, and if they're really trustworthy."

The appointment for my next statement had already been made when we informed Gerard we were going to testify against Wim.

Gerard was vehemently opposed to it. There was a case in the media that demonstrated that highly confidential statements didn't always have to be kept secret, even against the witness's wishes.

This changed Sonja's mind completely. Gerard had fueled her distrust of the Justice Department and the law so much, she didn't dare go through with it.

This changed my position as well, as I'd be left on my own, and I had to reconsider thoroughly. I canceled the planned meeting for making the highly confidential statements.

But I couldn't let go of it. There was plenty of reason for pulling back, but every time I met Wim and saw how he treated and talked about others, how he shamelessly referred to his previous crimes, something inside me seemed to explode.

By now the three ladies had gained my trust. Betty seemed driven but cautious concerning our interests. I figured Sonja herself should be the judge of that, and I asked her to talk to Betty about it. She agreed.

★ ★ ★

On March 29, Sonja came with me, and I told Betty we were both really scared that once our statements were put on paper, they would be used regardless of our wishes.

"That's not how it works," Betty said. "If we don't reach a mutual agreement on the use of these statements, they will be destroyed. It happens on a regular basis; there are many examples of cases that could have been wrapped up a long time ago. We had all the information, but eventually we had to destroy those statements because the witnesses didn't want to go through with it. Those statements never got out, either. You'll always have the possibility to pull out, until the very last moment."

But what about this case we'd seen in the media? "That was a completely different situation," Betty said. "The decision whether the confidential statements will or won't be used is entirely up to you."

"All right, we'll think about it," I said, to end the conversation.

We drove home. We didn't discuss anything in the car, afraid of bugging devices placed by either the Justice Department or Wim.

Once outside the car, Sonja said, "I don't know, As. I'm having doubts. Her explanation doesn't entirely convince me. It's happened in other cases. Why is ours different?"

"I don't think she can give any guarantees, she's got to deal with other people, too. The risk remains. In fact, we've already taken the risk, and all things considered, I think it's probably better if you go through with it. You want to refrain from testifying to prevent your children from ending up on their own, but that's your fate *now*—he's already started with you, and you know how it is: once he starts with you, he won't let go. Based on the past, I know how this is going to end, so I would actually do it, for the children's sakes. You should decide for yourself, though."

We walked to her house in silence. When we got upstairs, she said, "You're right. I know. I'll testify. We'll have to take the risk."

At that moment the lights in the room began flickering.

"Look," Sonja said. "Cor is here again. He thinks it's a good decision."

The Method

My decision to cooperate with the Justice Department didn't mean I put my fate willingly into their hands. My image of them had not changed, and I didn't expect to be able to fully count on them. How could I trust a judiciary when I knew corrupt officers were messing with its investigative system?

I'd be crazy to think they'd take over "the Wim issue" from me, so I didn't. I chose to cooperate with the Justice Department so I could make my own way, to play a double game. This way I could continue to see Wim regularly without running the risk of the Justice Department seeing me as an extension of him. Staying in touch with both the Justice Department and Wim would allow me to collect my own evidence, and then I'd see what my cooperation with the Justice Department would do for me.

Of course I was hoping Wim would get charged and prosecuted while he was in jail, since a prosecution with him on the outside would be extremely dangerous for us. Still, I didn't count on things going this way. No—should I end up facing an adverse investigative system, I wanted to have a plan B. I was going to collect enough evidence myself to force prosecution through a judge or supported by the media.

Whichever way it went, I had to take into account that a prosecution didn't guarantee a conviction. Wim would never surrender without a fight. Sixteen years of growing up with an insane father and forty years at the top of organized crime had turned him into a professional survivor, a master of self-preservation.

That's what we had to deal with.

He would throw all of his weight behind avoiding conviction. He would manipulate, cheat, and pressure any witness in order to remain a free man. The latter would be disastrous, for once outside, he'd have plenty of opportunity and ways to kill us. That's why we had to anticipate his defense and take into account what to expect from him.

Our advantage was in knowing him, and knowing what was coming. All through his criminal career, we'd been witnesses to, sometimes even involved in, Wim's cunning methods of "proactive defense."

The Heineken kidnapping had taught Wim that the extortion of wealthy people yielded a lot of cash, but it also taught him that kidnapping, holding hostages, and collecting ransom money involved a high risk of getting caught. Wim was done with kidnapping. He had switched to a more calculated extortion method: extorting without taking a person's personal freedom.

Wim still chose his victims based on their financial status, but as opposed to the Heineken and Doderer technique, he didn't grab them off the street, wrestle them into a car, and lock them up—he already knew his new victims.

They were his friends and family, people he visited at home and whose kids he played with, at whose table he ate meals cooked by their wives. They all thought he was their friend, and none of them could foresee that Wim would suddenly turn into a foe. On the contrary, they trusted him completely and believed him when he came by to warn them "as a friend" about the wicked plans of some scary criminals concerning their money, or their life, or their spouse's life.

"There's trouble coming!" he would tell them.

But not to worry, he knew who was behind it. As your friend, he would come to your aid.

With your best interest at heart, he was willing to act as a mediator in this conflict, which you probably didn't even know existed.

Then the "pay-up" began.

He was the messenger, so he was in complete control of what he told one party about the other.

"You were betrayed by your best friend. You'd better trust me." "You need to pay or they'll kill you."

The method enabled him to pit everyone against each other and play both sides. Thus, none of the parties would notice he was using them all and they were all his victims. Nobody noticed he was the one and only cause of the conflict.

Once they did notice, once they realized that their best friend had turned into their worst enemy, it was too late. They couldn't report him to the Justice Department, because they had their own crimes to conceal, including those committed in cooperation with Wim. If he was jailed for extortion, he'd tell the police about them, too, and he'd make sure they got locked up as well. If this didn't impress them, he'd make it clear that talking to the police meant the death penalty and he'd always find out through his rats. When his terror had made their lives so miserable that they were even willing to take that risk, he'd start to threaten their loved ones, and he ratcheted up his threats by showing up at their kids' schools.

In this way he improved on the classic kidnapping: he held people by fear without having to deal with the risks of physical kidnapping.

The most brilliant part of this extortion method, however, was the way he presented his role of mediator as his alibi. He didn't have any conflicts; they did. He was just passing on messages and helping out.

He linked a publicity strategy to his extortion business, covering his extortion for years. He'd make sure that the story of his "mediating role" was communicated to the Justice Department as well as to the criminal world and the media. He fed everyone his message about hoping to resolve the conflict—how could that be criminal? He explained all of his dealings with suspects and victims by saying, "I'm just trying to help." The Justice Department ought to be pleased with him!

Wim didn't care that some of the people he had "mediated for" were dead, or that some of them had pointed him out before their deaths not only as their extorter, but also as their future killer. Unlike extortion, liquidation was a crime that didn't require him to be in the victim's vicinity. He just had to give the command and could stay at a safe distance himself, preferably abroad.

He made sure his executioners couldn't point him out as the commander. He used intermediaries who'd never name him, for "they'd be in it up to their necks themselves." Wim knew that no one he'd involved in his schemes would confess to a murder, let alone multiple murders; that would land them in prison for life.

This was his usual strategy: get everyone involved, by force if necessary, and they'll have to be silent forever.

Any witness claiming to know Willem Holleeder had given the command could only have learned this from an intermediary, from hearsay—never from Wim himself.

Since this rumor was heard so often—he'd exclaim, "Every liquidation seems to have my name on it!"—Wim's defense was that these witnesses had gotten it from the media: "These accusations are really wearing me out."

He wasn't a perpetrator but the media's victim.

Before, during, and after committing his crimes, he'd always be collecting and tweaking information both within criminal circles and in the Justice Department. As he had told me, "Information can be both bought and produced." He did both through the use of his rats.

In this way he could stay informed about what he should guard against, and create his defense ahead of time by spreading disinformation, putting the Justice Department on the wrong track.

Meanwhile, he'd plant his stories within criminal circles so the disinformation he'd spread inside the Justice Department would be confirmed, and the other way around, making his story more credible.

He was very knowledgeable about the investigative methods used by the Justice Department, and he used them to his advantage. He made sure he couldn't possibly be incriminated by any traceable encounter, observation, visible contact, conversation, or telephone call. When he wanted to plant a false story, he'd talk about it on the phone or somewhere that was sure to be bugged. "Making taps," he calls it. He'd whisper or gesture the things he didn't want the Justice Department to hear.

He seemed to have succeeded pretty well, too; so far he hadn't been prosecuted for a single murder. And he'd managed to spread alternative scenarios that could help in his defense.

In this regard, we were hugely disadvantaged, and we knew he'd use his standard claim about our accusations: we got it all from the media.

At the same time, he'd try to chip away at our credibility by accusing us of all kinds of things and dismissing us as liars who'd benefit from getting rid of him. He'd do anything to raise doubt, for he knows a judge shouldn't just find evidence to be lawful, but convincing as well.

One thing Wim doesn't lack is persuasiveness. Within half an hour, he'll have your sympathy.

Within forty-five minutes, he'll have brainwashed you with his conspiracy theories.

Within an hour, you'll be doubting everything I've just told you. Within an hour and fifteen minutes, you'll be thinking, Surely this friendly, charming gentleman couldn't have done such things? Within an hour and a half, he'll have manipulated you into feeling sorry for him for getting screwed over by his sisters like this.

No, we couldn't expect Wim to surrender without a fight. So we had to come up with a way to show the world that his "credibility" was nothing but a carefully constructed facade, a rampart he'd built up around himself to cover his actions.

I knew Wim would deny ever having spoken to me about the liquidations, which was easy for him to claim because it was usually just the two of us. If there was one other person who knew, it had to be Sonja. He'd claim she took my side and joined the conspiracy against him.

"Maybe other witnesses will come forward once we've told our story," Sonja had said, but I knew we shouldn't count on it. He'd already cornered everyone who had anything on him. His fellow criminals remained silent for fear he'd start talking about their own illegal activities, and he'd corrupted every contact with decent people to make them susceptible to blackmail. Thanks to his charm, he could get in touch with the wealthiest, smartest, and most capable people. He'd use his social skills to make them forget about his horrible crime, and then he'd take the next step: he'd turn his criminal history—his disadvantage—into an advantage. Poor him, so much harm was done to him. He'd always been treated unjustly, he'd been wrongly convicted, and the Justice Department was ruining his life.

He was just a poor guy, not some vicious criminal, and believe it or not, even though they knew about his past of extortions and the liquidations he's associated with, some people grew to love him. Oblivious, they'd step into his web and come to his rescue. Registering a scooter, car, or a warehouse under their own names for him, renting a house: all of this is impossible for him to do without help, because the Justice Department had unjustly made it so.

Give Wim an inch and he won't just take a mile, but the entire road, and if he feels like it, everything you have. After you help him once, to him it's only natural that you'll continue to do so. If you don't comply with his wishes, this is what will happen: He'll turn into your enemy as quickly as he became your friend. The infatuation phase is over and he switches to enforcement, while threatening your loved ones. Going to the police is not an option, for he'll tell them what you've done for him and how this links you to his illegal actions. If you've done nothing for him that he can hold against you, he'll make something up. Because merely hanging out with him turns you into a suspect, and he'll threaten to add lies to it: "If you talk to the police, I'll drag you down with me." It'll be his word against yours.

No one, especially not people who are higher up the social ladder, will take that risk, and he knows it, for the higher the other's status, the bigger their fear of losing it. Reputations are easily destroyed.

Nobody would come to our aid if we took the witness stand. Since our lives were on the line, we couldn't confide in anybody else. If we were going to do this, it had to succeed the first time around; there would be no second chance.

Testifying meant anticipating his defense. We could only do this the way he himself had been doing it since the early nineties: by recording my conversations with him. It was the one way I could support my statements and show that he entrusted his secrets to me. That we shared these secrets.

"People won't believe us until they hear him saying it himself," I told Sonja.

The problem with our plan was that Wim had trained us to communicate in a way that made it nearly impossible to record anything.

Ever since the Heineken kidnapping, we haven't trusted anyone outside the family, and we don't speak to people we don't know. We always, literally always, keep in mind that we may be monitored by the Justice Department or an informant.

That's why communicating isn't just about talking for us. We communicate through mimicry, intonation, pauses, and silence.

We don't talk in any place that could have been equipped with recording devices by the Justice Department. So we never talk at home, not in, on, or near our cars or motorbikes, and we never sit at the same table if we go out. When we talk, we avoid people nearby because they might be undercover agents. We avoid the possibility of installed directional microphones by never talking in one spot, staying on the move. We only talk on the street, sometimes even covering our mouths with our hands, as we once discovered the Justice Department was using a lip-reader to monitor conversations.

We use nonverbal communication to inform each other of things so the Justice Department can't monitor it. We use gestures and eye movements. There are gestures for verbs and gestures to designate specific people. But by far the most important way to discuss incriminating subjects is by whispering into each other's ears. We never talk out loud unless we want to mislead the Justice Department and to *let* them monitor what we say. Same holds for every phone call. Because we know we're probably being wiretapped, we let them hear us so that the Justice Department will register our denial and lack of involvement. They'll never succeed in registering anything incriminating about us in a phone call. We only speak in riddles.

"You know." "That one, you know." "The thing, you know." "That thing I had to do, right?"

Threats are cloaked as well.

"You know what I'll do, don't you?" "You know what I'm like, right?" "I'll take a swing at it in the dark."

People have nicknames so we don't have to mention their names: Fatty, Longneck, Cross-Eyed. And Wim uses the all-purpose nickname Fucking Dog for whoever has aroused his anger.

This whole verbal, nonverbal, and hidden communication method has developed over time and is based on our shared history. After everything we've been through and shared together, our messages always come across.

Always factoring in the possibility of someone recording him, Wim, distrustful of everybody he speaks with, directs every conversation. He'll only discuss subjects of his choice. He'll determine the contents and course of the conversation, and block any other input. That's what he does with us as well, expecting us to toe the line. If we don't, he'll get suspicious immediately.

Every contact we have is dominated by rules that are set in stone; that's what we were taught, and that's the way we've done it for thirty years. The system is so complicated that it's almost impossible to get him to say anything incriminating about himself. I couldn't start talking to him in a different way without arousing his suspicion.

His observations are razor sharp. I was afraid he'd notice I was recording our conversations from my behavior, that I couldn't handle myself, that I would show an involuntary change despite my efforts. He would notice the smallest of changes and immediately attribute them to betrayal.

In his eyes, any deviation from your usual behavior shows you're hiding something or talking to the police. Even a tiny change is suspicious. All it takes is one faulty question. Or choosing your words wrongly, mentioning names, or talking out loud instead of whispering.

Bringing up a random issue is a no-go as well. If I were to just start talking about Cor, for example, it would immediately raise a red flag. That subject is off-limits. Many issues he is sensitive to—ones that could incriminate him—cannot be discussed.

This significantly limited the chances of a substantively successful recording.

Then there were technicalities. He might frisk me to see if I was wired. Search *me,* even though he trusted me. According to Wim, "checking isn't distrusting." But he'll distrust you the second you won't let him search you.

I was certain he would beat me to death immediately if he discovered I was recording our conversations. He'd know why I did it right away, realize what we had discussed, and know I'd sided with the authorities. He wouldn't take any risk and wouldn't let me get away.

I asked Peter de Vries for advice. He'd worked with hidden cameras and microphones before. Because he knew Wim only talked while walking down the street, he supplied me with recording equipment to be worn inside of a coat, with the microphone wired through the sleeve and attached underneath the coat's lapel.

I tried it at home. That didn't go well. The recording device was so large that Wim wouldn't even need to search me to find it. The wire and microphone were visible whenever I moved. It wouldn't work. I needed to find equipment that was invisible, that could not be felt by him, and that allowed me to move freely and behave normally.

Extorting Sonja

After his release in 2012, Wim worked to restore his standing in the criminal world, and by the end of the year, he was well on his way to regaining his previous dominance.

Using his remarkable charisma and boldness, he managed to turn his enemies back into friends. He assembled "gunmen" around him, past killers he thought he could trust.

The only thing he lacked was money.

He did have some, but not nearly as much as he was used to. He told us he'd once had forty million euros, but he'd left jail nearly penniless after the government recovered seventeen million euros from him—and he claimed former friends stole from him. In an attempt to generate some cash and "get back up," he invested in cannabis plantations and the cocaine trade.

But he had other plans, too.

Shortly after his release, he appeared on Sonja's doorstep. Instead of a sister, he saw two bags of money: Cor's money, and money from the American film adaptation of the 1985 book *The Kidnapping of Alfred Heineken* by our friend Peter R. de Vries. Peter had written the book based on interviews with Cor, and arranged for royalties to be split between himself and Cor. The book had done very well, and in 2011 it was turned into a Dutch movie. Wim had sued to prevent the release of the film, but he lost. It was said that he also threatened the film's director. Now there was an American remake in the works, and Wim was determined to either stop the production or get his hands on the profits. Sonja told him she didn't have any of Cor's money, but Wim didn't believe her. According to him, Cor had had considerable capital, which she'd inherited, so she had money and it wasn't hers to keep. It was his, for he bore the burden—making the gun gesture—and still risked prosecution. Why should she benefit?

Wim kept returning to Sonja's doorstep, asking the same question: "Where's the money?"

Her standard reply was "I don't have any money."

Early in 2013, though, when the press reported that Sonja had been sued for Cor's inheritance and had finally settled for 1.2 million euros, Wim had found his proof. "If you settle for one point two million euros, you gotta be loaded."

He concluded that there had to be money, and lots of it. Her denial only fired him up more. He wouldn't be "bamboozled"; she was going to pay him "or else she'd see what happened" (making his usual gun gesture).

Wim's extortion of Sonja had begun.

He started "sharing" with me how Sonja was a filthy whore and a selfish bitch.

"She's saying she's got nothing, but I don't buy it. She's a weasel, trying to keep everything for herself, but I'll find her out, all right."

That's what he wanted to use me for, to get information and to pass on information, since he knew she trusted me and that I was always in touch with her. To get me to take on this role, I'd have to cross over from Camp Sonja to Camp Wim. First, he had to get me out of my own reality and to see the reality he was showing me.

Every day he'd bring his reality to my door, trying to brainwash me. He'd talk to me, sometimes three times in one day, telling me I needed to know "the truth" and see "what a weasel" she really was.

He'd supply the craziest kinds of evidence.

"As, they're driving cars. Their closets are jam-packed with Gucci. Do you have any idea how expensive Gucci is?"

I knew how the cars had been paid for, and I only had to open Sonja's closet to see just one fake Gucci belt and two fake Gucci sweaters in there, but that didn't make any difference to him.

He applied the power of repetition, delivering the same message every day: "She's got money, and it's mine. She stole it from me." When he thought I'd taken in his view of reality, he took the next step to successfully induct me into his camp. Now that I'd finally "seen" how Sonja had fooled him, I should know that he wasn't her only victim; she abused me as well. "Assie, you should stop paying bills for her. She's just using you. She's using both of us, because she's got money, all right."

She was lying to him and lying to me.

"Why is she lying to you?" he asked, seemingly concerned for my well-being. "See what a filthy whore she is? She's lying, even to you, who does everything for her!" Here he was, caring enough to warn me about her. Because he recognized it, he was getting played by her as well! We were both being played! The two of us were buddies. Connected. We had to turn against her together.

I didn't react the way he wanted me to, though. I wouldn't be dragged into his conspiracy against her, because I knew how it would end. In dealing with him, it was important to stay neutral as long as possible, not to be sucked into his strategy: creating a conflict for him to use as grounds for extortion, extortion he justified by her so-called stealing from him.

He'll use such justifications to explain why someone should

commit to him, because he won't get his hands dirty on anything. He'll send his troops forward. Common soldiers, cannon fodder.

He'll get there when it's time to haul in the loot.

It took some prevarication for me to stay neutral about Sonja while still making him feel that I was on his side. My neutrality annoyed him, and I was increasingly nervous that he might see where my loyalties really were. But choosing his side just like that wasn't an option, either, since I'd be exposing myself to the risk of having to fix things for him that might prove disadvantageous to Sonja or myself.

I felt like a juggler trying to keep dozens of balls in the air. After making me listen to his complaints about Sonja and "his money," he renewed his attack on Francis: she'd been "talking" about him. She'd told one of his girlfriends he'd had Cor "done," and Sonja should pay for her indiscretion.

Eventually, he figured he couldn't use Francis's "talking" as a basis for extortion because it pointed too much toward the liquidation of Cor, and he was afraid he'd be prosecuted.

He moved on and found somebody else.

But that didn't mean Sonja was safe. Wim would be back as soon as he found a new reason to harass her. And it didn't take him long.

Richie

2013/2003

In 1993, when Sonja and Cor had a son, Cor was over the moon. He named his son after what he'd always wanted to be: *rich*. Richie was about two years old when he survived the first assassination attempt on his father. He was seven when Wim put a gun to his head to force me and Sonja to say where Cor was hiding so he could have him liquidated. He was nine years old when his father died.

After Cor's death, Wim claimed the role of the father whose murder he had directed. He demanded that Cor's family show him respect. Richie, who was suffering deeply over the loss of his dad, had to listen to Wim saying his father had actually been a "fat dog." He had to endure Wim insulting, degrading, and belittling his father while boasting about how great he himself was. Wim took pleasure in having beaten the man in whose shadow he'd always lived.

Richie instinctively loathed the uncle who was destroying the memory of his father. He was too upset to pretend to like him, respect him, or obey him. And he was too young to see the danger.

Barely ten years old, he was cold and unemotional toward Wim. Already, Wim thought of him as a pain in the neck. "Who does the little shit think he is?" he'd snort. "Thinks he's just like his dad? He'd better watch out, then. You know what I'll do, right?"

Yes, we knew, but for his own safety we'd never told Richie it had been Wim who'd given the order for the murder of his father. On the contrary, we'd denied the countless allegations that were made in the media, fearing Richie would run his mouth and retribution would follow.

But Richie had never asked us about it, as if there was no need, because he had known all along. He went his own way, avoiding Wim. This bugged Wim the most.

While Wim was in prison for six years, Richie grew into the spitting image of his father, both in looks and in character. He and Cor have the same face. He has exactly the same build, demeanor, and, especially, sense of humor. He's socially adept, a welcome guest wherever he goes. He turns life into a party, the way Cor used to and Wim never could because he can't feel any zest for life.

Richie didn't give a damn about his jailed uncle, even though Wim reminded him regularly that he was the notorious Willem Holleeder. Wim felt Richie didn't "show him respect," and it only added to his hatred for him.

Richie wasn't in the least interested in criminality. He was a talented tennis player and exercised intensively, something we'd encouraged as a way to keep him away from crime.

We knew it was very likely that, at some point, Wim would seek an opportunity to start working on Richie, and with his remarks about not letting children grow up so they can't take revenge in our minds, we worried about Richie's well-being after Wim was released.

So when the opportunity arose for Richie to play tennis in the United States, we sent him there. Finally he was at a safe distance.

He left behind his pride and joy: his small car, a VW Polo. Now that Richie was in the States, Wim had his eye on the car.

Richie

★ ★ ★

It was nine p.m. when the doorbell rang. "Are you coming down?"
  Of course I went.

A: "What's up?"

W: "Well, Assie, actually, I'm getting fed up. I've got to get around
    on my bike. It's raining, it's cold, I can't see, it's really danger-
    ous. But Sonja still has that kid's car, just sitting there. Why
    shouldn't I use it? Why doesn't she just say I can use it? I can't
    register a car in my name. Why hasn't she given the car to
    me? They get to drive around in cars, and I have to be on the
    scooter in the cold? How did they pay for those cars, any-
    way?"

A: "But, Wim, you already have a car, don't you? The one that's
    registered to the garage in Haarlem?"

W: "So? What about it?"

A: "So can't you drive that one? Then you won't be cold, either."

W: "No, Assie, that's not how it works. She should have loaned
    that car to me! Isn't that normal? We are family, right? It
    doesn't matter whether I've got another car somewhere. She
    should have given the car to me right away."

A: "Can't you ask her to lend it to you?"

W: "No, Assie. Listen to me, Assie. I shouldn't have to *ask* any-
    thing. She should have offered it to me. She knows the
    weather is bad and I have to ride the scooter through the cold
    and the rain, doesn't she? Why couldn't she just hand over the
    car to me? Drives cars herself while making me use the
    scooter? If I fall off that scooter, you'll see what I'll do to her.
    I'll crush her jaw. I'll knock the teeth out of her mouth. You
    know she's got money, don't you?"

The fact that he already had a car didn't support his accusation of Sonja, so he left that part out entirely. It didn't matter. An argument didn't have to make sense; it just had to serve Wim's goal: to find a cause for conflict that would justify his extortion of Sonja.

Richie's compact car was merely a stepping-stone to the real issue: money.

Later that evening, I hurried over to Sonja's to tell her, and I asked her if it might be better to just give the car to Wim so he wouldn't use it as a reason to start with her.

Sonja wasn't planning on lending him the car, though. "I don't want him driving Richie's car, As. He's involved in drugs and shady business, and I don't want Richie's car tangled up in it. He meets his drug clients, and if the Justice Department sees Richie's car, they'll think he's involved somehow, or they'll seize the car and Rich won't have one when he gets back. I just won't do it."

The following day, he was on my doorstep again.

W: "Assie, it's a bloody shame! They're cruising in their cars and I
    have to face the elements on a bike. They've got houses to
    live in. I can't even register a house in my name. So, she's got
    money. Why didn't she tell me? You can't have a house and
    cars if you don't have money. She's got money. But she's not
    entitled to it. Who does she think she is?"

I tried to postpone Sonja's doom for as long as I could. "How do you know you can't borrow the car? You haven't even asked her yet," I kept telling him. "You're mad at Sonja without even knowing whether she'll let you borrow it."

I knew he had no intention of asking her, for if she said yes, the matter would be solved and he'd have to come up with another reason for the conflict.

I pretended not to understand, and he realized he couldn't get me to buy in to his line of reasoning without him actually asking Sonja the question.

Two days later, he was back.

W: "I asked her today to let me borrow that car. Just to see what
    she'd say. But she won't give it to me. Filthy whore. She just
    won't. Because she won't have me driving it. Because the Jus-
    tice Department would seize it. I don't care about the fucking
    car—I can go by bike just as easily. I just wanted to see if she'd
    hand it over. But I'm not done with her yet. This is just the
    beginning. I'll have that cute little car incinerated so the kid
    won't have it, either. Nothing for me, nothing for him."
A: "But if you just talk to her, I'm sure she'll give you the car."
W: "No, I'm done talking to her."
A: "Then I'll go tell her to give it to you."
W: "No need. She's no longer allowed to give that car to me."

He had no intention of solving the conflict. As long as there was conflict, something to blame her for, he could justify retaliating any way he wanted: through betrayal, manipulation, threats, extortion—and, eventually, murder. Sonja had pampered him his entire life. She'd shared a lifetime of joy and pain with him, been through everything with him. The aftermath of the Heineken kidnapping, traveling to Paris at least once, sometimes twice, a week, always doing his laundry and ironing, getting his groceries, cooking his dinner.

None of that mattered. It was all meaningless. Forty years of loyal service erased by what Sonja had "done to him." From now on even the smallest bump in the road would be her fault. Everything he'd brought on himself was Sonja's doing. Sonja was "a nail in his coffin," so she had to pay up.

It was only natural, right?

Sonja had officially gone from friend to foe. This was the moment we'd all been dreading, and the reason we'd tried to comply with his demands as much as we could. From then on, he'd be at my door every day, displaying his theatrical indignation toward Sonja. The extortion had begun.

Sonja and I had to try to stay ahead of him for as long as we could, meanwhile gathering evidence against him so we might be able to reach our goal just in time: making him pay for Cor.

In one respect, there was an upside to this misery. This could be my chance to make his motive for killing Cor clear to the Justice Department. Why else did he feel entitled to the inheritance; why did he "bear the burden" while she "got the benefits"?

If we could both record our conversations with him, the extortion of Sonja—horrible as it was to endure—offered an excellent opportunity to link past to present and capture Wim's past crimes in his present-time statements.

I bought Sonja some recording equipment.

"I usually attach it to the front of my bra, right in between my boobs. Then I put some tape over it, to keep it in place," I said.

"Like this?" Sonja asked, and in one go, she was wired.

Sonja was ready to rumble.

Giving Out the Confidential Statements

"How should we do this?" Sonja asked. "An entire weekend is a long time. We can't stay away that long without him noticing." Betty Wind had estimated it would take at least two full days to write down our statements. Getting away and staying away unnoticed for two entire days was a real issue: it would never work. Wim would notice immediately and become suspicious.

The day we were supposed to meet was a Sunday, but Wim didn't do weekends; he didn't differentiate between days, as he'd never had a regular job. Whether it was a Saturday or a Sunday, he'd be at my door just as early as any other day of the week.

Thus I couldn't rule out running into him on my way to the meeting point where Michelle and Manon were going to pick us up. I'd tell him I had to respond to an urgent call from a client in Roermond in two hours, so I had no time for "a stroll" or a cup of coffee.

Then I'd drive toward the highway in case he followed me on his scooter, and then change direction to pick up Sonja.

I could get away with this fairly easily, since my job gave me some space. Things were more complicated for Sonja. She didn't have a job to use as a front, and he came to her door at the strangest moments. Especially when he couldn't get through to me, he'd drop by her house. She couldn't give him a plausible explanation for her absence. Where would she go this early in the day?

We agreed that I would pick her up at Francis's house, because Wim didn't know where Francis lived.

Sonja would drive there at seven thirty a.m. and park her car there. Leaving her car at home would strike Wim as odd. Sonja, leaving without her car? Who with, and what for?

If she ran into Wim at this early hour, she'd tell him she was going to help Francis out just like the day before, because her daughter, Sonja's granddaughter, Nora, was sick with a virus. He'd let her go then, scared that she might be contagious—his heart condition made him terrified of catching anything. We'd arranged that if he demanded that Sonja come with him immediately for one of his usual urgent errands, she would call me and I'd let my phone ring so she wouldn't have to speak to me. On that cue, I'd call Francis to call her mother and urge her to hurry up because Nora was seriously sick. Francis would do this right away, without asking questions.

Our kids don't ask questions. The word "him" is enough for them to know it's serious. They know we never mention his name on the phone.

If he met me at Francis's place or on my way there, I'd tell him I had already dealt with the urgent issue with my client so I wasn't in a hurry anymore and was going to see Francis's little girl, as she was so worried about her. This would match Sonja's version of events.

We still had to come up with an explanation in case he saw us getting into a car with Michelle or Manon. I said I'd handle that by saying they were two of my basketball friends with whom I was going to watch a tournament. Sonja was just coming along; she didn't have a social life of her own, anyway.

I often belittled Sonja in his presence, the same way he did. He liked to hear it, because it made him feel I was loyal to him, not to Sonja. That way, I remained worthy of his goodwill.

The scenarios we'd come up with would also be valid if we didn't see *him*, but he saw *us*. This happened sometimes. He'd ask about your day with vague interest to check if your reply matched his observations. If your answers didn't match, you were hiding something.

We were supposed to spend the night at the interview location. This would be a problem if he dropped by in the middle of the night. I often switch off my doorbell and he's used to that, but that couldn't be done at Sonja's apartment. How would she explain not answering the door?

Fortunately, when we got back, we could check her security camera system—which registered anyone at the entrance—to see if he'd been there the night we were gone. If he had, she'd say she'd been knocked out by sleeping pills. He'd buy it.

The next thing we had to figure out was how to handle our phones. What should we do when he called? For he would definitely call, not once, but ten or fifteen times in a row if he didn't get through to us.

I could get away with it rather easily by claiming I was working, but here Sonja was in a fix, especially if her phone was switched off for an entire weekend.

If she wasn't home, he'd call her. "Where are you? What are you doing? Come over here, now!" It always had to be NOW!

"Wim, I can't right now, I'm busy."

"Busy? See you in a bit!" and he'd hang up and switch his phone off so you couldn't call back and were forced to go, because if you didn't show up he'd go haywire and start looking for you everywhere, making a scene.

So it would be best to avoid any form of contact so he wouldn't be able to order us to come. We decided to switch our phones off. In between interviews, we'd check the situation and if things were getting out of hand and he'd called often enough to make him suspicious, we'd have to go home.

That's just the way it was.

I couldn't possibly tell people at the office I was going to make statements against my brother to the Justice Department, not only because, being criminal lawyers, we are always on the opposite side from the Public Prosecution, but also because I couldn't burden others with this kind of secret. And of course, we couldn't take the risk of anyone letting on to someone else what we're doing, however accidental or well meant it might be. Nobody could understand how fatal just talking could be for us. It can't be fathomed by any normal person.

That's why the weekend was the safest possibility for me. On weekdays, there'd often be crises that required my attention, and if people at work couldn't reach me, they'd panic, and everyone would start to wonder where I was and why I didn't get in touch with the office. Although the work would continue over the weekend, at least the office telephone wouldn't ring.

But Michelle and Manon said it would have to be Sunday *and* Monday; there was nothing to be done about that. This was incomprehensible to me. I felt I shouldn't be the one adjusting to their schedule; they should adjust to mine. I was giving them something, but I wanted to do it safely and without raising all kinds of questions at the office.

It was the first time I was dealing with the difference between civil servants and entrepreneurs, and it wouldn't be the last. Meeting on weekends was often a no-go, and so were weeknights. It had to be office hours all the time, and the moment it was five p.m., an internal alarm clock seemed to go off and people wanted to leave.

The plan was set. We would leave from the designated location on Sunday at eight in the morning. I asked a colleague to take my urgent client calls on Monday, so people at the office wouldn't be questioning my whereabouts.

Amstelveen, across from shopping mall Westwijk. They were already there when we drove up. I parked my car in a residential area so it wouldn't stand out; after all, it would be there the whole weekend, and who knows whether Wim would speed by on his bike. He went everywhere on that thing, and he'd always show up where you least expected him.

"Good morning, early birds! It's a long drive to where we'll be taking your statements, so make yourselves comfortable," Michelle said cheerily.

My God, how perky, like this was some kind of field trip. They didn't have the slightest notion of the pain it cost us to get away unseen, not a clue of how difficult this trip was for us.

I felt extremely grumpy all of a sudden. It happens three times a year at the most, but when it does, it's bad. I looked at Sonja, and she could see it in my eyes right away.

"You will behave, you hear me?" she snapped at me.

But that wouldn't be easy. Once I'm in one of these moods, I can't just shake it off. I tried analyzing where this had come from so suddenly; maybe it was a premonition not to go through with this.

I shot a let's-go-back-glance at Sonja. She shook her head and I understood: No, we're pushing through. Behave.

She was right. I had to try to pull myself together.

In times like these, the only thing that can change my foul mood for the better is food.

The love of food is a major thing Wim and I had in common. We had our special places for all things edible, and it didn't matter if we had to drive the extra mile to get them. We'd drive across the city, to the Rivierenbuurt quarter to get the best pastry, to the Jordaan for the best sausage roll, and to the Gelderlandplein shopping center for the finest fruits.

I pulled out the buttered cheese sandwich I'd brought with me.

Meanwhile, Sonja was chatting with the girls and diverting their attention from me. I declined their friendly attempts to start a chat with me, gesturing that I couldn't talk with my mouth full. I wasn't up for chitchat yet.

An hour and a half later, we arrived at the location where our interviews were to take place. To our amazement, we were confronted with two more civil servants from the Special Witness Protection Program. I hadn't seen that coming: another set of interviewers, two men. They introduced themselves, and I immediately dubbed them Columbo and Briscoe.

I hadn't thought about the way the statements would be taken. If I had, I might have anticipated this. But I certainly wasn't prepared for another set of interviewers. What were these strangers doing here?

We were used to Michelle and Manon—they were young, pleasant people—but these two were typical police officers, from Amsterdam at that. I already envisioned them leaking at Café Nol on Westerstraat after a night out drinking.

I did not feel like doing this at all. I could see that Sonja was having the same reaction; she looked at me and shook her head no. She would not talk to these people, for sure.

I took her aside.

"As, I'm not sitting down with these two men. I don't know them. I just won't."

I felt exactly the same way. My mood, just slightly lifted by the cheese sandwich, dropped all the way down again.

"Where are the restrooms?" I asked.

"Through that door." Columbo gestured. Sonja sauntered out behind me to deliberate.

"This was not what we agreed on, right? Two more people. It's not how it should be."

"No," I said, "I'm not happy about it, either, but the damage has been done now. They've already seen us."

"It doesn't matter. I'm not talking to those two guys. It doesn't feel right; they look like proper cops. I'll shut down."

"I get it," I said, and then, reluctantly, "I'll talk to them then. We can't throw in the towel at this point. Maybe my mood actually was a bad omen. But you told me to push through, so there's no going back now. We should have done that at the beginning. We can hardly say we won't talk to them and tell them to take us a hundred and fifty kilometers back to Amsterdam. They've booked rooms, installed equipment, made time for us. It would be extremely rude, Box. You can't stop the leaking anyway; you can only hope it won't happen."

Sonja did have a point, though, and I didn't understand why Betty had organized things this way. How can you expect two people who've kept their silence all their lives to tell their life story to complete strangers? This would be the first time in our lives we would be speaking about our misery.

We walked back.

"Sonja will go with the ladies, and I'll talk to you," I told the men.

"All right, let's get started," Columbo said, and Sonja and I went to two separate interview rooms.

Prior to our interviews, we had to sign an agreement stating that we wouldn't discuss the making of our statements or their contents with others. If we did, all agreements would be void, and the Public Prosecution Service would be entitled to use our statements and their contents without our consent. Meaning we couldn't discuss this procedure with anyone; we couldn't even talk about this life-altering process with our children or mother. It's not as if we would do that at this point, since "they can't tell what they don't know," but our children would definitely have to tell us how they felt about our action at some point: if they didn't agree, we wouldn't go through with it.

These were the thoughts that went through my mind when Briscoe cleared his throat. "Astrid, this is the tape on which we'll be recording the interview. Are you ready? We'll start the tape now."

The Threatening of Peter

After making our statements, Sonja and I were totally drained.

For two days, we'd gone through memory hell. The grief about Cor that we'd been suppressing out of fear for the last ten years turned out to be as intense as on the day he'd died. The denial that our brother was his murderer had been blocking our mourning process: every single day we'd had to make sure not to betray him through our behavior, actions, or the things we said for fear of a repetition of what he'd done to Cor.

After two days, we didn't just feel exhausted and empty; we were also glad we'd finally told the truth.

We expected Betty to snatch the statements from the hands of her employees the very same day and to start reading them immediately. So two days later I called and asked her if she thought the statements provided enough relevant evidence to use against Wim. We needed to know. If not, we wanted to get off this emotional roller coaster as quickly as we could.

She said she wanted to discuss it with us in person, and we made an appointment for May 1, 2013.

Before we got there, though, the next catastrophe occurred.

APRIL 25, 2013

I've been out and I had my phone switched off the entire evening because I didn't want him bugging me. The mere sight of his number on the display makes me feel tense.

On my way home, I switch my phone on to check if anything crazy has gone down. The missed calls come flooding in. Wim has called a number of times; I know something is up. Sonja has called, too, confirming my suspicion.

I don't return Wim's call, knowing I'll have to show up somewhere right away.

I call Sonja. She'll probably know what's going on.

Sonja answers the phone and tells me Wim went berserk. "Why this time?" I ask.

"First he called to bully me, and then he drove over to Peter's house to threaten him."

It was unusual for Sonja to be speaking negatively about Wim. We usually don't badmouth him over the phone. This worried me right away. "Okay, and now?"

"Peter has filed a report."

"Oh, God, that's not smart. Does Wim know?"

"I don't think so," Sonja says.

"This is going to be bad."

I know there's no way he'll put up with this. For him, talking to the police calls for the death penalty. Peter doesn't know what he's gotten himself into.

How am I going to solve this?

APRIL 26, 2013

The morning after, Wim calls me early and says in his usual manner, "Meet me at the Maxis store in Muiden."

He doesn't know I've already heard what happened last night, and I am well aware that my seeing Wim is of vital importance to Peter. I get in my car and drive to Muiden.

When I get there, he's waiting for me. He knows Sonja calls me whenever there's trouble, so I say right away:

A: "Did you fall out with Sonja?"

W: "And with Peter. I went to his place last night."

A: "Yeah."

W: "He's called Stijn Franken all stressed out because he feels threatened."

A: "Yeah."

W: "I went over to his house last night to tell him: Listen, you're not using my name, you're not using my character, you're gonna take it out and if you don't, you'll see what I'll do to you. His bitch was there, too, and he said, 'I feel threatened.' I said, I don't threaten, I just do what I say. I'm done with you, you're taking my name out, my character. I will fuck up that movie, I'm fucking done with it."

Wim was after Peter about the American film being made based on Peter's book. He was being played. How could they put him in a movie everybody is profiting from without talking to him first? He should get money out of it, too. I try talking Wim down.

A: "Why don't you talk to Peter again?"

W: "If I go there and he says no, I'll just gun him down. Another one bites the dust."

I'm starting to sweat bullets. If he finds out Peter talked to the police and filed a report, it would only add to his list of reasons to kill Peter.

I'm really worried about Peter. I have to let on that Peter might file a report, so Wim can get used to the idea and won't blow up entirely if he gets the message.

A: "What if he files a report?"
W: "Well, he'll just have to do that."

He is confident that Peter won't have the guts to actually do it; he knows how much he scares people. Nobody dares talk about him to the police, and those who do come to regret it.

What was Peter thinking, filing a report?

Meanwhile, I've been talking to the police for quite some time now. Once again, I'm afraid he'll see it written all over my face.

Right now, his focus is entirely on Peter, so he isn't paying attention to me. Not in the least, since I'm the one actively trying to work out the situation in his best interest.

I try to get Wim to talk to Peter. He refuses. It's all on Peter, and that's what he'll say if the police interview them.

W: "I'll tell them he's banging my little sister. It's only natural it's pissing me off, right? Do you really think they can't see that?"

To Wim, every interaction between a man and a woman is about sex, one more way in which he resembles our father.

A: "Well, Wim, if that's what you say, they'll commit you to the asylum."

W: "What for?"

A: "What do you think? They are adults, they're free to decide who
they're banging, right? You can't be the one deciding it for
your fifty-three-year-old sister. You're not her husband, you're
just her brother. If you bring that up as a reason, it will sound
really crazy. You won't win. By the way, you know it's not
true, either."

W: "It isn't? Didn't Thomas claim that, too?"

A: "Oh, Wim, you really have to bring up Thomas now? Come
on."

Poor Thomas. Making statements against Wim cost him his life.

Wim has often bitched about those statements, about how
they had been used as supporting evidence leading to his conviction. Now he is using them to his own advantage. It disgusts
me.

I try to prepare him for Peter's report.

A: "What if he does file a report?"

W: "Let him! Then what?"

A: "You'll get more hassle."

W: "What can he do? I'll just say, 'Yes, I went to his place, I asked
him to leave me out of the movie. I can't afford a lawyer because I'm broke, I can't sue him, that's why I told him
myself.' Done. And if he says 'You threatened me,' I'll say he
might have taken it that way."

A: "What did you say, though?"

W: "Doesn't matter! I'll take out all the shit he's giving me on
Sonja. Listen, I'm in the right. As, they can't make a movie
about me and the others, keep the money for themselves, and
not pay the people it's about."

A: "Hmm."

W: "It's just not right!"

A: "No, but you can talk about it, can't you?"

W: "No! 'Cause, Astrid, how many times have I told you things are going wrong?"

A: "Hmm."

W: "Assie, I'll tell you this: I can't handle this. I'm losing my mind here. This shit is . . . [incomprehensible] I won't accept it, you know? [Gun gesture again.] Yeah!"

A: "Calm down, please! There's no reason to lose your mind. Nothing's up, and everybody means well."

Wim gestures me to come outside as if he's going to tell me something that can't be said indoors.

W: "If I go to him and say, 'Listen, how can we fix this?' and if he says, 'I don't care, I've already got my money' . . . If I took this step . . ."

A: "Yeah?"

W: "There's no way I'm leaving with my tail between my legs. [whispering] I'll shoot him to death."

A: "Yeah, but—"

W: "It's going down, 'cause I'm fed up!"

A: "No!"

W: "Astrid, I'm through!"

After our talk at the Maxis store, I go over to Peter's.

Once again, Wim has burdened me with information that forces me to get involved. I tell Peter how Wim is threatening to kill him. He should be prepared for the worst, but he must never say that I warned him.

Peter hears me out and feels uneasy about it, but he stands firm behind the report he's filed. Wim has gone too far, and Peter will wait and see. What else can he do? The damage is done.

With a knot in my stomach, I drive to the office to get some work done. Damn Peter and his principles. Why won't he yield a little, just once? He's so hardheaded. I feel he is being unwise, but at the same time, I admire his taking a hard line with Wim.

I've been afraid to do that for more than fifteen years. Peter just did it. Why couldn't I? Has he brainwashed me this completely? Am I this afraid of Wim because his terror resembles that of my father during my childhood?

Whatever it is, I have to keep my eye on the facts: Cor, Endstra, Thomas; they showed what Wim was capable of. My way of dealing with him might not be the bravest, but at least it isn't suicide.

That same day, I hadn't been at the office for more than an hour when Wim called me again and told me to meet him. "Come to where we were last time."

I drove back to the parking lot at the Maxis store.

"He filed the report, that pervert," he said in a chilling tone. "As, I need to know exactly what he told the cops. You go and listen."

His lawyer, Stijn Franken, had told him that if he was convicted based on Peter's report, he'd get in trouble regarding his parole, and it meant he'd be serving his three years' probationary jail sentence after all.

All because of Peter.

He whispered into my ear that if he had to do time, he'd hire a gunman before he went in. Peter would go, as Thomas had.

I had to warn Peter and see what I could do.

"You'll go now?" he asked.

"Yeah, I'll call him from the car to see if he's home, and otherwise

I'll find him someplace. It'll be fine. I'll let you know when I've talked to him."

"Okay, talk to you later."

Peter was at home, and I drove over there. I was pondering what to tell him. I wanted to protect him, but I had to be wary of what I said.

Of course, we'd already confided in Peter a long time ago, so he knew what Wim had done and what he might do again. I just couldn't fathom Peter's reaction to this stressful situation, and I didn't want to cause him to panic, making him unpredictable. For all I knew, he'd get so scared he'd let on to the police that we'd been making confidential statements. Call me paranoid, but I couldn't take that risk, and in the moment I already regretted ever having confided in Peter. I felt so worried.

I parked the car right in front of Peter's house, and he came to the door.

"Sorry, Peter, it's me again."

I told him that Wim was extremely nervous about his parole and that he was making threats. I felt it would be inappropriate to ask Peter straight out what exactly he'd told the police, but I did get a general idea of what he and his wife, Jacqueline, had said. I decided to downplay their statements a bit to Wim to keep him from hiring a gunman for Peter.

That evening, I reported to Wim. He was at Maike's, and I spoke to him on the corner of her street. Wim had to report to the police the next day at ten a.m. in Hilversum. He'd been summoned for an interview at the precinct, but he still feared getting arrested in the meantime. "Let's see where I have to be tomorrow. Drive along with me," he said.

We drove past the precinct and afterward we hung out at Maike's place. Wim remained enraged and agitated. He thought it was a shame Peter had gone to the police. Wim's double standards are striking. The second something is done to him or he's got the slightest suspicion in that direction, he'll scurry to the police. Like the time he stood on Westerstraat with my mother and a gunman appeared to be coming at him to kill him. He left my mom standing there and drove straight to the main precinct to file a report. But the rules he imposes on everyone don't apply to him.

Naturally, Sonja got all the blame. The logic behind his conclusion was hard to fathom. But then, his aim is not to reason; he just wants to put the blame on somebody else. Whatever misery he causes, it's never on him. In that respect he's just like his old man. It's always someone else forcing him to threaten, abuse, and in Wim's case, extort and kill as well.

"All right, good luck tomorrow." And I said goodbye.

The next morning he called me early, at seven a.m. He wanted to see me and told me to come to Maxis in Muiden at eight. He told me he was getting pretty scared about his parole being withdrawn and the possibility of being held there. Wim had figured out what to tell the police to prevent imprisonment. He was still planning to tell them he'd been at Peter's because supposedly Sonja was having sex with him. He didn't have the faintest idea what a weird impression this would make.

I knew he'd be released if I came to his aid now. Just four days before, I'd been making confidential statements with the exact goal of putting him away. But I also knew Peter would be in big trouble if Wim had to go back inside. I didn't know if he'd made arrangements for Peter yet, but I didn't dare count on the opposite. I had no choice but to help Wim.

"If you want to walk out of there, you'd better admit to it, talk

Peter's story down a bit, and tell them your version of what went down."

The day before, the very word "admit" had caused an outburst of rage, but in his stressed state of mind right before the interview, he seemed to listen to my idea. I thought he should resolve the fight with Peter before the interview started.

"Just call Peter and talk about it so you can say it's all been re-solved during your interview," I urged him.

"You call him and see what he wants," he said.

It was one hour before the interview. I reached Peter in time and told him Wim was in the car with me, and I really wanted them to sort it out together.

"Can I just put him on the line?" I asked with sweaty palms, thinking, Please don't refuse.

To my great relief, he said, "Put him on then."

Wim acted really nice on the phone, of course taking the piss out of himself, for this gives people the impression he knows himself, and he told Peter it wasn't meant that way.

That settled the issue.

Wim told his story to the police and pointed out how they'd resolved the issue. The police wanted to hear this from Peter himself and called him. Peter confirmed it, and Wim could go home.

He called me right after his release.

"Would you come to that same place?" he asked.

I went to Muiden, and we spent the entire day together. I'd done well in advising him. For now, the parole issue was solved. I'd rather it had been different, but this seemed to me to be the safest solution for everybody. We concluded the day at Maike's house.

"I'm heading home now," I said.

"I'll walk you," he said. He'd managed to stay out of jail, and his fear of being inside again had been replaced by smugness.

Outside, he told me, "See, that's how it's done: scare them first, talk to them later. Now I want to see Peter about those movie rights." I couldn't believe my ears. He was going to keep extorting Peter. And he had involved me; he'd trapped me by calling on my protective reflex toward Peter. Now I was someone who could get close to Peter to carry his messages. I had to tell Peter that Wim didn't want his character to be in the movie and that this was in fact his reason for being upset. Wim forbade me to say it was about the money, for that would turn it into extortion.

There were some advantages to Wim asking me to take this position. I'd try to record the extortion. It may sound opportunistic, but when disadvantage is all you've ever experienced, you learn to see advantages where you can.

APRIL 29, 2013

The next Monday morning, the misery continues. Wim calls me to order me over to the Viersprong in Vinkeveen. When he comes walking up to me, I can tell he's upset. After the initial tension regarding his parole lifted, Wim apparently realized delay didn't necessarily mean cancellation.

W: "Did you talk to Stijn yet?"
A: "No, why?"
W: "Well, the parole thing. If I am convicted, I'll get trouble with this parole business. The fucking trick he pulled on me, that

piece of shit. He's playing games—why can't he just shut up!
I'm not sure if he'll blab, act all smart."

A: "Should I go see him again?"

W: "I think he wants to go through with this criminal case. As if it
isn't enough everyone is getting shit over that fucking movie,
I should go inside for three years over it? It's the best promotion there is for that movie. You know what I'll do, right? Not
just some threat. If I have to go inside for three years, he'll get
it. My children get hurt, he gets hurt! Astrid, I can tell you
this, I gotta do what I gotta do, and I will do it, too! [whisper-
ing] Assie, if I get put away for three years…[gun gesture]"

A: "No."

W: "Yes!"

A: "No, don't! Just find a solution."

W: "I'll try to fix things with Peter. It works for him if both parties
are kept undamaged. If he really wants a fight, that's fine with
me; I'll speed things up and arrange it tonight."

I immediately rush back to Peter's to try to get him to change his
statement enough so that Wim won't suffer any consequences.

However, Peter is not the easiest person to deal with, and he sure
as hell won't be scared. I'm stuck between two strong egos. Peter
won't take anything back, and I feel nervous about his reaction. If
Peter digs in his heels and I take that message back to Wim, he'll
have him killed.

I'm worried Peter isn't realizing how serious this is, that Wim actually will carry out his threats. Then again, if anyone knows what
Wim is like, it's Peter—this won't make him revise his statement,
though.

Speaking with Peter, I can tell he's willing to bury the hatchet,
but he won't retract his version of events. I propose they meet up

to talk. Peter consents, and Wim's lawyer, Stijn, arranges a meeting for the next day.

I beg Peter to comply with Wim's wishes. He says he'll do his best to meet him halfway, but no more. He'll approach him calmly, willing to talk. I go back to Wim and tell him everything will be fine.

APRIL 30, 2013

After the meeting, Wim asks me over to tell me what happened.

I arrive at Sandra's, and Wim is lying on the couch. "He's not happy, is he?" I ask her.

"You think it's me?" she asks.

"Never, you're a darling."

He grunts, "Hmm, come with me." As always, we go outside to talk.

W: "I called him yesterday, or rather, he called me. He thought it wasn't that bad, or at least he thought it was a laid-back conversation."

A: "Yeah."

W: "So, he was glad we did this."

A: "He was?"

W: "Yeah."

A: "Yeah, he's also written to Stijn that it was a good talk, he's okay with it."

W: "That's good then, right?"

A: "And Stijn wrote a letter on your behalf."

W: "And that I apologized, this apology stuff again, that's fucking bugging me."

A: "Yeah, well..."

W: "It's bugging me, because, well, it makes me wonder: What
the fuck, that retard files a report for no reason at all, and
then they make me apologize?"

A: "Well, Wim, if that's what you gotta do to prevent three years
inside, what's the issue? What's bugging you?"

W: "I guess that's true. Yeah, Stijn tells me, 'It's almost impossible
for them to give you those three years. They can't give you
three years if the problem is gone.'"

That was the only reason he'd apologized—with the utmost reluc-
tance. He still wasn't happy about it, but it was worth it. According
to Stijn, they couldn't give him the three years he was facing, so he
could drop it for a while.

Wim's Arrest

"WIM HAS BEEN ARRESTED!" SONJA EXCLAIMS. "WAS IT BECAUSE OF OUR statements?"

"I have no idea," I say. "They didn't say, but I assume they won't inform us beforehand anyway."

I call one of the women from the CIU and ask why Wim was arrested. "Is this happening because of us?"

Strangely enough, she claims she doesn't know, either.

"How can you not know? You're part of the investigation unit, aren't you?"

"No," she says, "they never tell us in advance, either." She'll have to look into it.

I tell her I really need to know if it's because of us, since then I'd have to reconsider my position. What should I tell people at work, for example? Imagine if everything we'd told suddenly appeared on the news. I could forget about my job.

The suspense was unbearable: this could be the moment our lives would change drastically, the moment all the dangers we'd have to reckon with would present themselves.

I'm a nervous wreck. I need to know what he's been arrested for, and soon. In the meantime Stijn has already called me, and I can't be speaking to him if it's about cases in which I'm testifying myself. It doesn't feel right, and it would hurt our case, as well.

I check to see if Wim's girlfriend Sandra has heard anything. At this point, she doesn't know about our statements to the Justice Department.

Sandra has spoken to Jan, the guy from the garage where Wim was picked up and asked to come along—no arresting unit. Nothing had happened at Sandra's place, either, no kicked-in doors, no house search, none of it.

It seems this operation isn't focused on him in particular, so the arrest is not related to the cases about which we've made statements.

This is readily confirmed by our CIU contacts. The sense of relief that the moment hasn't come and our lives won't be turned upside down just yet is immediately followed by disappointment. Why haven't they arrested him for the liquidations yet?

It turns out that Wim was arrested along with others on suspicion of extortion. His arrest is not linked to our statements, and we should act as normal as we can.

This means we can't deviate from our usual pattern: visiting, bringing clothes to prison, putting money in his jail account so he can buy stuff there. We have to pretend nothing's going on, as if on the day of his arrest we hadn't been hoping he'd finally be prosecuted for Cor's murder. We have to pretend we're not talking to the police.

Our only advantage is having some peace and quiet for the time being, and we need it badly. The tensions have worn us out.

With him inside, I finish making my confidential statements. It's nice not to have to be so alert on my way to the appointed location.

We've become grateful for small favors.

Wim's Arrest

★ ★ ★

I'm in my car when Sandra calls me. After forty-four days, he is already being released. Once again, he's a free man.

It's all starting again.

Part IV
Diary of a Witness

2014

The Order Is Issued

WIM HAS SANDRA CALL ME AND ASK IF I'LL COME AND SEE HER—WHICH means him. As soon as I get there, he takes me outside. He wants to know how Sonja reacted to the two messages I was supposed to pass on to her.

The first was about how he has to ride his scooter when it rains and the visibility is poor, so he runs the risk of having an accident. That is her fault because she won't give him Richie's car. The message is "If I fall off that scooter and I'm hurt, I'll kill Francis and her son, what a fucking tramp. So I have to ride like this? You tell her. Tell her that I'm really mad. That I don't care, that she'll have to wait and see, but that if I fall off, I'll kill one of her kids."

In the same conversation, he repeatedly threatened to kill Sonja herself. I delivered the message.

"And?" he asks.

"She can't hand over the car. She's sold it."

This really gets him going. She doesn't do what he tells her to? While he is threatening her children? He's surprised. He figured Sonja doesn't take chances where her kids are concerned. That's the regular pattern and he's used to it: she does what he tells her to. And that would have happened now, if Sonja and I hadn't agreed not to give in so we could record his reaction.

"Who did she sell it to?"

I tell him she's not going to tell him. "Because you'll go and see the person."

I see him thinking: More disobedience from Sonja? What is she up to?

I tell him that I have delivered the message about killing her and her kids and that Sonja replied that she just doesn't care anymore because she has been terrified her whole life.

Then I tell him Sonja's reaction to the second message, which was that if Francis's earlier remark would lead to his imprisonment for the murder of Cor, he would pull Sonja down with him, and he would tell the Justice Department that she had him kill Cor.

Sonja's reaction: "Why do you think Cor lived so long? Because I always warned him."

He didn't expect this. He's quiet for a while. "Fucking tramp, isn't she?" he says, sounding surprised.

"No, but I get it now. She has played a double game all this time," I reply.

He can't believe it and mutters, "No?!"

I see doubt in his eyes. He never saw through Sonja's double role in all those years. He's totally unhinged. He can't believe that Sonja has had a hidden agenda all this time and didn't always live by his rules. At the same time, he knows like no other what a double game is.

"Can you believe this bitch?"

He suddenly realizes he hasn't been in charge all this time and may not be now. When she talked to Cor about him without him knowing, who else did she talk to? He has experienced this before. The threats became too much for his victims so they resorted to desperate measures and went to the Justice Department. Is it possible? Sonja, who had remained silent all this time?

He feels he is losing control and wants to avoid every chance of being played by Sonja in the future. "I want you to tell her one more thing: Go nowhere near my family... and tell her she means as much to me as my little brother Gerard."

Wim and Gerard haven't seen each other in years. Wim has written him off. He says it's a matter of time and money before it's his turn (gun gesture).

So now he has also written off Sonja, and I understand her fate. "Tell her I'm done with it." Which means, Look over your shoulder and fear for your life.

It makes him insecure that he has just found out that Sonja has played her own game all these years. It means that she may also try to establish her own position and betray him to the police.

His face shows a tortured look. He stops, stands still, then bends over and whispers in my ear. "If she talks about Cor, she'll have a problem." It's the only time I have heard him say Cor's name. I do hope my equipment has recorded this, I think while he keeps talking.

But I want more than this reaction on tape. He and I know exactly what he means, but somebody else listening to the tape won't. I have to make it clearer for the listener what we are discussing here, what we are talking about. But I don't want to clarify it myself, because he could later say that I provoked him and that his statements on tape aren't worth anything. So when he says about Sonja that she's a bitch, I just say briefly, "You'll get into more trouble because of her."

He and I know what "trouble" is: being convicted for Cor's murder after all.

Those few words of mine were enough to get him back to discussing the way he treats snitches to the police: "I'll tell you, As, I just have to take care of that immediately."

He made his pistol gesture with his hand. It's a sign that makes him untouchable to the Justice Department. For his whispering I have more or less found a solution by using the bugging equipment, but I can't record a gesture. And I can't record the meaning we ascribe to the gesture. So I confirm its meaning in my own words: "No, you shouldn't do that, Wim. You'd never be able to live with that."

His reaction is typical. "Yes, I can. I can't live with it if I don't." I need more, so I point out the risks of another liquidation in the face of the Justice Department.

"And you know then you'll end up with another loose end," I say. "I don't care."

He doesn't say, "What do you mean, 'loose end'?" or "What are you talking about?" No, a loose end doesn't interest him and he is willing to take the risk of hiring a contract killer—and having a possible witness. His determination scares me, and I try to lessen the threat to Sonja. If he gets his way over the car, he might not judge her so harshly. He might be more lenient toward her.

But it appears to be an idle hope.

"You have to tell her that she *cannot*, she is not allowed to anymore! It doesn't matter anymore. And tell her also that I know she hasn't sold it."

I get frightened, because I've heard those words "not allowed" before. That's what he said in January 2004, the year Endstra was liquidated. Endstra "was not allowed to pay anymore."

The message is loud and clear, but Wim takes it further and stretches the parallel with Endstra. He thinks Sonja is already talking to the police. "Take it from me: people who act like that talk to the police."

"Well, I would be very surprised, Wim. How would she end up there? It's impossible. I don't believe it."

He stops me by standing in front of me, and bends toward my ear: "I don't care, you know. [Whispering] I've already given the order."

My pulse quickens. "Okay."

"It's fine with me. If that's what she will do. Bye [pistol gesture]."

I went home immediately to find out if I'd been able to record his voice, and better yet, his whispering. I asked Cor to help me, as I often did. He was always there, in the background, with everything we did to get Wim sentenced for his murder; he always gave us the strength to continue by sending us a sign. Call it superstition, call us crazy, but if we were down or lost, something always happened that made us feel that he was there and doing his utmost to support us. Sometimes it would be a rose inexplicably left on the doorstep of Sonja's house in times of terrible stress; or it could be a particular song, a gust of wind through the room, the lights going on and off. That convinced us he was still there.

And now I needed him again, badly.

"Let it be successful, please let it be a success." My prayer was answered; I could hear the whispers. I even heard him say Cor's name. Finally, he mentioned a name. Would this at last be enough for a conviction for Cor's death?

I was happy with the recording, but at the same time very worried about its content. He'd already given the order for Sonja?

The way he stood there in front of me, the look in his eyes, and the coldness in his voice, the whispering.

I had to see her immediately.

But first I needed to find a spot in the house where I could keep this recording, so vital to me, without anyone being able to find it.

In the end I decided to take the recording to Sonja's to let her hear what he had said.

★ ★ ★

"Sis, you really have to watch out from now on," I told her when I got there. "He said that he has already given the order for you."

"You're kidding," said Sonja. "Why?"

"He's afraid you might talk to the police."

"Does he know?" she asked in shock.

"No, I don't think so, but he's afraid. He sees a connection between talking to the police and the extortion of the film rights. Or he said it to throw sand in my eyes on purpose, and knows full well that we have already talked."

"No, because then he wouldn't say anything to you about it," said Sonja. "And now? What should I do?" she asked, panicked.

"He must never get the impression that we talk to the police. But you know how he is—if he thinks it, then he has found confirmation in his own head."

"What should I do?"

"Act as normal as you can. If you start behaving differently all of a sudden, that's his confirmation that you talked."

"As, I can't handle this any longer," she cried softly.

"I know," I said. "I do have some good news, though." I tried for a light, joking tone.

"What's that?"

"I have it all on tape, so if something should happen to you, I can let them hear him giving the order."

"Well, at least that's something," she said flatly.

The Pit

AFTER FEELING TERRORIZED FOR MONTHS, SONJA AND I HAVE AGREED to meet with Wim. We've come to the agreed-upon meeting place. From here, we will follow his car. He's driving ahead of us toward a dark park.

Sonja is scared. Shortly before, Wim had asked Mom for Sonja's current address—she wasn't sleeping at home, for safety reasons—but she had refused to give it to him, afraid that he would do something to Sonja. Wim was furious with "the old one," she was a fucking bitch. Earlier he had visited Sandra. She was sleeping, and when she woke up, a man wearing a helmet was sitting on the edge of her bed, staring at her. He scared her and asked for Sonja's address. She had contacted us immediately.

After seeing my mom, he came to me. I didn't know it, either; I never look at house numbers. We were all on alert.

Wim asked me to call her because he wanted to resolve the conflict about the film rights. Sonja and I meet him at the agreed-upon place in Laren, and he gestures us to follow him. He parks in a neighborhood on the edge of a moor.

S: "Where's he taking us? He's not going in that spooky forest, is he?"

He shows us where to park. We stop the car, get out, and walk toward him. He's on the side of the road pissing, as usual. A conversation follows about a buddy who was arrested with eighty thousand euros on him and whether this might affect him. Sonja walks behind us, because she can't know what Wim and I are talking about.

W: "Nice out here, isn't it?"

I don't like it at all. I find it a very scary place, unsafe, but I try to keep the mood easygoing.

A: "Lovely! Good choice! Nice place."

As if he doesn't know that Sonja is following us like a slave, because he specifically insisted she come, he says to her:

W: "How did you get here?"
A: "Ha-ha, just popped up out of nowhere."
W: "How is that possible? I suddenly see you again."
S: "Yep, it's me again, that pain in the ass."

Then the question:

W: "Hey, what's your house number where you live?"
S: "Why, it's two twenty-six. You should know that by now."
W: "I keep forgetting. Two twenty-six."
S: "Will you come to my door again?"

And then, pretending to be funny:

W: "No...it's for when I come and get you."
S: "If you want to come for me, yeah."
A: "Ha-ha."

I'm still trying to keep the mood light, but I don't trust it. What will happen here?

S: "Yes, that's it."
W: "I have to know that."
S: "Yes, I thought as much, I think. Hey, what's going on here?"

I keep laughing loudly because I'm so nervous. We're in a secluded place. I don't feel comfortable at all in this leafy environment. He's toying with her fear, playing with his prey. Things could get really serious all of a sudden. I'm always afraid that I won't see it coming. Then he says to her, smiling:

W: "Come here. I have this spot here."
S: "Yes."
A: "Ha-ha."
S: "I wouldn't be surprised with you. I swear, you're mad..."

I hear panic in Sonja's voice, right through her faked lightness.

A: "Ha-ha."
S: "Yes, really, I do, you know..."
W: "Dig."
A: "Please don't think that I'm playing a game here, Box."

I'm afraid Sonja thinks that I set her up. She does think so, briefly.

S: "No, yes, I will—"

W: "Both of you, dig."

S: "Now I'm really starting to get scared, you two..."

W: "No need, you won't feel a thing. Two seconds' work."

A: "Are you kidding, you're my darling sis."

S: "I don't care anymore..."

W: "Yeah, it doesn't matter anymore, but when it gets closer,
everything's different."

Another threat. I keep laughing. We keep walking. It's pitch dark,
I've never been here. He knows the way. He starts moaning about
the film again. I don't like the location. I try to act silly.

A: "Ouch, I almost stepped into your hole, Wim."

S: "Ha-ha."

W: "No, that's farther along."

They're supposedly jokes, but under these circumstances... What is
he going to do?

A: "Can we please stop about those film rights?"

W: "Why stop? Why do we always have to stop, when it's your
fault?"

A: "Hey [and together with Sonja] 'your fault'—both of us? Ha-
ha."

I keep laughing, but I can think only one thing: that I am exposed,
that he's onto me. He realizes I am unconditionally faithful to
Sonja. He counts me among his adversaries; I'm persona non grata.
Desperate to get away, I say,

A: "Hey, piss off. I'm going to my car. You fight this out between
    you."
S: "No, you're not leaving me here alone with him, you hear?"
W (jokingly): "Come on, I have one pit, just one."

Relief again. I'm still in his good books. He keeps talking. Peter
extorted him, and so he reported him.

W: "Just have to tie my other shoelace."

He kneels. I'm overcome by a weird feeling of panic. I look around
me.

A: "I meant to say, is this some kind of signal?"

He just laughs...

W: "I'm looking for this pit...I'm just looking..."

Pff. I'm relieved.

A: "You need more light? I have a little flashlight somewhere. My
    guess is you're in the wrong forest; this is the gnome forest."
W: "Well, I'm not going to start digging again. We'll come back
    next week."
S: "I'm not coming back here, that's for sure."
W: "Let's just forget about this, but don't think you're smart now,
    okay?"
A: "Is it solved now?"
W: "We'll stop. Let's try and act normal. No more lies, Boxer. And
    when I say do something, then you do it. Got time tomorrow?"

Now the cat is out of the bag. She has to do something for him, something he doesn't want to do himself. This theater of fear was conducted so he could be sure she wouldn't refuse him. He can use her again for a while.

While we're leaving, he drives past our car. I open the window and he calls out—as some kind of finale to this horrible evening—"Boxer, I will leave the pit open. I'm leaving it open, you hear?"

The Counterattack

THE THREATS TO SONJA REACHED THEIR PEAK IN MARCH 2014: SHE went into hiding again at Francis's.

We couldn't think of anything to do other than tell Wim that she had taped all the conversations they'd had—as insurance on her life. And that if anything should happen to her or her kids, or to Peter, those tapes would end up with the police.

She'd land him with a life sentence.

I passed that on. He was briefly disturbed. He hadn't seen this coming. He concluded that Sonja is so stupid that she would have had to do this with someone else. She couldn't have thought of this, couldn't have the proper equipment.

Usually when somebody does something he doesn't like, he explodes. But it's different when it's really about something that can get him into trouble. Then he remains cool and collected, analyzes the situation right away, and thinks up a strategy. A counterattack.

After I told him, he stopped and stood still, right in front of me. His eyes seemed to look right through me.

My heart beat in my throat. God, he was onto me! I had pushed this game too far; he would frisk me on the spot and find the recording device.

I thought I might vomit.

I started talking, knowing that contradicting him is no use in these situations. Of course, yes. She is indeed too stupid to act alone. She can't even transfer money electronically, let alone anything involving technical equipment. She'd have to be doing this with someone else. But who?

W: "With Peter. They thought of this together. They're playing a game with me."

Oh, God. I couldn't have Wim suspecting me, but I didn't want Peter to take the blame. I felt guilty. Poor Peter had no idea how deep in we were. Sonja and I had chosen this strategy, but beyond helping with the initial contact, Peter had nothing to do with it, and now he was going to get the blame.

A: "No, I don't believe that. Peter wouldn't do that."
W: "What about Francis?"
A: "Certainly not."

I felt these denials made him trust me more. I was clearly the only other person who could have helped her, but I didn't take the bait of trying to divert attention away from myself.

He relaxed.

W: "You'll see to it that I get those tapes. I'll see you tonight."

Thank God, I was safe—for now. As long as he can use me, I thought, I'm okay.

That morning had had such an impact on my nerves that I couldn't handle using the bugging equipment that evening when I met up with Wim again to discuss the tapes. But the conversation is etched in my memory.

We took off from Sandra's and walked through East Amsterdam.

A: "No, she says she has them [the tapes] in a safe place. And she's not going to tell me where, because when push comes to shove, I'm with you."

W: "What a fucking bitch. I knew it. Is she talking to the police?"

A: "How should I know? Why would she hide those tapes if she is already talking to the police?"

W: "She is talking to the police. I don't care. You know what I'll do to people who talk to the police. But with her, I'm going to take a different approach. I'm going to let her die really slowly. Really let her suffer. First her children, her grandchild, then her. I won't have her shot. I'll have her tortured. For days."

A: "Well, she says that if something happens to her or her kids, the tapes will go to the police. So that wouldn't be wise. It won't be any good to you."

W: "I don't care. Is she abroad?"

A: "Why would she be?"

W: "I don't know what she's up to. She is doing this with Peter."

A: "No, I don't believe that. He wouldn't dare."

I had to deflect suspicion away from myself. I told him Sonja had betrayed me as well.

A: "She says, 'I taped you, too. All the messages he gave, that you passed on, that he would have my children shot dead. Peter and me. I've got it all. And more, because I have been recording for a long time.'"

W: "So she's going to hang you, too. The bitch. She's going to
hang you, too."

A: "How? I only delivered the messages. I was merely helping. I'll
just deny that you told me. Then it stops with me."

W: "She's going to hang you. She's a dirty traitor. How long has
she been recording?"

A: "I don't know. She won't tell me. But keep thinking straight.
Think about what you've said to her, what she can do with it.
You never make a slip."

W: "I just acted a bit angrily. But of course, I have no idea how
long she's been recording and whether she talks to the police.
What she'll say to them. I need those tapes. And I'll get them.
For sure. I'll just drag her off the street and torture her until
she tells me where they are. I'll break every bone in her body.
Cut her to pieces."

A: "Get a grip!"

W: "Get a grip? I will! She had it coming. She should have expected
this."

A: "I'll go search her house, see if I can find them."

W: "Yeah, start searching. The fucking bitch. This has to be solved."

I got the feeling that we'd overplayed our hand. He was so eerily
relaxed; this wasn't going the way we'd hoped. I had to turn things
back, but how?

I went back to him.

A: "Well, I've spent hours with her, and I think she's bluffing: she's
got nothing. She's not well. She's just threatening."

W: "You think?"

A: "Yes, I know her like no one else. She can't get anything done.
She can't even switch on a computer. She's a moron."

If I wanted to come across as trustworthy, I'd have to tear her down to the ground.

A: "But I get her, she's afraid of you, afraid you will have her children killed. She hasn't got a clue what to do next. It's a leap in the dark."

W: "She is scared, isn't she? She should be."

A: "I think she really regrets saying this. She was nervous as hell."

W: "I understand. She knows what I'm like. Or she's in it with Peter, she does have tapes, and they are playing games."

A: "Well, I don't see why."

W: "You don't know, do you? You don't know what they're up to."

A: "Well, I think they're bluffing."

W: "Really?"

A: "I'm sure of it."

W: "Well, we'll see."

Annulment

By now it had been a year since we had made our statements to the Justice Department, but nothing had happened. Everything was the same. Meanwhile I'd had to intensify my relationship with Wim, and it felt like a noose was tightening around my neck. I could hardly breathe. All this time, I had told myself that the Justice Department would take action at some point, but I hardly believed it myself anymore.

Sonja, who had to suffer through all the threats, was just as frustrated.

"As, we are being played for fools," she said. "He must know somebody, somebody in the Justice Department, who protects him. Fuck them. I quit. It's worse with them than without them. Every day I hope they'll do something, and every day I'm disappointed. It stresses me out."

She was totally right. They weren't doing anything, and they couldn't explain why it was taking so long. We'd been exposed to danger for more than a year, and they were leading us on. Maybe it was time to back out, focus on controlling the damage.

We talked to Peter about it, and he agreed with us: the Justice Department showed no decisiveness whatsoever, and the risk our statements would leak remained real. He supported us in our decision to annul the statements. We'd rather be alone in this than not taken seriously.

We scheduled a so-called exit talk. Betty said she couldn't share with us why everything was taking so long, that she wanted us to "stay aboard," but that she understood that we'd lost faith. She would give the order to annul our preliminary statements.

I immediately doubted our decision. Were we not running a greater risk of our statements leaking the moment we had them annulled? If the Justice Department thought we would still cooperate, the responsibility of a possible leak was clearly still with them.

Besides, these statements also provided me protection by justifying my many meetings with him. I wanted to continue recording what he told me without being seen as his accomplice by the Justice Department.

In the end I felt it was best to hang on to the preliminary statements and the contact with the CIU. That way at least one judicial department would be aware of the true reasons why I kept seeing him. Should I be arrested because of him, at least I would have witnesses on my side.

A couple of days after the exit talk, I called to ask if they had annulled the statements yet.

"No? Good. Don't do it. Maybe someday they will come in handy," I told Manon.

I'll Kill Him

THE BELL RANG. AND THERE HE WAS AGAIN.

I felt all the energy drain from my body. I felt so tired. I wanted out, but I was so deep in. This would never come to an end.

We walked down Maasstraat, and during his monologue, he laughed about how he had frightened Sonja again. "She's so scared, really scared."

I walked next to him and looked at that grin on his face. Somebody who enjoys hurting others so much has no right to keep on living, I thought.

Enough is enough.

I am going to kill him.

Sonja was at the gym. They also had a physiotherapy practice, where I had my first appointment.

Sonja was having coffee, and she joined me.

"Today I am going to blow him to pieces," I told her. "I'm getting my weapon later."

"Don't say that. You are doing no such thing. You can't do that to Mil, to the little ones. They will lose you."

But even that didn't outweigh my feelings, which screamed for an end to all this. I didn't want to depend on others anymore, didn't want to keep looking for another way to stop him. "I'll do it myself. I should have done it much earlier."

Liquidate or be liquidated was an essential part of our lives. Cor was Wim's target; Wim was the target of Mieremet, Endstra, and Thomas van der Bijl, among others. We lived with that imperative, and it had taught me what was needed to avoid liquidation and what was needed to execute one.

Know where somebody is going to be, and know when. It's impossible to wait for hours on a street corner until someone arrives at his house; it's too conspicuous. And being conspicuous means running the risk of attention from the police or vigilant citizens, and the possibility of being recognized later. It should be done relatively quickly. Arrive, do the job, and leave.

In and out, as Wim said.

Knowing where the target is and when sounds obvious. But it's not easy, and it's the reason so many liquidations rely on betrayal. That betrayal is often by someone close: somebody says where the target lives, where he goes, what his habits are, the locations he visits regularly, and when he goes there.

The where and when was never my problem: I saw Wim when he wanted. Every day I had the opportunity. All I had to do was show up for an appointment, get near to him, and take him off-guard. For an untrained shooter like me, that last part was the most important.

I know how to handle a weapon, but I can't shoot to kill from five meters away. I would have to be as close to him as possible and, without him noticing, put the gun to his stomach and pull the trigger.

I needed the element of surprise so he wouldn't have a chance to resist. A shot in the stomach wouldn't ensure a fatal end, but it would take him so much by surprise that I'd have time to fire my fatal shots. That's how I had thought it out, and, by way of practice, had visualized it.

"You shouldn't do it," said Sonja.

"I don't know why not," I replied.

I really had no reason not to do it. It was as if I didn't have a moral compass. Just like him.

When I thought about it, I felt no repulsion or fear. I felt nothing at all. I thought it self-explanatory: he was a malignant growth that had to be removed. I understood he was capable of killing because he didn't have that moral compass, either. The only thing that had stopped me all this time was my daughter's words: "Mom, I don't want a killer for a mother."

She apparently had a moral compass and absolutely didn't want this. I tried to understand her, but I honestly couldn't grasp it, rationally or sensibly. Sonja understood Miljuschka very well. She didn't want it, and couldn't do it, though it would be more logical for her to do it. It was about her husband, her children.

It was a discussion we'd had before. I thought she should stand up for her children, whatever it took. But she couldn't.

"I'll do it," I said, ending our conversation. "At home there's a bag of clothes for you to bring me when I'm at the police station." I would not try to get away with it; I'm not like him. I would take responsibility and turn myself in. I realized that I would go to prison, but that prospect was way more attractive than to go on living with him.

I walked up the stairs to my appointment with the physiotherapist. It was the last thing on my mind, but the man was always swamped, and I was there with Sonja's help. She'd explained to him that I desperately needed treatment, and he had specially squeezed me into his busy schedule. No way I could cancel.

After my appointment, I'd pick up a weapon, a small revolver, just right for me. I would have to avoid any police stops, or they might find the gun before I had used it.

I knocked on the physiotherapist's door.

"Hello," a tanned, muscular man said. "Are you Astrid?"

"Yes," I said.

"I'm Vincent. Please sit down." He gestured to the treatment table.

I did, and he asked me where it hurt. "In my calves," I said.

"Your calves are your second heart," he said. He felt them. "I see why you hurt. There's a lot of tension in them." His hands started the treatment, and I could hardly stand the pain.

"Astrid, you're at a crossroads in your life. Your calves keep you from going a certain way, and that tension creates your pain. Maybe you should follow an entirely different road."

I thought, What is he on about? He can't know what I'm up to, can he? "What do you mean?" I asked.

"Maybe you should let go of everything happening in your life right now and look at it from a different perspective. We are all energy. And sometimes this energy is disturbed by the energy of others."

Stay with your own energy, he was saying. Don't let it get distorted.

I felt caught. Why was he talking about this? Was he trying to tell me in a roundabout way that he knew what I was up to and that I had to give up on it? I got the jitters. "I'm just a bit tired," I said. "And I am so busy."

"You're tired because others take away your energy. You don't have to solve everyone's problems."

Wow! That last one hit me. I had to be crazy. Why do I make such an effort to help others? To help Sonja, Peter—why? Let everybody solve his or her own problems.

Vincent had, just before the fatal moment, changed my mind.

Sonja was waiting for me downstairs. I went to her.

"I'm not doing it. I'm not going to prison just because I so desperately want to solve things for everybody. You don't do anything, the Justice Department doesn't do anything. It's not my problem. He's your husband; they're your children. You solve it. If he threatened my child, I'd do it immediately, but it's your call."

"I'm glad," Sonja said. "I'm glad you won't do it."

She was sincerely happy. She'd rather have the terror continue, not being able to do what was necessary to end it. I didn't understand her. How different she was from Wim and me.

I drove home. I had been on the verge of killing my brother, something I should have dreaded. But it felt righteous. An eye for an eye, a tooth for a tooth. You hit me, I hit you back.

Now, in hindsight, I think, I wish I'd done it. I would have been free sooner, I would have gotten maybe nine years and been out in six for good behavior. Young enough to build a new life.

Now I've got a life sentence, whether he's ever convicted or not. The regret will go on forever.

Sandra and the Women

WOMEN PLAY AN IMPORTANT PART IN WIM'S LIFE. HIS MOTHER, HIS SISTERS, and his girlfriends—all the women in his life have a function.

I'm his sounding board, Sonja is his jack-of-all-trades, and Mom is, well, the mother; if he feels like he wants it she has to take care of him like a child. The part his girlfriends play depends on what Wim needs at any given moment. A car, a scooter, a house, or a financier.

Wim has at least four women, and they all want to believe they're the only one. He rotates between them constantly. He tells them he's in danger of being liquidated and that he can't stay in one location for too long. He has to leave, for his safety. And as a loving woman, you're not going to make trouble, are you? You don't want him to get hurt, do you?

That he might have more than one woman never occurs to them. It's sad to behold, all these women he deceives, all wanting to understand him and sympathize with him. Often lovely women, totally brainwashed by him.

Even when they catch him and see the reality for what it is, he somehow manages to make these women believe that they shouldn't have doubted him in the first place.

How could they be so nasty to him? They should be thankful that they can still apologize to him.

We're also living with all his different women. He has been using us for ages to be able to continue his polygamist lifestyle.

My mother was trained not to let her behavior arouse my father's jealousy. At the beginning of each relationship, Wim's girlfriends have no idea what he expects from them, but he teaches them quickly.

Their first lesson is: Wim is jealous. Without any reason, they often protested, but Wim didn't think so. It wasn't that he was jealous—they behaved like sluts, and he wasn't going to accept that.

The second lesson: When Wim is jealous, he can barely control his aggression. He screams and hits. They wouldn't accept that! But...maybe Wim was right, and it was their fault. So they stayed with him.

The third lesson: To control his anger, they had to steer clear of any situation that might make Wim jealous. So in his presence, they were transformed from spontaneous girls with a worldly outlook into nervous types who only had eyes for him. If they walked beside him, they didn't look around; they watched the ground. Whenever they went out for dinner or a drink, they sat opposite Wim so he could make sure they would only look at him and nobody else. No, looking at other men was not allowed, let alone talking to them.

The sooner the girls learned what was and wasn't allowed, the better. It was always heartbreaking to see such a girl getting scared when she found out she'd apparently done something wrong and had to deal with the consequences.

We helped them learn the manual to Wim as quickly as possible. "It's best if you don't wear that blouse. Wim wouldn't like it."

"That sweater is way too tight—it reveals everything."

"Those men are staring at you. We have to get out of here." They felt our support and confided in us.

"Please don't tell Wim," they would say when they'd accidentally run into a male acquaintance.

"No, of course not!" we'd say.

If there was trouble, they let off steam with us.

"I was on the phone with Wim when I saw all these little bugs creeping down my crotch," Martine told Sonja at the kitchen table one day, while I sat there listening. "I swear, Sonja! I see them teeming before my eyes."

"No—really? Bugs?" said Sonja.

"Yeah, bugs!" Martine said, still in shock. "So I called the doctor. You know what they are? Crabs!"

"Crabs?" Sonja asked, not familiar with the word.

"Pubic lice!" Martine replied.

"Pubic lice? What's that?" The combination of the two words didn't ring a bell with Sonja.

"They're little bugs in your pubic hair, down there." Martine clarified by pointing at her crotch.

Sonja suddenly realized and shouted, "Yuck—bugs? Where did you get those from?"

"Your brother!"

"Oh, really? How did he get them?"

"He is sleeping around!" Martine raged.

Apparently Wim's girlfriends thought that because Wim didn't want them to sleep around, he wouldn't do it, either. And he didn't, he would say, throwing his hands in the air, with these innocent, wide eyes. Even when the irrefutable evidence was crawling in Martine's lap, he shouted that they must have come from her. He hoped for her sake that she hadn't infected him, because then she'd have a problem. He was going to see a doctor for a checkup and didn't want to see her for a while.

Wim's girlfriends couldn't prove that he saw other women. Unsure of their own observations, each could only doubt herself and thereby became an ideal partner. Ready to be controlled by Wim.

In 2003, Wim introduced Sandra den Hartog into our lives. She was the widow of Sam Klepper, who was assassinated in October 2000.

In 1999, Rob Grifhorst was about to rent a luxury apartment on Van Leijenberghlaan when Wim visited him. He had to give up the apartment because Wim's friends Klepper and Mieremet were about to move in there. Wim already lived in the building: after he had left Beppie, he went to live there with Maike. The apartment was located across from the police station. "Very safe," Wim joked.

Klepper and Mieremet moved in—their wives lived in Belgium— and Wim brought his new best friends fresh bread for breakfast, with the best meats and cheeses, as he used to do with Cor. After breakfast, he'd go out with Mieremet to show him the real estate he had invested the duo's millions in, through Willem Endstra.

Wim increasingly got closer to Mieremet, whereas Klepper got more and more involved with the Hells Angels. It was similar to the division that had taken place between Cor and Wim; Mieremet and Wim focused more on the upper world, while Klepper, like Cor, preferred to spend time in the underworld.

On October 10, 2000, Klepper was assassinated on his way out of the apartment building, in broad daylight. Wim and Mieremet were having a sandwich near the new RAI Convention Center when it happened.

Sonja and Cor were in Dubai. My mother was taking care of Francis and Richie in Sonja's house. When I heard the news about Klepper, I immediately understood that Mieremet's posse would think that Cor was behind it as revenge for the attempt on his life, especially because he "happened to be" abroad. Making sure you are not there when the deed goes down is the best alibi.

But there was another reason why I thought Cor might have had something to do with it. Sonja lived in fear of being killed along with Cor and leaving their children alone. After the first attempt on Cor's life, she had wanted to make it official that I'd look after Francis and Richie, to avoid other family members making claims.

Cor had no will, though; he wanted nothing to do with that. He believed that you would attract death if you made one.

But this changed just before they went on vacation to Dubai. Cor had a will drawn up. If he and Sonja were no longer there for the children, they'd be handed over to me. "That's all right, isn't it?" asked Sonja.

"Of course. You know that."

I was surprised that Cor had gotten over his superstition. He was wise to do this, I thought then. But after Klepper was murdered, I immediately wondered if he had had a will drawn up because he knew what was going to happen, was expecting revenge, and, as a result, wanted to have the care of his children arranged. All this together made me think that Cor might have had something to do with it.

I was afraid of revenge. I had a clear memory of Wim's stories about Mieremet's gang killing our whole family if they didn't get their way. I was scared to death that the kids would get hurt, and I knew Sonja would be just as scared when she heard what happened.

I couldn't reach Sonja to ask her what to do, but I knew she'd count on me if it was about the safety of her kids. I drove over to my mom's to discuss it.

"Have you heard anything?" I asked.

"No, what?" she replied.

"They killed this Klepper guy."

Immediately I could tell she was scared. She too realized that because of all that had happened over the last couple of years, this might put the kids in danger.

"Yes, so I'd rather move you away from here. You never know whether they'll suspect Cor is behind it, and they might come to Sonja's house. You'd better take the kids to your own place. They won't come to your house because Wim belongs to them. I'll come to you, with Miljuschka."

I picked Miljuschka up because I didn't want to leave her with the sitter under these circumstances, and drove to my mother's house, where she was waiting for me with Francis and Richie.

"Are you sure it's safe here?" my mother asked. "Wim might stop by, and he'll see the kids here. I'd rather not have them with me here."

"But I can't take them home with me, either, because he'll come there, too. I'll take them to a hotel until we know how things are," I told her

I told the kids that we were leaving.

"Where are we going, Assie?" Francis asked.

"We're going on a holiday," I joked, and they understood their questions wouldn't be answered. We were going, period.

I started my search for a safe place at a hotel a little bit out of town in Badhoevedorp, but they had no rooms left. At the next hotel, I got the same message, and again at the next one. I drove the kids from one place to another. I didn't want to call the hotels ahead of time. I didn't want the police listening in, hearing we were on the run, because that would only look suspicious. But no matter where I tried, there was no room. I don't know what was going on that day, but every hotel we stopped at was booked.

It was getting late and the kids were dead tired when I made one final attempt in an ugly, filthy little hotel on Surinameplein where you wouldn't even let your dog stay: the Belfort Hotel. I took the kids into the hotel with me, because in Amsterdam I wouldn't leave them in the car alone.

"Do you have a room for four, please, sir?" I asked the man behind the desk, who looked as scruffy as the hotel itself.

"No, miss, just one single room left."

"Oh, that's fine!" I said, relieved, because at least we had something.

"No, miss, the number says it all: it's a room for one person and not four," he said coldly.

I saw myself leaving and spending the night with the kids in the car. "But, sir," I begged, "please, I'm here with three kids and there are no rooms left anywhere. Please put us up for one night?"

"How were you planning on sleeping, miss? There is only one bed. The number says it all: a room for one person," he repeated.

Tears were filling my eyes at this lack of empathy, and I started sobbing uncontrollably. I was tired and frightened, and I lost my grip on myself. "Sir, I don't know where else to go," I cried. Richie, also tired and tense, started crying with me.

That did it for this insensitive jerk, and he cried out, "Okay, okay, but you'll have to pay for four persons."

"No problem," I said, and I counted out four hundred guilders on the desk. "First floor, last door," he said while he shoved the money in his pocket. "Here's the key."

I walked up with the little ones, locked the door, and stood in the middle of a doghouse: filthy, no larger than two by three meters, no shower, just a dirty little sink.

Rich threw himself on the single bed and never left it. Miljuschka tried to join him but ended up on the floor with Francis and me. The three of us were spooning, stuck between the bed and the door.

Meanwhile, I tried to reach Sonja to find out if Cor was behind all this, but I couldn't get through. It was the middle of the night when she finally called me.

"Glad you called. I couldn't reach you all day," I said.

"No, we were on a jeep safari," she replied. I had to suppress the irritation in my voice. I was a nervous wreck and she was on a safari.

"Did you have a good day?" I asked.

"Yes," she said, "a great day!"

From the way she said it, I knew that she already knew. To be sure, I asked if Cor, too, had had a nice day. "Him particularly!"

"I'm here having a good time with the kids," I said, so Sonja knew that I had brought them to safety.

"Yes, Mama told me."

"Do you need me to do anything?"

"No, nothing special. Will you take them to Mom's again tomorrow?" She meant that I didn't have to do anything out of the ordinary.

"Yes," I answered. "Sure?" I asked her.

"Very sure," she replied.

"Cor, too?"

"Yes, Cor, too," she replied.

"Okay, sleep well. We'll talk tomorrow."

Without referring to Klepper's liquidation, she had told me that Cor had nothing to do with it and thought that I could safely leave the kids with Mom.

"Was that Mom?" asked Francis, who'd been listening in.

"Yes, all is well, go back to sleep. We have to get up early and get you back to school."

We were spooning again, with Miljuschka in the middle. Francis bent over her and softly whispered in my ear, so Richie couldn't hear, "I don't want to go home, Assie. I want to be with you. I'm so scared they're coming for us."

"Me too," said Miljuschka, who'd overheard Francis.

* * *

Cor may have had nothing to do with Klepper's death, but that didn't mean Mieremet's gang wouldn't hold him responsible. Mieremet had lost his best friend and probably had no use for a thorough investigation into the killer. Just the suspicion of Cor would probably be reason enough for Mieremet to take his revenge on somebody close to Cor.

After all the threats against the children, I was not entirely sure they were safe, and I decided to keep them away from the obvious locations. With Richie that appeared impossible.

He felt the tension in the air and was so hard to handle that I took him to my mother's. I kept Francis and Miljuschka with me. I searched and found another hotel, on Churchillaan.

I desperately dreaded the moment I had to see Wim again, and that moment would inevitably come. I was with Francis and Miljuschka in our hotel room when he called.

"I have to go out for a bit. You have to stay here. Keep the door locked and open it for no one. I'll be right back," I told them, and went out to see Wim.

I assumed that Wim would put the blame on Cor and would hold him responsible for the death of his friend. I expected a lot of aggressive shouting about that "cross-eyed fuckface" with all the re-lated threats, including toward the children.

I immediately showed my respect for the loss of his friend, hop-ing to alleviate his anger. "So sorry for you, Wim," I said, as mean-ingfully as possible.

He didn't react as I had expected; he was totally indifferent. Ac-cording to him, Klepper was a fucking asshole, and he had deserved it because he'd had a lot of others "done." I was totally taken off guard. I had always thought that Wim would betray us for these new friends. And now he talked like this? He didn't care one bit that Klepper had been assassinated.

"Should I be worried about Sonja's kids?" I asked him. He seemed surprised, and said I shouldn't worry at all, because this had come from "our side."

Our side? Wasn't he with Klepper and Mieremet? I could only interpret Wim's remark to mean that Wim and Mieremet were involved in Klepper's death.

Wim didn't flip out about Cor and didn't threaten him; he didn't even mention him. It was clear that he made no connection between Klepper's death and possible retribution by Cor.

He didn't in the months that followed, either. Wim still wanted Cor dead, but the reason had not changed. At no point was there any talk of retribution for the assassination of Klepper. It was still all about "taking everything away" from him.

Not long afterward, I met with Wim at the car wash in Aalsmeer. He only had a minute, he told me cheerfully; he was busy picking up money from Klepper's wife—he was going to "protect her."

At some point after Cor's death in 2003, Wim asked me to have a sandwich with him at Sal Meijer's on Scheldestraat, where I was confronted with Sandra. She needed a different accountant, and she had hired the same one I had. I had to go there with her so she wouldn't be alone. In 2004, he introduced me to her kids. They were having problems with the tax department and the Justice Department about their father's inheritance, which they didn't see one penny of.

Sandra was a classic victim of Wim's "negotiating role." He told Sandra that her husband had been liquidated by Sreten "Jotsa" Jocić, a serious criminal from the former Yugoslavia, and that he would stand up for her. He would protect the lives of her and her children and work on solving the conflict. The conflict could only be solved by paying lots of money, or so he told her. But Sandra wasn't interested in money; she would pay anything as long as it would save her kids. Vulnerable and totally emotional after the death of her husband, she fell prey to the man who declared that he would unselfishly risk his life for her and her children against this terribly dangerous Yugoslav.

It was Wim's dream scenario. He'd take care of her and her capital. Her money became his money, and her life became his property.

Sandra's initial reaction to the death of her husband was that Wim was behind it. The media tended to think the same thing. But before long, Sandra, brainwashed daily by Wim and totally isolated from people who could offer a different perspective, was totally in awe of this knight in shining armor, and he took her husband's place. She had no idea whatsoever that she was bringing a Trojan horse into her family.

When Wim was doing six years for different kinds of extortion, she got her own six-year sentence: house arrest, as Wim demands of his women when he's inside. From prison he controlled her daily routine, her contacts, all her doings. She was only to occupy herself with him; she was only to have a small number of contacts designated by him, and that was basically just us. We were ordered to visit her so she would see people sometimes. He knew that we wouldn't dare open Sandra's eyes. We were her chaperones.

I didn't expect to like her, but after a while, I let go of the whole "Klepper-Mieremet stigma" I had imposed on her. Sandra was naïve but actually really nice. Her kids were sweet and well behaved. "She can't help what Klepper and Mieremet have done," Sonja had said to me before. And she was right. She couldn't help it, as we couldn't help what Wim did, either.

All of this produced the insane situation in which our Richie—who had been shot at by the Klepper, Mieremet, and Holleeder combination—went to the birthday parties of the Klepper kids; the same Klepper that Wim had killed. I got sick of going to these things, seeing these four innocent children who'd all lost their fathers. Wim was the only survivor and ruled over both families.

In Sandra's house, there wasn't one single photo of her deceased husband. Wim wouldn't tolerate it. The only photo of him had been moved to the storage shed. It was as if he'd never existed. I was curious to see how she'd react when I mentioned this. But she acted as though it was quite normal; she was never out of character. What I didn't know at that point was that she'd never say anything negative about Wim because she was convinced he had sent me to question her. And she wasn't entirely wrong.

During Wim's time in prison, Sandra got into trouble with the tax authorities. She had to pay additional taxes for the millions that Sam Klepper had invested with Endstra. Endstra should have had to give it back to Sandra; in reality, Wim had taken that money. She had nothing, but she was still liable for the taxes. When she visited her knight in shining armor, she got a rude awakening. He made it clear to her that he had no time for her problems. In the meantime, Wim couldn't afford a woman who'd say "the wrong things" about him. I got the order to stay close to her, keep an eye on her, go with her to all her appointments with the accountant, and make sure his name wasn't mentioned.

I thought it best that Sandra knew where she stood, so I told her that I was only trying to "help" so as to make sure that Wim stayed out of all this.

"It seems to me that I don't really have a choice in this," she replied. "Do you think I dare say anything about him?" I was surprised. It was the first time I heard her say anything remotely negative about Wim.

* * *

In January 2012, when Wim was released, he didn't care about Sandra anymore and had hardly any time for her. She was almost broke, and what she did have had claims against it. He started investing more time in Maike. He still had a future with her. Plus he was busy with his own security, and with his other women, including Mandy from Utrecht, who'd waited six years for him.

Sandra's house with the garden facing south was the main reason he held on to her. A house in Amsterdam, close to his contacts, was useful to him; he could stay there when he needed to see them instead of having to drive back and forth to his apartment in Huizen.

In March 2012, Sandra asked me if I knew someone named Mandy. It was a question I could not possibly answer truthfully. We were there to keep the calm in Wim's harem, not to stir up unrest.

But over the years, Sandra had won not just my sympathy but also my respect. Sandra had been a gangster girlfriend her whole life and never had to earn money; she'd just had to spend tons of it. Until now. The house arrest Wim had imposed on her meant that since Sam's death, she'd lived in isolation, totally controlled by Wim. At the same time, with him in prison, she'd been less under his influence, and it was clear to her where she had ended up. Her capital had become his capital. She had nothing left, and as a result could expect nothing from him. She'd have to find a job. But how and where? She secretly took a course to become a nail stylist. When she was almost done, she told Wim what she'd done and that she was ready to work. He was livid, but she calmed him down, arguing that she needed a regular income. He had no legal income, so how could he provide for her?

Wim, who wasn't too keen on providing for her anyway, agreed. As long as she understood that in addition to her job, she'd have to be available to Wim twenty-four hours a day. Should he hear sounds on the phone other than the ones at her job, or should she not pick up the phone, or if she was seeing another man, he'd make life hell for her. But she held her ground.

I found it sad to see how Sandra was abused and dismissed. It would have been better for her if she had a life of her own, but that's not the way Wim works with women. Once you're his, you'll never get rid of him unless he wants to get rid of you.

I decided to tell her the truth about Mandy, but only if she promised me she wouldn't tell Wim or let on that she knew. Not even in an emotional moment during a fight or while making up. Sandra swore on her kids that she wouldn't. I took a risk by telling her the truth. Not many betrayed women could have stayed silent, but Sandra kept her promise. And this occasion increased our trust in each other.

Later, Sandra asked me to confirm what Wim had snapped at her in anger: that he had had Sam killed. "Do you know anything about that?" she asked, trembling with emotion.

Now that she was asking me straight out, I thought I couldn't keep quiet, I couldn't do this to her any longer. But I wasn't going to discuss it with her, not inside the house, at any rate, not out loud, and certainly not before I frisked her for bugs. I thought I could trust her, but she could still be in cahoots with Wim, or she could still want to do him a favor in a moment of weakness.

"First take off your sweater and bra," I said, and frisked her for equipment. I searched her trousers, but there was nothing there. "Come on, let's take a walk," I said, and took her outside.

"And?" she asked.

I stood in front of her and nodded. That's all I had to do.

* * *

Sandra called me. Wim had totally flipped out at her youngest son, Mitri. He had left her house ballistic and had even left his key. She sounded very upset. "I have agreed to meet your brother at Café De Omval. Will you please be there, too?"

"He called me, too," I said. "I'm on my way. You come in later. I'll have a word with him first," I said.

Several months earlier, Wim had left her. "It's all due to that fucking kid," he told me. "Fries eggs during the day, the whole house smells, and I have to be in it. Every time I come in, he's there in the living room, on his PlayStation. He irritates the hell out of me, that fucking kid. Just like his dad."

But despite his swearing never to return, he'd always be back in her house in a matter of days, lying on her couch waiting for her to finish work, pretending nothing was wrong, and ordering her to give him a foot massage. She just couldn't get rid of him.

He stood there waiting for me at the café. Next to his scooter, with that aggressive look. He started raging as soon as I reached him.

"You know what he does, that weasel? He jeopardizes my life! He is such a little liar, always lying."

"So what's happened?"

"So he's sitting there in the living room, like he's a king. And he's wearing this Excalibur T-shirt. I look at him and think: Excalibur? It was a new shirt. Know what that means? That he's been around the Hells Angels! And you know what that means? That they'll find out where I am, that they're getting information from him. Know how dangerous that is? Through that fucking kid! The weasel. I've really had it. He's out."

"Wim, slow down a bit. He's a kid; you can't really throw him out, can you? Where's he going to go?"

"I don't care, to his aunt's. Let him sleep on the street, but he's got to go."

"No, that's impossible. And he's not going to say anything about you. That kid knows he shouldn't talk."

"Listen, they will just question him. He won't even notice. He's with them. He really has to go. Thinks he's smart."

"Okay, what now?"

"Now I'll have Sandra come over and I'll tell her that he's got to go."

"You can't ask a mother to do that. He's her child."

"When he's out late, he's not a child, and now all of a sudden he is? He's not a kid. No, he's leaving. I'm not leaving there, I'm not going to be chased out by a little brat. As, it's a lovely house. I can sit in the garden all day long. I'm right in the center of everything. I'm not leaving. If she doesn't kick him out, she'll have to live with him somewhere else. I want to keep that place."

"Well, Wim, it's not that easy. How are you going to rent that place?"

"She should keep it in her name!"

"That's impossible."

"Oh, so he's won? But he won't. You know what I'll do."

Sandra arrived, and Wim immediately started yelling at her. She couldn't say a word, overpowered by his verbal violence. She tried to walk away three times, but Wim shouted her back.

"Sssht, Wim!" I said. "Take it easy. Cops are driving by—you don't want them to stop!"

"I don't care," he shouted. "Let them stop! I've had it, Assie. So I have to hit the street because of a fucking kid. Wait and see. His turn will come. Then I'll do him, just like I did his dad."

I froze and looked at Sandra.

★ ★ ★

To Wim, I did my best to encourage the thought that it was for the best that he didn't go back to Sandra's house. They would never get back together.

"Know what it is, As? Sandra has really changed since I got out. Before, she could think like a criminal, but that's gone since she started working. That woman has gone mad. I just think it's a waste of that house. Now I have to find another bitch where I can spend time in the garden during the day."

Wim easily resigned himself to the fact that he wouldn't live with Sandra any longer, but he didn't forget what Mitri had "done to him." He would get what was coming to him.

Sandra knew Wim well enough to be terrified. "I don't know what he's up to now that he's not here with me," she told me. "When I see him every day, at least I can check his mood, estimate what he's up to. He'll definitely harm Mitri, and then he'll come to the door with tears in his eyes, telling me how sorry he is and asking if he can help me. I'm sure of it!"

I tried to comfort her. "I'll keep an eye on him for you, and if he's going to do something to Mitri, he'll tell me and I'll just tell you." She was right, of course; Wim was not letting it rest.

"Wim, you can't pop Sandra's kid," I told him the next time he brought up "the fucking kid." "That woman has done so much for you all these years. You really can't do this."

"Okay, because of Sandra I won't do it," he said. "But I'm not giving up on this, I really can't. He offended me to the bone. He's still going to get it. Not yet, because Sandra will think it's me. But in a while. In town he'll run into the wrong person, who'll beat the shit out of him."

I told Sandra that for now Wim wouldn't hurt Mitri because that would be too conspicuous, but that she should be on her guard. She was shattered. "He's killed my husband, taken all my money, and now he's threatening my child," she said. "How brilliantly this man has insinuated himself into my life and done so much damage."

"You're not the only one. He's left a long trail of damage. We feel he has to pay for what he's done."

"Me, too!" said Sandra.

"And we're really going to make an effort," I said.

"How do you mean?"

I doubted if I should tell her, but I took the gamble: "I'm going to testify against him," I said.

"Then you won't live long," she said immediately.

"Maybe you're right."

"Aren't you afraid of his rats?"

"I will keep being afraid of them, but I'm starting to know the people I've talked to a little, and I think they're okay. I've been working on it for a long time, and it hasn't leaked yet, so..." Very carefully I asked her, "How would you feel about it?"

"You mean, do I want to commit suicide, too?"

"Yes, something like that." I smiled.

"Well, why not? I always wanted to die young and pretty," she said.

Sandra was a weird chick, but she had a very strong character. When she said she'd do something, she did it.

That night, we took a stroll with Sonja along the Bosbaan. We were walking along there, the three of us, when a man walked up to us. He laughed at us and said, "The Three Musketeers!"

We looked at each other, scared.

I said, "What was that? Was it a cop? Did they bug us?"

"Nah," said Sonja, "that's impossible."

"But he's right," said Sandra. She put her arm in the air, pretending to hold a sword, and shouted, "One for all, and all for one!"

"One for all, and all for one!" Sonja and I repeated after her. It had been a long time since we'd last laughed. Her cynical humor was a welcome addition.

Fred Ros

I GET A CALL FROM MICHELLE, AND SHE ASKS IF WE'VE GOT TIME TO TALK to Betty. She'd like to see us tomorrow, but I've got commitments and I don't feel like showing up there whenever they see fit. I've made time for them on so many occasions, totally reorganized my schedule, and it has gotten us nowhere.

"No, Friday doesn't work for me. Sometime next week, maybe." Could we come on Monday, because they'd really like to see us. I wonder why the hurry all of a sudden. It has been eighteen months now, and I've never noticed any sense of hurry before.

So we make a plan to meet on Monday, September 15, 2014.

SEPTEMBER 12, 2014

On Friday morning, we find out that Fred Ros, the man who was convicted of killing Thomas van der Bijl, has made statements about that murder, among others. He points to Dino Soerel as the direct contractor, but adds that Willem Holleeder was behind it.

Now I understand why Betty wanted to see us, and I understand the hurry.

It's a big news story, but I don't hear from Wim.

He doesn't call me till after noon, and he wants to meet at the Viersprong in Vinkeveen. I assume then that he knows about the Ros statements. I get in the car and drive to meet him. I hide my equipment in my clothes; I want to record what he has to say about this.

When I see him, he's in very high spirits, and I ask him:

A: "Do you know yet?"
W: "What?"

He doesn't know.

A: "That Ros has testified."
W: "Oh, fuck. Fucking hell. Oh, that's bad. I don't even know the guy."

I'm disappointed at him saying that he's never spoken to Ros. I want to record something useful. At the same time, it's clear that he's not happy with the news about Ros. He wants to know where I got it from.

A: "It's on the Internet, everything."
W: "What?"
A: "That he is a Crown witness who has testified against you. He testified against Soerel, Akgün; he talked about liquidations, Cor, Nemic, and eh... what's his name, Thomas."
W: "Cor, Nemic, Thomas."
A: "Yes."
W: "What did he say about me? I've never spoken to this man."
A: "I don't know."

He wants to see what's on the Internet; but as always I have my cell phone switched off when I'm with him. He lets me switch it on, and I read to him from my screen.

A: "He also made statements about the killings that aren't part of the Passage file and also mentions the name Willem Holleeder. He's said to be involved in the assassination of his former companion Cor van Hout in 2003. Holleeder has been linked to at least three liquidations but was never prosecuted."

W: "So he talks about Cor? Is that what they're trying to get me for?"

A: "Well, obviously. I'll switch it off now."

W: "I've never talked to him."

A: "Well, good."

W: "In prison I told them that I did not want to be in a cell near him."

While Wim was in prison in the Penitentiary Institution in Rotterdam for extorting Endstra, Fred Ros was put in the cell next to him. Ros was being held in connection with the Passage case, the same one for which he'd now become a Crown witness, after an appeal. Wim immediately asked for a transfer to another prison.

W: "When he was put next to me in prison, I said at once, I have never spoken to this man, and I have no intention to at this stage."

He is so clever. From the beginning he has avoided the danger Ros could present. He instantly suspected him of working with the Justice Department as an informant. He wanted to prevent at all costs that Ros could say he had spoken to him, and from the moment Ros was moved into the cell next to his, he never set foot outside of his cell.

W: "I have an appointment with Stijn, tomorrow at three. He has
    received some statements."

He now understands why Stijn asked him to come over and is irritated at Stijn for not bringing this up immediately. Stijn had mentioned a box of statements coming in, but he never said they were Ros's. Surely this can't wait! We need to see him at once.

We drive there, although we haven't been able to reach Stijn to tell him Wim wants to see him now, and there is a good chance Stijn is no longer at his office because it's late.

And he's not there.

We call his partner, Chrisje Zuur; maybe she knows where he might be or where we can reach him. But she can't help us. Wim will have to wait, and these circumstances make him very tense.

To reduce the tension a bit, we start scanning the Internet for more news. He wants to know more about the contents of Ros's statements, but we can only find generalities.

We drive back to my house and end up in Beatrixpark. Wim is afraid of being arrested. We talk mainly about Cor's assassination. For years there has been speculation about who was riding the motorcycle. I tell him I recall him saying that Ros wasn't the one. Wim confirms that.

I try to put him at ease. If Ros wasn't riding that motorcycle, how can he make a statement about the liquidation? He wasn't there, was he? How could he incriminate Wim?

Wim keeps going on about how he's never spoken to him.

W: "At one point I said, 'I want to speak to the warden.' So I spoke
to him, and I said, 'You have put this Fred Ros here [in the
prison cell next to his]. I have never spoken to him, and I'd
like to keep it that way.' "

A: "So you don't have a problem. Others can say what they like
about you."

He trusts my legal judgment and has calmed down, but his unease
about the possibility of arrest remains.

SEPTEMBER 13, 2014

The Ros case is a crisis situation to him, so he's back the next day.
"I see you're still here," I say, referring to the fact that he's not been
arrested yet.

He asks me to see Stijn Franken with him. Stijn apparently had
gotten a sense of Ros's statements. At his office, Stijn appears to be
less optimistic than I am pretending to be about the repercussions
for Wim, and, understandably, much more careful about what he
says.

He wants to take his time rereading the statements.

SEPTEMBER 14, 2014

The next day Stijn, Chrisje, Wim, and I meet at a hospital somewhere in the Gooi area. We can speak freely there.

Wim walks and talks with Stijn. I walk and talk with Chrisje.
"He's just lucky, again," I tell her. "This Ros thing is going
nowhere."

After further reading of the statements, Stijn is also convinced, but Wim remains tense. He had a girl make a reservation at a hotel so he can choose where to sleep. I tell him not to take any chances, but that I don't expect an arrest because it would have already happened by now. They have no reason whatsoever to wait—if they have a strong case.

SEPTEMBER 15, 2014

Wim is convinced now that he'll get away with it. "God is with me," he tells me. And he only sees Ros as an advantage. After his earlier panic, Ros had become "exactly what [he] needed."

I get the distinct impression that he has made a pact with the devil.

That same day, Sonja and I meet with Betty. She asks if we are aware that Ros is testifying against Wim. Of course we are.

"But it's not enough. Wim has never spoken to him, so that's not going to work," I say. I tell Betty what I've been through with Wim this weekend, including the reason why Ros became a Crown witness: he was no longer going to be getting paid to keep quiet by his former friends.

She's taken aback but gets ahold of herself. "I would like to know if your loyalty has returned to Wim."

"It's still the same, it's not with Wim," I reply. "If you want him convicted, you'll need us."

"And that's exactly what I don't like," she says, worried as always. "I still think it's too dangerous."

"We are both still willing," I say.

Sandra's First Meeting with the CIU

IT'S VERY DANGEROUS FOR SANDRA TO BE INTERROGATED WHILE WIM IS still out there. He's not living with her anymore, but his control is still very tight; he checks her whereabouts twenty-four/seven, and he will notice right away and get suspicious if she's not around for a couple of hours. Sandra takes the gamble anyway. She has a credible story ready should he ask where she's been.

It's September of 2014. We have agreed to meet at ten a.m. at the Bosbaan restaurant, and we'll leave from there for the location where we'll introduce her to Betty and her associates. Sonja and I are waiting for her at a table outside. When she arrives, the tension is palpable.

"Are you still coming?" I ask her.

"Yes, I'm coming."

After introducing her to our people, we leave her behind. A couple of hours later, we meet up again.

Back at the Bosbaan restaurant, she walks to her scooter, and lingers there.

"What's she doing?" I ask Sonja.

"What do you mean, 'what's she doing'?"

"Why does she keep lingering there? The coffee is here. Can you tell if she's carrying bugging equipment?"

"As, are you mad or something? She's just been with the cops. What are you on about?"

"That may well be, but you can never be sure whether the Nose is playing games with us. He may have sent her. I don't entirely trust her."

"No," says Sonja, "you can trust her. We're all so screwed up because of him; he makes us mistrust everyone."

Sandra comes back and I ask her, "What was it you were doing there?"

"I just needed a moment to myself. It was all pretty intense today."

"Okay. I'll tell you honestly, San, when you do something like that, I think, What's she doing and can I trust her? I hope you won't hold that against me..."

"No, I understand perfectly well. I still have the same with you two. That's because I've always had to mistrust everybody; he plays people off against each other."

"I get the same feeling. Call me paranoid, but I am scared to death that you're still on his side."

"Oh, my thoughts exactly. You don't want to know how I felt when I got here this morning. I was so scared he might be here, too, that you two were in cahoots with him and that he would be here. I thought if that were the case, I would drop dead from fear, on the spot."

"Horrible, isn't it? What he's done to our trust in humans," I say. "I'm afraid that's our life. It is what it is."

Sandra is on the level as always.

The Attempt in Amstelveen

DECEMBER 8, 2014

Sonja had just left, and I was alone on my couch, dozing off, when the phone rang. My secretary was sobbing, totally freaking out. "I thought it was you," she cried. "My sister called me to see if I had seen the news yet, because they said that Holleeder's sister had been liquidated. You have no idea how I felt—I really thought for a moment that you were dead. Damned media!"

And she went on like that for a while.

Francis had also called me before Sonja left, saying that a woman in Amstelveen had been liquidated and asking where Sonja was. But she was still with me, so it wasn't her. It wasn't Francis, and I had checked on Miljuschka right away, too.

We don't call each other all the time for nothing. It's because we know that this can happen at any time. Whenever we hear sirens, see emergency helicopters, hear on TV that someone has been assassinated, we check that it's not someone in our circle. We've been doing that ever since the first attempt on Cor. But whereas we used to count on it happening only to one of the men, we now bear in mind that it could also happen to one of us women.

People were really frightened, and I got several messages and phone calls inquiring if we were still alive. It was a weird experience; for a moment I thought I had an insight into the future. I was a living witness to the news of my own death, or Sonja's. I was witness to the grief my death would cause a lot of people.

To Sonja and me, it was a very awkward situation, and it happened at a time when we were well aware that this could be our fate if it became clear we had testified against Wim.

And then he called.

He laughed. "Ha-ha-ha-ha. The press thought it was Sonja, didn't they? Well, it could have been."

"That makes you laugh?" I asked.

"Yeah, it's funny, right? It could happen to her."

He was such an imbecile. Such a twisted mind. Talking like that, over the phone, no less, he had a nerve.

I can't remember the rest of the conversation, I was so mad. I do remember him calling Sonja to ask if she really was alive.

The malevolence of this man never ceases to amaze me.

DECEMBER 9, 2014

The next morning, he came to my door early. "Call Sonja, tell her to come over."

I called her and asked if she wanted some coffee.

He wanted to step up the pressure on his extortion scheme, and yesterday's event came in very handy. We were inside waiting for her.

S: "Morning. Looking cozy, this early."
W: "We're going to buy you a bulletproof vest later."

S: "Oh, get lost. Really?"

W: "Sure."

S: "Why can't you act normal, you idiot."

W: "Well, what do you think?"

S: "What?"

W: "You think this can't happen to you? That this Boellaard, who is a psychopath who walks around with a gun... if he is having a bad day, that he won't kill you? He also shot dead that customs officer. He's just an imbecile, right? You make it all seem so easy with your friend Peter. But that's the reason why I should buy you a bulletproof vest. You are seriously in danger."

He used his familiar trick: I only want to help.

This time he was trying to scare us with his associates, Meijer and Boellaard, unaware that we'd already worked things out with them. They wanted money from the film, too, and tried to get it from us. We told them loud and clear that there was nothing there except for Cor's debt and that they should take it over because it was about their Heineken kidnapping. I had really had enough: these guys were trying to extort a defenseless woman and her children and at the same time as invoking their intense friendship with Cor. What kind of a friend are you, to do that to his wife and kids? Take over Cor's debt from the period that you made money with him; be a real pal, or a man at least. That did it; the two men lost the appetite for pursuing their plan.

S: "I'll go and see that guy."

W: "Who?"

S: "Boellaard."

W: "What will you do? Are you being smart?"

S: "No, I'm not being smart."

W: "You're being smart. You think he'll go for that?"

S: "I'm not being smart. But why would this guy hurt me?"

W: "Because you've got the film dough, Box. And because they feel they've been had and didn't care for the movie, either. We've discussed this more than a hundred times. And you can pretend to be really tough about all this, saying, 'I'll go and see him . . .'"

S: "I'm not playing tough!"

W: "Because if you are playing tough, it's your responsibility, right, and what happens then is also your responsibility, because you are not going to get me into trouble because you think you're acting tough."

S: "I'm not acting tough."

W: "It's all right to be tough, but yesterday you weren't all that tough."

S: "But I—"

W: "If they come for you tomorrow and blow your brains out, then what? I'll have to take care of it. You and your Peter. It could happen, I'm telling you. Because do you really think . . . See, these people are afraid of me . . . Do you really think they are two morons who don't have the guts to do anything? Really, Son, they shot at the police, everything. They killed that customs officer. Do you really think they're crazy? That they'll do what you tell them to do because you say like . . ."

S: "Do as I tell them?"

W: "Because you say . . . 'Get lost, because I'm Sonja Holleeder.'"

S: "Nothing like that. I didn't say that."

W: "You didn't? But what are you saying?"

S: "What am I saying?"

W: "Yes, how do you see things? Because when you get killed, I have to act."

I was so glad to have these recordings because they show exactly how he goes about things and the reason why the Justice Department can never catch him. He uses somebody else's name, so he can use as his alibi that he only wanted to give a warning. He won't say that he's the extortionist or the killer. No, it's always somebody else, people who don't even know they're being used as his alibi. The conversation continued on the street, where he publicly berated her.

W: "Why do you have to screw up my life with that Peter of yours? What have I done to deserve this? I have to go to court. I have to go to jail because you and your friend Peter decided that. You've had me sign something, I don't even know what. I really don't. Doesn't really matter...But don't go acting tough with your 'I'll go and see him,' you and your big mouth."

S: "No, but I mean—"

W: "No, because you know, you can't do anything."

S: "No, I can't."

W: "You know, you have no idea what you have caused. That is just a sleeping cell. Because anything can happen. And you can go on acting tough..."

S: "I'm not acting tough. But I don't think they're going to hurt me."

W: "You know what it is? Whether they're Cor's friends or not, it's one big misery because of your behavior. Everybody feels cheated, and they are ganging up on me, for you, because you and your friend Peter made that movie. And everybody was looking forward to that movie, and hoped to make some money. And you're walking like a priss..."

S: "I'm not walking like a priss..."

He knows himself well, and he knows when to accelerate, slow down, pull the reins, or loosen the reins. He never loses control; he only scares people to achieve his goal. Because later on, after we leave Sonja behind—savagely berated—he says, when I point out to him the judicial status of the film rights, he says, "But, As, I don't care about the judicial aspect. Judicially it's totally sound; the thing is, people feel they've been had."

He was extorting, and the tragic murder of a woman with children in Amstelveen—he used that event to intimidate his victim.

Wim Arrested After Statements Made by Ros

SONJA AND I ARE IN AMSTELVEEN MALL WHEN MY PHONE RINGS.

"Wim has been arrested based on statements made by Ros," I hear someone say.

The impact of the message was so huge that I can't remember who called and what else this person said. I just remember, "Wim has been arrested."

Finally!

Since my last meeting, on November 27, 2014, we haven't heard from the Justice Department and I have lost hope that he'd ever be arrested.

But now what?

Are they going to use our statements and—more important—does he know yet that we've testified against him?

By the time Michelle calls, we are feeling very tense and insecure. CIU wants a meeting on December 17 to discuss if they could use our statements.

This is the moment for us to decide. Are we going to testify against him publicly? If we decide to do it, we can't go back to how things were.

* * *

Now that it's all so real, I start doubting. I wonder if I can do this to him: no more prospects of freedom. Getting old and dying within the confines of prison walls. Alone, without family and friends.

I decide to ask my therapist for advice.

"You must be crazy," she says. "Why would you do that, testify? You're messing up your whole life! Everything you've worked so hard for. You shouldn't do it. You couldn't live with yourself if you did." That last remark hit me right in the heart; I don't know if I can live with myself if I convict my brother for life.

At the last moment, I call off the meeting. I'm in doubt. Almost two years I've been waiting for this moment, and now I'm not sure.

That afternoon I tell my best friend—who has been a witness to my life for twenty years—what my therapist has said and that I therefore had called off my meeting with Betty.

"That woman is out of her mind," he says. "She doesn't get it, the misery you've lived with for so many years. Easy for her to say. I'm not saying that you should or shouldn't—that's your call. But I know your life, I've seen it up close, and your life sucks, big-time. It couldn't be any worse. And if you feel guilty about what you'll do to him, just listen to the tapes every now and then. Then you'll know exactly why you did it."

Part V

Women Floor
Holleeder

2015–2016

Prison Visit

2015

PETER CAME BY. HE HAD THE FRED ROS STATEMENTS WITH HIM. THEY revealed that Ros had heard who it was that had spoken about the whereabouts of Cor to his killers. A video made of the moment right after Cor's death had appeared on the Internet. According to Ros, the informant could be seen in the footage. Apparently he was one of the two people seen running around.

Sonja and I have always wanted to know who the informant was. We knew this footage and started watching immediately. There were indeed two people running around: Adje, Cor's half brother, and Bassie, a friend. Could it have been one of them? And which of the two? Ros gave no definite answer. We found it hard to imagine.

Adje was out of the question, but with Bassie, something awkward was going on. It was Bassie who was driving Cor around that day. He picked up the car just at the moment Cor was shot on the pavement. Bassie said getting the car out took a bit longer because two other cars blocked it.

We'd stopped thinking Bassie was a suspect after Wim once told me smilingly that he'd given him a hiding in public because he "had betrayed Cor." This display was a typical diversion on Wim's part. By publicly blaming him for "giving Cor away," Wim proved his own innocence. We assumed Bassie was innocent, too, a victim of Wim's manipulation tactics.

But now we were in doubt again.

"If we want to know who the informant was, we'll have to get it from Wim," I said. Sonja and Peter nodded in agreement.

If Wim would tell us, it would mean that he knew the killer. But then, it wouldn't be enough just to talk to him. How could I prove what we had discussed during that visit? Wim could easily deny the contents of that conversation.

The only solution was to record the conversation. But how? Wim was in a guarded prison: how could I smuggle my bugging equipment in? To enter the Penitentiary Institution in Alphen a/d Rijn, you have to pass through a metal detector, and there was metal in the recording equipment, even if only a little.

"How will you do it?" Sonja asked.

"I'm going to remove as much metal as possible," I said, and I stripped the equipment. I bought a handheld metal detector to check whether the remaining metal would set off the detector. It did. I had to hide the last bit of metal in a place that wouldn't get noticed.

"Son, get us some condoms."

Sonja came back, and I wrapped the stripped device in toilet paper and put it in the condom.

"Here, put it in your vagina and we'll see if it still goes off." Sonja went to the bathroom, and when she came back, I moved the metal detector in front of her crotch to see what would happen. There wasn't a sound! I made the same tampon for myself and tested it. It remained silent again.

"That's a good sign, at least," I told Sonja, "but I don't know how they've adjusted the metal detector at the prison."

In my experience as a criminal lawyer, I knew conditions could vary. In some prisons, I pass the detector with keys in my pocket without setting it off, while others react to the underwire in my bra. I had some experience with this prison, but they could adjust the scanner any day and there would be no way to tell. We couldn't afford to be involved in a riot at the entrance in case they found metal on us.

"We have to wear pants with an iron button near the crotch," I said. "That way if the scanner goes off, we can tell them that's the cause. But there shouldn't be too many buttons, or the pants will set it off for sure; then we won't get in. Look in your closet."

We tried on all the pants and tested them with the manual metal detector.

"I'm wearing these," said Sonja.

"Yeah, those are good. I'll wear these, then." They were jeans. I wasn't too happy about them, because I don't like jeans and never wear them.

"You think he'll notice me wearing jeans all of a sudden?" I asked Sonja.

"I guess, but we don't have many options. They'll have to do." Okay, so much for the pants. Now for the shirt to stick the equipment on or in. Finding a shirt that could disguise the equipment wasn't easy; for days I had been experimenting with various items of clothing. I was used to going outside with him to talk, and I always wore a coat. This time I could hardly sit there wearing a coat; it would be too conspicuous.

During the summer, I sometimes wore a dress I had rigged up, but it wasn't a thing to wear on a prison visit. And he knew me through and through. He knew exactly what clothes I always wear, because he and I share the habit of wearing the same outfit every day. A clean version every day, but always the same outfit. If I were to suddenly wear something different, he would be immediately suspicious.

Furthermore, I knew from all the earlier visits that we would be whispering and would be seated very close together. A situation where I couldn't walk away or turn away if I thought he was looking at something.

In the bright light of the visitors' area, any discrepancy would stand out, every bulge in my shirt would be magnified. If he were to see anything at all "off," he would discover the equipment at once.

And then there was the issue of the whispering. If I stuck the device under my bra strap, it wouldn't be close enough to my ear to catch his whispering. It had to be hidden near my shoulder.

I had tried various shirts, cut them up, sewn the stuff in, and eventually I found a shirt that would have to do. But recording the whispering would still be really difficult, so I looked for an alternative. I found one in a spy shop in southeast Amsterdam: a watch that could record. I got one for myself and one for Sonja.

If I dared to wear it, it just might work. I know from experience that when I'm whispering to him in prison, I usually have my arm around his neck. My wrist would be near his mouth, so I'd presumably catch the whispering clearly. The only problem was that those watches are strikingly large, and he knew I never wore one.

I took a gamble: that his trust in me added to the stressful situation would make him blind to the minor wardrobe changes. When he saw me, he would be counting on my support and not aware of even the possibility that I would betray him that day.

The moment had come to enter the prison. Wim's latest flame would be there, too, and we'd given her a head start. She was already in and couldn't be witness to anything that might go wrong with us at security. I was very nervous. Theory is totally different from reality. I couldn't afford to get caught, so Sonja, who had already lost Wim's trust, served as a guinea pig. She passed through security without a beep. That was good. The watch also passed. Security had no idea that this was bugging equipment. Now me. Phew! Not a sound! We went upstairs to the visitors' room.

We were inside.

I knew there was a toilet by the entrance near the visitors' room. There I would have to get the rest of the equipment from Sonja, inconspicuously. Cameras are everywhere and the two of us in there at once would be too conspicuous. So she went in first, took the device out of her vagina, and left it on top of the toilet cistern. I went in after her to get mine out and to attach the equipment as invisibly as I possibly could.

Of course Wim has his own room to receive his visitors in private. We say hello. He could strangle me on the spot.

He grabs me by the shoulder, and I feel his hand trembling. I feel his fear about the message I have come to deliver to him. How terrible. I feel so mean. To extract from someone—in his deepest misery—information about who really set Cor up: such treason. How can I be so evil? I feel like throwing up.

Sonja sees my doubt; she blinks her big eyes and looks at me firmly. It means, Go on. She's right: We've come this far.

I take a deep breath and try to act naturally.

W: "How are you?"
A: "Good."
W: "Yes?"
A: "Yes. So here we are."

I start about Ros's statement at the door, before we even sit down.

A (whispering): "That Ros guy, he is pointing to someone."

W: "Yes."

A: "He pointed to someone in the footage, and now they're busy with the informant, to finally arrive at…"

We are sitting next to each other. He puts his arm around me, whispers in my ear.

W: "One more time."

A: "The informant, who told on him…in Amstelveen."

W: "Yeah, but how?"

A: "Well, Ros says that the guys in the footage—"

W: "Yes."

A: "On TV, okay, what you can see is…the guy who is really running up and down…he's the informant."

W (softly): "The informant of what?"

Wim has no idea what informant I'm talking about. I put my arm around his neck and whisper in his ear:

A: "Of Cor's murder."

W: "Can't be."

I don't understand. I repeat what Ros has said. I let him see my doubt, but he is adamant.

W: "No."

A: "This is his [Ros's] statement; he got it from Danny."

Wim shakes his head.

W: "I don't have a problem there."
A: "I don't know that?"
W: "No."
A: "No? [Whispering] The moment it happened..."
W: "No."

I ask him three times, but he says no, three times. He's sure about it. He has no problem with Ros's statement.

Wim turns to Sonja and the girlfriend.

W: "Why don't you just talk a bit, you two?"

As always, when Wim wants to talk with his visitors unimpaired, the others have to make some noise, ambient noise that covers our conversation and ruins the recording.

Wim explains to me why it's not an issue—because between the "lurer" and him, there was a middleman. He doesn't know the lurer, so he can't name him. He calls the informant the lurer: I hadn't used that word.

W (whispering): "There was a person in between but I don't know
     him..."
A: "Sure?"
W: "Sure."

Wim wants to know how many people were seen running in the video.

A: "Two of them, that's all."
W: "Well, then."

Neither of them—not Adje or Bassie—was the lurer, according to Wim.

Wim wants to know if the guy next to Cor during the shooting was visible in the video. "No," I tell him.

The one next to Cor was also hit and was lying on the ground, invisible in the footage. I'm surprised at his question.

I make up that Sonja will also be interrogated about Cor's murder. We had agreed on that beforehand. I'm still not sure who the informant or "lurer" is and steer the conversation to one of the guys running around in the footage. I indicate that I'm afraid that if Bassie is the informant and is questioned, he'll crack.

A (whispering): "Because Sonja was also asked to come in . . .
       Bassie . . . that he started talking . . ."
W: "No."
A: "No?"

Wim whispers into my ear. The way I think it happened, with Bassie, is not the way it happened.

So it's not Bassie. Or Adje. But then who gave Cor away? I steer the conversation back to Bassie.

A: "He is a nutcase, isn't he?"
W: "Yes, but he's peanuts. Really."

But he still hasn't told me who it is. I give it one more try.

A: "Last one, and then I'll go—"

Wim wants to know again what can be seen in the footage.

A: "I looked at the footage and saw Bassie running around."

W (whispering, then loud): "I was really scared."

A: "Yeah, me, too."

W: "I'm thinking: What are you on about."

A: "I was also scared because I'm thinking: Well, that…umm."

I explain to him again that I'm scared the lurer will start talking.

A: "Afraid that—"

Then Wim explains why that's impossible. The lurer was next to Cor, and he's dead. It's ter Haak.

Now I understand why Wim at first didn't get which informant I meant.

Now I understand why Wim knew that what Ros said was impossible.

Now I understand his question about whether the one next to Cor was visible in the footage.

Now I understand why he was so sure that Bassie was innocent.

Now I understand why he knew that neither of the two people running around was the lurer.

Wim conceitedly looks around the visitors' room, as if he's proud that they can't hurt him with a dead informant, and I immediately get the feeling that ter Haak was deliberately killed. I see Sonja looking at Wim, then at me, inquisitively.

I nod inconspicuously; I know who did it.

I don't want to talk inside the prison, afraid that someone will record us on the security system.

We walk outside. "And?" Sonja asks.

"It's not who we think it is. It's somebody else."

Back in the car safely, I tell her what she has wanted to know for years: "It was ter Haak."

That Robert ter Haak was the lurer, according to Wim, doesn't mean that he was aware of the role. I wasn't able to ask Wim that question, because it would arouse his suspicion at once. It's feasible that he was trapped, maybe by a middleman. One thing is for sure, and that is that justice has to be done for his brutal assassination. He had died in the hospital a few hours after Cor, mowed down by the same spray of bullets.

That night Sonja says to me, "As, you shouldn't feel guilty about Wim. He is a monster. He wouldn't hesitate one second to do this to you."

Mom's Blessing

WE HAD TOLD OUR KIDS MUCH EARLIER WHAT WE WERE DOING AND THAT we might eventually be testifying. Although we had promised the Justice Department not to tell them, it was impossible to keep it a secret from them till the last moment. Our actions would have an enormous impact on their lives, and they had every right to think this through and not be confronted with it suddenly. If they thought we'd better not do it, we would quit immediately.

They were witness to our doubts, the times that we decided not to pursue it, and the times we decided to go ahead with it. But now was the moment when we had to make a choice.

We pointed out again that there was a strong possibility that we'd have to pay for this action with our lives.

Francis said at once, "Do it! He's going to kill Mama anyway, so she'd better be one step ahead of him."

Richie totally agreed. But that reason didn't cut it for me. My position toward Wim was different: I was his ally. How could I justify to Miljuschka putting my life at risk without yet being in acute danger, like Sonja?

"You know what the consequences are if I do this, sweetie?" I asked her.

"Yes, I know, Mom," she replied softly.

"I have to decide now."

"Yes..."

"I can't think of a single reason that outweighs the risk I'll be taking. I shouldn't do it, because I know how this is going to end, but still..."

"I understand, Mom. Sometimes you've got to do the right thing."

We already knew Gerard's point of view on the matter. Sonja and I had asked him back in 2011, before Wim was released, if he'd testify if we did. But back then he'd said: "You're not going to survive, so why do it? What's the point?" That was still his position. "What's the point of all three of us dying? At least I can take care of Mom when you're no longer here."

There was still someone else who needed to know.

"We'll have to tell Mom," I told Sonja.

She agreed, and we decided to drive straight over there.

"Are you nervous?" she asked me.

"Yes, kind of. We have been working on this for more than two years, but if Mom is against it, we can't pursue it. In that case we've had all this misery for nothing, and we're facing many more years of it. But hey, it's her child. She decides."

"And you know what she's like."

"That's why I'm afraid of her reaction. She has always buried her head in the sand and justified his behavior."

We arrived at my mother's house. She was waiting for us at the door, always glad to see us.

"How nice of you to come by," she said. "Make yourselves comfortable. Tea?"

"Sure, Mom," I replied.

"I'll have some, too," said Sonja.

I got straight to the point. "Mom, we'd like to talk to you for a bit."

"What is it now?" she asked.

"Yes, well," I said. "We're going to testify against Wim."

"Testify how?"

"Well, tell what he has done."

She immediately looked worried. "That's not very clever. He'll never accept it."

"I know, but it has to stop sometime. You know that it's Son's turn one of these days, and I don't want to wait for that," I said.

"Then you should do it," she said resolutely.

Sonja and I looked at each other in surprise. Was she throwing in the towel that easily?

"But be aware that if we do it, chances are that he's going in for life," I said.

"Let's hope so, or he'll be chasing you."

Sonja and I again looked at each other in astonishment. This was her son. "Do you know what you're saying, Mom?" I asked to be sure.

"Assie, what do you think? He is threatening Sonja, he is threatening my grandchildren! That is unheard of! Do you think I don't know what he is made of? I am scared to death that he will get you. I would much rather have him inside prison walls. I wouldn't know what to do if anything happened to you. I would rather hang myself!"

"Okay, I'm glad you support us. For a minute there I was afraid you wouldn't."

"Wouldn't? As, he has brought nothing but trouble to everybody. And now he wants to get at my child and my grandchildren? He's my son, and it hurts to say it, but he's an animal! I've had no life because of him, right? Always visiting, always with those crazy women of his. Always shouting and cursing when things don't go his way. I didn't even dare maintain a normal relationship with Roy, afraid of him running into Roy and kicking him out the door."

My mother had met Roy a couple of years after the divorce. He dropped by the fruit stall where I worked, and my mother got to talking with him. Every week he came back and asked how she was doing. He was a tall, handsome man of Surinamese descent. They started seeing each other.

Wim didn't like that. He didn't want his mother to date a "negro."

It was a disgrace. She anxiously kept it a secret from Wim for thirty years. She didn't have the chance to have a normal relationship, and now she was alone.

"Did you know that Wim was responsible for Deurloostraat?" I asked.

"No, you never told me. Really?" she asked.

"Yes, it was him."

"What a bastard. I still see it happening, right in front of my eyes. It's been so long, but it still keeps me awake sometimes. Then I'll see, bang, bang, bang, there on the car window. I hear Son screaming, Richie crying. I see Cor's blood everywhere. I'll never forget it. That's all I needed—how is it possible?"

"But, Mom, let it sink in a bit what I'm saying: When we testify, chances are he'll get a life sentence. Do you realize what that means? That you'll never be able to visit him, never be able to call him, because he will use any contact with you, in any way, to track us down. Do you understand? When you say yes, you will be saying goodbye to your eldest son. Can you do that?"

I saw tears in her eyes.

"See, you start crying at the mere thought."

I started crying, too, and said, "Son, we won't do it!"

My mother was trying to control her tears. "But, As, it's not so strange that all this saddens me so much, is it? It saddens you, too. I will have a lot of sorrow for the rest of my life, but it has to be done. This has to stop."

"Are you sure?"

"Very sure."

"Will you think of me as a traitor?"

"You, a traitor? Why? For helping your sister? Because you stand up for your nephew and niece? Are you crazy? You're no traitor! He's a traitor! He's got the Nazi blood of your grandfather."

Apart from my mother, there was one more person I had to take into account in our decision to condemn Wim to life in prison: his son Nicola.

If I'd had the least idea that I'd hurt this little boy by taking his father away from him, I might not have done it. Maike and her mother raised him, and Wim called him his "white source" (legal money source) because he was the heir of Maike's father, a wealthy real estate tycoon.

Maike, whom Wim still considered part of his harem, had called to meet me when Wim was arrested and nobody knew of our role as witnesses. During this meeting, she asked if I'd help her to stop Wim from seeing Nicola. She was terribly worried about what would happen if Wim was released, and she hoped that he'd stay behind bars for good.

I figured that it wouldn't be too traumatic for Nicola if Wim were put away for longer, and that I wouldn't be robbing a little boy of a loving father if his father got a life sentence.

That relationship was no reason not to testify.

The day before it was made public, Sonja and I went to see Maike to tell her what we had done. For Nicola's sake, we wanted her to know beforehand so she could be there for him if he needed her.

Use of Preliminary Statements

From mid-December 2014 until March 19, 2015, we had been going back and forth about using our preliminary statements. Now, finally, we had decided to go ahead and use them.

The plan was that on March 20, 2015, the statements would be handed to the court, the district attorney's office, and the defense. Finally, after such a long and nerve-racking experience, the moment had arrived. We were fully prepared for that day, and then came the message that it was called off! It was an incredible blow. My nervous system couldn't take much more.

It was rescheduled for Monday, March 23. On Wednesday, March 25, there would be a pro forma hearing, and I knew that Stijn Franken would ask for Wim's release, a request that, I thought, had a chance of succeeding. The statements Ros had made about Wim's involvement in the liquidations were second- or third-hand at best. If our statements were presented by March 23, they would be just in time.

In the meantime, we had informed the press based on the understanding that all parties to the trial would be familiar with our statements. The *Telegraaf* and *NRC* newspapers were going to publish our interviews on Tuesday, March 24.

But on Monday, March 23, at 12:08, I got word from Betty that the handing over of the statements was off again. The statements would be issued later.

Postponed again? I called Betty to ask for the reason. She told me it was too early, due to our safety and the measures that had to be taken. I told her that we couldn't wait, because we had already alerted the media. She asked me to cancel the press; there could be disastrous consequences if the papers published the interviews before the preliminary statements had gone to the court, the lawyers, and the district attorney's office.

But we had no intention of blowing off the press. We wanted our statements to go public on the agreed-upon date. The publication of the statements would increase our safety. By now an unknown number of people already knew about our role as witnesses, and the chance that Wim would find out had increased.

The DA didn't want to jeopardize our safety, but we hadn't been safe for a long time. Not safe from the moment we'd had our first meeting with the Justice Department, and certainly not safe during the two years we, knowing we had testified, had to go on seeing Wim.

We were totally worn out by the stress and didn't want to spend any more time in uncertainty. We'd just have to see what would happen: on Tuesday, March 24, we would stand up to him, with or without the district attorney's office.

I told Betty that we knew what we were doing and also knew the consequences. That was our choice, and I said to her, "I discharge you of all responsibility regarding our safety. Don't worry. It's our decision, and we'll do it with or without you."

That same day, just before five p.m., I got the message that it was a green light and that the statements were available to the court and defense. No later than tomorrow, but it could well be today, Wim would know that we'd stood up to him.

I had been imagining this moment for two years, how it would mean a turning point in my relationship with my brother. The moment he'd hear that his little sister had been trying for years to get him convicted. His little sister, to whom he had entrusted his fear of a life sentence, would now get him condemned for life herself. It still makes me cry, how it must have felt to him, like a knife straight through his heart.

Women Floor Holleeder

On Tuesday, March 24, 2015, our story appeared in the media. It started early in the morning.

"Women Floor Holleeder" was the *Telegraaf* headline of an interview with Sonja and Sandra. That evening, my own story was published in *NRC Handelsblad,* and virtually every TV show broadcast it. I had to be in Assen that day for a hearing and hadn't realized how huge the impact of our story would be.

That day and night—after the sound clips played on the *RTL Late Night* show—Willem Holleeder was exposed, and his true identity was revealed.

It seemed as if a wave of relief swept over the country: everybody had guessed as much, but nobody could lay a finger on him. Willem Holleeder had done all the things the Justice Department had suspected him of doing all these years.

Luckily, the thing I was afraid of—that people would react with anger and call us traitors—didn't happen. Far from it; I think that that day alone, we received some three hundred messages of support from familiar but also unfamiliar people. And really, every message made a difference. One in particular. John van den Heuvel, a crime journalist, sent it through to me:

Dear Astrid and Sonja,

I would like to express my admiration for your courage in saying goodbye to Willem Holleeder in this way.

I have deep respect for the three women who, under such enormous pressure, have nevertheless decided to make a statement; in my opinion you belong to the backbone of the Netherlands.

I know from experience what death threats and the ensuing fear can do to people; that one can feel desperate and powerless, always living under pressure and constantly being alert because "the unknown" can strike violently at any moment. But you have made a difference by showing character.

Do think back to the Heineken-Doderer kidnapping for a moment. You may remember the codes that were used to communicate: the eagle (Holleeder c.s.) and the hare (Heineken c.s.).

The roles are reversed now. You have morphed from a fearful hare to a free-flying eagle.

I hope with all my heart that you and your children will be able to enjoy wonderful and safe flights, because you fully deserve them.

With kind regards, Kees Sietsma
Leader of the so-called Heineken team (1983)

That evening Sonja and I sat at her dining room table, opposite each other.

"Do you feel it, too?" I asked.

"Yes," she said.

"But what?"

"It feels like the day Cor died," she said.

"Yes," I said, "I feel exactly the same."

We'd gone back in time twelve years, to the source of our grief, and it was as if only now were we ready to deal with that grief.

Consequences

IT HAS CHANGED ME, THE STEP I TOOK, AND THE KNOWLEDGE THAT I won't grow old.

I used to spend my life solving other people's problems; it gave me an identity, personally but also professionally. But when someone starts talking about his problems now, I think, Stop whining and deal with it.

You can still deal with it.

My problem, though, is unsolvable. There will never be a solution, but there will be an end, a bloody end.

It won't take long before he has room to get an easy revenge. Did I do right? That question keeps coming up. No, I didn't do right. But I had no choice. It's the way it is.

We—Sandra, Sonja, and I—each got a bracelet from Liesbeth, Sam Klepper's sister, a bracelet with a four-leaf clover. She understands that we could all use a bit of extra luck.

When we're together, we regularly talk about who's going first. Actually, we all agree that I'll go first, because he didn't see my treason coming, and he'll hate me forever for that.

He took me seriously, asked for my advice, trusted me, and I betrayed him. He really can't stand for this. I feel that a bulletproof vest could be useful, but Sandra would rather "go" straight away.

We discuss this on the couch at her place. It seems suicidal, but she's got a point. What if you survive by wearing the vest but end up in a wheelchair?

Better get it right away.

That's true, but I'll get a vest anyway.

My eye rests on Sonja's arm, and I notice she's no longer wearing the bracelet. "Where's your four-leaf clover?" I ask.

She's scared stiff, her face turns red, and she gasps for air. "Oh, God, where is it?" she asks.

I know what she's thinking; we're both superstitious, and I understand why she's so frightened.

"It's there, on the couch," I say.

Relieved and happy, she puts it back on.

"You thought you were first, didn't you?" I ask.

"Yes," she said. "I thought: This is a sign that I'm going first, that luck has abandoned me."

"That's what I thought."

Less than a week later, I discover that I have lost my four-leaf clover.

Car Wash

On May 30, 2015, the story appeared in *NRC Handelblad* about the lurer. To involve my mother in what we were doing as much as possible, which she'd insisted on after we came out with our statements, I went to her house to bring her the newspaper. On the way there, I stopped off at the car wash.

I parked my car in a stall and got the coins from the machine. Coming back, I saw a car drive toward the stalls, coming in from the wrong direction; two young men were in it. They drove past me and reversed. They looked at me while doing so, as if they wanted to be sure of my identity. They parked two stalls away and stayed in the car.

Meanwhile, I had foamed my car. One guy kept looking at me while the other one bent down and appeared to take something from the floor. Something wasn't right. I wanted to leave, but first had to spray the foam off my car or I wouldn't be able to see through the windshield.

That same moment, a second car parked next to the car already there. A slim guy wearing mirrored glasses got out and came my way. I froze inside and hurried to get the foam off.

I had to get out of there.

The man walked up to me and asked, "Are you Astrid?"

At that moment I felt the blood drain from my face. I immediately thought of a line that was used at the Mieremet liquidation. "Are you Johnny?" When he said yes, they opened fire, and the assassination my brother had wanted for so long was accomplished.

I didn't know what to say.

"Are you Astrid?" he asked again.

I said yes and expected my life to be over then and there. "I am Makali," he said. "How are you doing?"

"I'm doing well—how about you?"

Makali, I knew that family name. He could be a client of one of my associates, but I didn't recognize him. He was being friendly so I assumed he wouldn't hurt me, but the other two guys were still there in the car, and he walked in their direction. Maybe he just came over to check that I was the right one to kill, and they would soon open fire?

I threw the hose down, got in my car quickly, and drove away as fast as I could, the foam still on my roof. I was shaking all over. This is what he's always aiming for.

"He's so scared," he'd always say about his targets. "They know what I'm like, they know what I'll do, and if they see someone running at them toting that thing, they know: it's over. And then they think: I wish I hadn't done it."

Yeah, I know that, too, I know what you're like and what you're going to do. I will also know, the moment they come running toward me toting that thing: it's over. But I won't think, I wish I hadn't done it. Because I know, brother, that when they set fire to my coffin, you'll be slowly rotting away in your cell, without the celebrity you've known, because I have taken that away from you. Without the privileges you've always had, because I have taken those, too, and you may wonder: What is worse? To set me on fire, but count on me coming back to haunt you? And when all your victims and I come to visit you in your cell, without surveillance, you'll run out of oxygen.

What happened that afternoon gave me a reason to talk to my daughter. I would be seeing her that evening.

"Sweetie, this afternoon I thought for minute that my time had come. You know that could happen any moment, right?"

"Yes, I know, Mom," she said. She bit her lip, but tears were flowing anyway.

"That's why it's important to talk about my funeral and how you'll go on without me."

I couldn't stop myself from crying, either. But I pushed through it, because today had shown yet again that I needed to talk about this with her as soon as possible.

"I don't want an open casket so people can see my soulless face. I want a closed casket. And I want to be cremated. Nice and warm. I can't bear thinking about lying in cold earth. Just set me on fire, a full urn, and put that in a cozy room. Nice flowers, a couple of framed pictures, nice and warm. Not a grave you need to visit, which you won't anyhow. No, I'll be here at home with you and the kids. That's what I want."

"Me too, Mom," she cried.

"Okay, sweetie. And you need to go on without me. You have to stay who you are. You have had enough experience to know you'll always return to yourself. That's you, so I'm not worried about that. And the little ones soon won't know any better. Point out a star and tell them I live there and that I am with them every day."

We both cried.

"But I will miss you so much, Mom," she whispered through her tears. "Your voice, your scent." She stood up and started collecting pieces of clothing. "I need to keep your scent. I need to have as many items as possible with your scent still in them. At least I can smell them when you're not here anymore."

My heart broke. What a life. Death almost feels like a reward to me, but I have to leave behind such sorrow.

Still, I have to discuss this with her, because I don't know how much time I have left. And, of course, it's not the first time we've talked about it: before Sonja and I decided to use our testimony, we discussed the consequences with all the kids. But we also told them we'd run the same risk if we didn't testify. They knew that risk.

I explained to them that I was going to die either way, and I'd rather my death mean something. If he was still out there, having fun, despite all the victims he's harmed, my death would be pointless. Now when I die, at least I will have had the satisfaction of bringing out the truth about him and knowing he will pay for the suffering he's brought on Cor and many others.

"You just go to bed now. Tomorrow things will look different," I said to Miljuschka. "I'll be here for the time being."

Together Forever

I'M IN THE CAR WITH SONJA WHEN BETTY WIND TELLS US IT'S OFFICIAL: Wim will be prosecuted for Cor's murder. Now, two years later, the thing we had hoped would happen has become reality.

Sonja looks at me, tears running down her cheeks, and I feel my own tears coming.

"Together forever," she cries.

"Together forever," I reply.

It's the text we had engraved on Cor's tombstone and which is symbolic of our mission: justice for Cor, for Richie, and for Francis.

"You'll finally have your peace, sweetie," she says to Cor.

Shooting Lessons

"GIVE ME A GUN LICENSE SO I CAN DO SOMETHING WHEN THEY COME FOR me," I tell our witness protection officer in July. But it's against the law, so she won't agree to it. In other words, I should let myself be butchered like a lame lamb.

I tell Sandra, "Then we'll have to go get a gun license ourselves."

"You think they'll admit us to the shooting club?"

"If not, we'll make trouble. We're no different than other people. I don't feel like just being shot. I have reached the point where I will accept what is coming to me without fear or grief, but it's ridiculous that I have to surrender without a fight. I can't live with that passivity; it will just give him as much power over me as he ever had, because he doesn't have to abide by the law and I do. I'm always the loser. So no matter what, I want to be able to do something to take out at least one of them when I see the gunmen. I will not just be butchered."

"Me neither," says Sonja.

"Then we'll do something about it."

Sandra has researched a way for us to be able to defend ourselves: we'd take SPEAR defense training and shooting lessons. On July 24, we are going to have our first lesson at the shooting club.

Sandra has not listed our surnames, but we'll have to show our identity cards, so it won't be long before this will become public. When we walk to the club I say, "They will be scared shitless when they see my surname."

It always remains to be seen how that will pan out. That's why I try to postpone giving my last name as long as possible, preferably until I have spoken to the person and they can see for themselves that I'm not scary. That is my plan for today.

We are already in and were chatting with two nice, naïve ladies. We have been connecting well before I need to show my identity card. I think it highly unlikely that they will refuse us after all this, but you never can tell.

The instructor comes over with a serious look on his face. "You're here for the introduction class?"

"Yes," we say, as bland as possible.

"Well, let's get started."

A few days later, Sandra sends me a message saying that she'll be at my house at eight fifteen a.m. and asking whether we should take her car or mine. I'd forgotten about it for a minute, but we had a meeting with our SPEAR trainer at nine that morning.

I first want to know what we're looking at. If I have a bad feeling about the trainer, I'll say goodbye without telling him who we are and why we want this. If the impression is good, I want to know beforehand if he'd be willing to keep this a secret. Somebody walking around using our names and our situation for their own benefit does not help us: we really need to keep our preparations secret.

We arrange to meet at the Hilton in Amsterdam. Sandra shows him the table where I'm already sitting; he comes up and introduces himself.

My first impression is good. Posture, voice, energy, I like him right away. His short introduction is also good. Not a guy who thinks too much of himself, overestimates himself. I feel no irritation at all. So I decide to open up and tell him who we are and what our goal is. "The reason we are interested in your training is because we are women testifying against Willem Holleeder. We expect to be executed in the short or long term and don't want to resign ourselves to it."

The poor guy needs to catch his breath; he was not prepared for this. He's being treated to an announcement, on a Sunday morning, that he could never have imagined.

"Okay, that's extreme," he says, and gets a grip, "but it's doable. You seem to take the situation quite lightly."

I smile at him.

"That's because," I say, "we accepted it the moment we took this step. We know this will be the end for us. He will never accept this betrayal. The three of us know that the only thing keeping him alive is the thought of revenge. He always told us that if he gets a life sentence, he'll commit suicide. But he'll wait until he's butchered us all."

"So you know it's going to happen, just not when?" he asks.

"Yes, and as things are now, we still have time to take your classes. But I won't take a year's subscription"—I laugh—"unless you reimburse me for any unused lessons!"

"I think that the lessons will help you, but you should know that if they really want to get you, they'll always succeed and this training is not going to stop them."

"We know that. We don't ask for a money-back guarantee. We are under no illusion that we'll survive because of your training, but we have to have dignity to be able to fight back. Maybe we can collect evidence—maybe DNA under our fingernails—that will help the police arrest the perpetrators and find a link to Wim. We don't want to die like lambs, and we can't bear the idea of him escaping punishment because of a perfect alibi, as happened with Thomas van der Bijl."

"Still, heavy stuff," he says, "but let's just get started next week."

"Good," I say, "let's do it. My sister will be there, too."

All three of us leave the Hilton, and on my way to the car, I tell Sandra: "Well, that's all we can do."

"Yes," she says, "but maybe it'll help."

Dying II

Sonja and I are walking on Scheldestraat when I run into Netteke at the ice cream parlor. I remember her from the Palmschool, where we had our English classes during grade school.

She was the strongest girl in her class, and her classmates had decided that she should fight the strongest girl in our class: me.

Poor Netteke, cheered on by her classmates, she had just enough courage to fight me. She followed me to the cigar store.

I wasn't aware of her mission and thought she also was going in to buy something.

"Hi," I said when I turned around and saw her standing there.

"Hi," she replied timidly, and dashed out of the store.

"She followed you because she wanted to fight you!" my friend Hanna, who was there with me, said excitedly.

"Oh," I said, unimpressed.

"Yeah, but she didn't dare. The chicken. You know her father is in prison? I'm telling you. In England!"

"Oh," I replied again, not getting what one thing had to do with the other.

Netteke was from the Jordaan. Of course people talked about her father being in prison, but that was more of an observation than a judgment. The Jordaan was the bottom of society; you were lucky if you could feed your family. It wasn't the way you earned your money that mattered, but how much.

Netteke was the first girl I dared take home with me. In the daytime, when my father was away, we'd eat butter cake at my mother's table. And so Netty met the rest of my family.

"Your brother works?" she asked the moment we were outside and saw Wim driving up in a Mercedes.

"I don't know," I said.

"You don't know?"

"No," I said. I really didn't know.

"My father knows your brother," said Netteke, in a conspiratorial kind of way, and I quickly did the math. My brother drove an expensive car without me knowing if he had a job, and he and her sketchy dad knew each other.

Netteke was trying to say my brother was a crook.

My father once had different plans for Wim. He wanted his eldest son to be an honorable, respected citizen, and the job of a policeman fitted that description perfectly. His eldest son should join the police force.

My father had enlisted him, and Wim had an interview the next day. That evening my father, in his own special way, went on to "instruct him" to behave decently and be polite. He went about it a bit too diligently, and Wim ended up with a black eye and a fat lip. He refused to go to the interview like that.

Maybe Wim's life would have turned out differently if my father had left him alone that one time and he had gone to the interview.

But what Wim did for a living, and in what way that was criminal, I had not the faintest idea. I saw only parts of his life:

Wim with Cor, smiling, at the dining room table my mother had spread with bread, sandwich fillings, and steak she had to get for them, after they'd come back from the gym in their expensive cars.

A visit to the house of his Surinamese girlfriend, who was a showgirl and who showed me all her makeup and glittery underwear.

The day he took me to the red-light district, where he bought me a milkshake with whipped cream on top at an Italian ice cream parlor and I had to wait for him to come back.

The brown chunk of something he showed me as a little girl, which I later understood was hash, because many kids at school smoked it.

From these fragments, I couldn't see Wim doing anything nasty or wrong. On the other hand, my father, shouting out loud that Wim was no good, did something nasty and wrong every evening.

"How terrible," Netteke says at the ice cream parlor, when I tell her about Wim and how we've testified. "So what happens now? And how do you deal with this?" she asks.

She doesn't use the word "death," but her meaning is clear. Indeed, how do you deal with it, and let me name it: an approaching death. I act unconcerned, and in the meantime, I scan the environment for possible contractors: that's how you deal with it.

"You try to stay alive as long as possible, that's all."

The conversation is a painful reminder of what different directions our lives have gone in since those childhood days. She lives, whereas I just survive. Still, I don't think of myself as less happy. I just enjoy other, slightly smaller things.

"So you've got a nice life?" Netteke asks. "What is it you do?"

"I really like to have my cup of coffee around here in the morning." She looks a bit pitying. Was that my idea of a nice life? I saw her wondering.

"After that I eat a yogurt," I say, "at a place near here. And in the evening, Japanese food, as often as I can. I love that."

"You do anything else apart from eating?" she asks with pity in her voice.

"No," I say, "actually, that's the only thing that makes me happy. The small things in life, you know."

"But why don't you just leave?" she asks.

"I don't like it abroad. I don't even like a holiday abroad. What am I going to do there?"

She doesn't understand. "You're not even fifty, and you don't find life worth living?"

"I'm actually quite tired of everything. I don't feel like running away anymore."

I also don't want to have this conversation. It doesn't make me happy. I will never be able to explain satisfactorily why I just have to accept my death. I can't even fathom it myself. I don't know why I've done this; I only know I felt I had to.

I steer the conversation in a different direction. "How is your mother?"

"Well," she says.

"Good," I say. "Well, I'm off. See you soon," I lie.

Farewell to My Job

I HURRIED TO GET TO WORK ON TIME FOR A WITNESS HEARING scheduled for nine a.m. at the courthouse. Always aware of the risk that the distance I have to walk to my car entails, I walk down the stairs cautiously. I'll never know what will happen at the end of those stairs. I'm always prepared for a gunman waiting for me there. Not that I can do anything about it; I have to use those steps no matter what.

If the gunman's there, I'll always be too late. It's just a weak spot that is hard to avoid. Once you're in the car, you have a chance, although that also depends on the car you drive.

I hurry to my car, which is quite a ways away because I'd had to park around the corner. No spots in front of the house.

The more meters I have to walk to my car, the more vulnerable I am, and the higher the risk I run, especially now that I can't see my car. If the car is on my block or in front of my door, at least I can see if I'm being waylaid. If the car is around the corner, that's a lot more difficult. I know that a gunman would know the direction I walk to my car. Your car is a focal point, just like your house. Draw a line between those two points and you've got your walking direction. Turning a corner makes you more vulnerable, you don't know who'll be waiting for you.

I'm in a hurry, and you can't afford to be if you need the time to adapt to the situation.

This particular Monday in August 2015, everything's going wrong. Aware of the danger that may lie around the corner, I first run to the other side of the street so I can see the block my car is parked on before I walk there. My car itself is out of sight; it's hidden behind a big bus. That's not good, and my first thought is to wonder if this was done on purpose. Has someone deliberately blocked the view of my car? And what, or rather who, is in that bus?

I'm halfway to my car, and I see a person who doesn't fit in with the street. He's just standing there. From my side, I can see that he's looking at my car.

I slow down and walk closer to the houses. He hasn't seen me coming yet; at least, he doesn't act like he has. I disappear into one of the many porches. It doesn't feel right. I'm sure he was standing there waiting for me.

I don't want to wait on the porch for too long, in case he did see me and will come for me. I consider ringing the bell of one of the apartments in the porches, to pretend I don't feel well and to ask for a doctor. The chance that a poshly dressed and unwell woman asking for help won't be let in is not so big.

But I'm in a hurry as well, that damned hurry. I need to get to that hearing. Maybe I'm seeing ghosts, and what kind of explanation will I give to the judge, clerk, and witness for my arriving late? Explain to them that I thought I was going to be killed? That I had to make sure not to take any risk of getting shot? How would that look? I can't very well say that, now, can I?

What should I do? I can't go to my car, that's for sure. I decide to walk back to the corner I came from. Meanwhile I call Sonja to ask where she is.

"I'm on my way to you, to clean your house," she says.

"Can you come pick me up?" I ask. "Someone is standing near my car."

"Of course. I'm on my way."

"How much longer?" I ask. "I'm in a hurry; I need to get to court."

"Ten minutes," she says.

"Okay, please hurry, I may just make it in time. Drive up to the entrance of Coffee Company. There's a lot of activity there, and I'll just get in and you drive straight on."

To be safe, I call Sandra. We always warn each other when we see something suspicious.

"San, I have this guy standing near my car. I don't trust it. Son's picking me up. But you be careful, too, when you walk out your door."

"I will," she says.

Sonja's pulling up, and I get in. "It can't go on like this."

I am just in time for the hearing. It turns out the witness wasn't delivered by the police, so I can just go home. All that stress for nothing. To me, it's the last straw.

If I want a chance to survive, I have to live like he did, the way he survived for so long.

"They have tried to kill me a hundred times," he told me last year. He probably exaggerates, but I knew there were people who at least had planned on popping him.

Thomas van der Bijl, who openly said to Teeven that he couldn't manage to have him killed.

A group of people, among them Kees Houtman, who tried and failed during Christmas 2005, but were still at it.

Willem Endstra, who had tried through several different hit-men, attempts he told me about himself, when they were pending.

That time Srdjan "Serge" Miranovic's son came to see him in Kobe's Restaurant with a loaded gun, an attempt at retribution for his father's death.

That one time someone (probably hired by the Mieremet clan) had actually tried to kill him on Westerstraat when he was with my mother. He meant to report it.

Or that time we were in a restaurant on Van Woustraat and this guy with dead eyes reached for his pocket.

I truly believe he has escaped death on many occasions. So often that it probably feels like a hundred times to him.

He had survived all of them, and he was helped by his practice of having no regular patterns, no regular place to go to, no fixed address but various places where he stayed: in Huizen, in the house a doctor friend rented for him; at the Newport Hotel, where he stayed with Nicky; in Utrecht at Mandy's and Maike's places; in Amsterdam, in the western part with Marieke, a new young flame; and in the Jordaan, at Jill's. And then there was Sandra's house. And Mom's.

He could not be linked to one residence. He had no normal job with one fixed address. He met in public bars and restaurants where it was so crowded that no gunman would ever open fire there. He never made an appointment far in advance; he would always change or cancel plans at the last minute if the feeling wasn't right.

No car in front of the door, but a garage where Sandra's son, the one he hated so much, had to take his scooter out for him when he needed it and put it back in at night. He wouldn't do that himself; it was too dangerous. And when the scooter was in the garage, no one could see if he was there.

So waylaying him was not an option. He only had a phone to call, not to be called. He was unreachable by anyone, and, with the battery out, not traceable.

★ ★ ★

With me, it's a different story. I live in my one apartment, where I always sleep and have to leave from; my car always in front of or near the house or my office. You know where I am. And most of all, my normal job, my fixed office address, where anyone can find me at any time of day.

That aspect of my life in particular forced me to adapt to a pattern I couldn't escape. I didn't have to sleep at home, and using other means of transportation wasn't a problem, either, but my job—that could kill me. I couldn't cancel or postpone hearings at the last minute. They were planned months in advance and were fixed. These were often cases where clients were detained, and postponement meant that they would be held longer, maybe needlessly. That was in contradiction to the responsibilities of my job as a lawyer.

I couldn't arrange for my visits to prison at the last moment, or visit my clients without warning. It doesn't work that way. They know when I'm coming. I prepare cases with my clients; it's a collaboration that takes planning, so everybody knows where I am. Not only my clients, but also fellow prisoners, their families, and the prison staff. All of these people have scheduled contact with me, and it takes just one hungry person who wants to make a buck to give me away to a gunman.

It's impossible to be a criminal lawyer without running into people who have dealings with Wim.

And what if Wim comes out of the ESP and goes back to the Penitentiary Institution, where he can chat with other guys? Guys he can easily use to his benefit? Guys who are often a bit mentally handicapped in some way and can be easily persuaded to do the weirdest stuff for their idol?

Things would only get more dangerous. I love my job. But it also connects me to a world that I know gives ample opportunity to track me down and give me away. I had already had one scare at work.

This was when it had just come out that we were testifying, and it involved a client with a certain background who could be dangerous to me. That day I was in a hearing with him, and I got a very uneasy feeling.

To be on the safe side, I wore my bulletproof vest in the car. The time I was to arrive was known, and it would be very easy to approach me on the stairs of the courthouse. As a lawyer I don't have to pass through the scanner, so when I'm inside, in the toilet, I can replace my vest with a tunic. After the hearing, I replaced the tunic with a vest again, that I wore invisibly under my clothes, so that I could walk back to my car at least sort of protected. Nothing happened.

But fear of some professional situations made it hard for me to function. If some clients wanted to come to a hearing against my advice and would not come in, that made me suspicious. Then I would think: Do you want to point me out so that after the hearing I'm an easy target?

When I made an appointment outside my office or court, I would change the location just before, or would go there half an hour early to complicate the situation. I had to be on guard. But I grew tired of it, and it took all the pleasure out of my job. And I knew that the regular pattern imposed by my work would be the end of me. I didn't want to give up. I wanted to keep on working, but it was irresponsible.

That same day, the day Sonja drove me to the hearing after I saw the strange man standing at my car, I texted my partner, with whom I'd worked for almost twenty years, and told him I was quitting.

My partner, with whom I had celebrated Christmas and New Year's Eve for twenty years. My partner, who'd been through everything with me—Cor's death, the prosecutions, my role as a witness—and who's always been there for me. My partner, whom I had never once kissed on the cheek, nor had he kissed me on my cheek, because we functioned as men with each other. And we were both against unsolicited and above all unwanted physical contact. We both detested socializing, and if we really couldn't refuse, we'd go to a party together. My partner, the only person who's never lied to me or anybody else; you can't even catch him telling a white lie. It's almost corny, how trustworthy he is. My partner, whom I texted that I was unable to speak to him, because after reaching this decision, if I heard his voice, I could only cry.

Twenty years together, every day, and now nothing. Being alone. Again, my brother was dictating my life. The person who—next to my family—was most valuable and dear to me, I had lost now, too.

That same Monday, I informed my colleagues and my secretary, who had become my friend. We cried together, afraid of the inevitable separation, angry at the unfairness of the misery laid upon us.

I couldn't even face my partner after my decision without my heart exploding from grief. Seeing him at our office, knowing that we wouldn't sit together anymore, made my stomach turn.

That afternoon I left the office and he walked past me, both of us silent, not able to say anything meaningful, till we turned around and embraced each other. We were both sobbing.

"I love you," he said.

"I love you, too," I said, and then we parted and walked on quickly.

The grief was too immense to touch, or to even come close to.

I had to get out of there quickly so as not to succumb. We were never emotional, no matter what kind of drama took place—we both thought it too complicated. The only way we dealt with sorrow was by working even harder so we couldn't think about the pain. But I was way past that.

Tuesday, I handed over all my cases. Thursday, I did my last hearing. That Friday I was unemployed for the first time in my life. Saturday and Sunday, I emptied my office.

Now I live surrounded by bulletproof windows and doors. I've lost not just my job, but a part of my identity.

Wim Hears Us Testify

Today is the first time we are being heard as witnesses in Wim's case, which is named Vandros. We have asked the judge to prevent Wim from having visual contact with us. None of us can bear the thought that he'll manipulate us with his eyes. We know that he can intimidate us with nonverbal communication that others won't see or understand. We are afraid to implode, to freeze.

That first hearing, I'm emotional more than anything else. I feel terrible with Wim sitting close to me, and the glass wall between us makes no difference. I'm aware of his presence and feel constrained by it. His close presence feels like him crawling under my skin.

That's how long he's owned my spirit.

I don't dare say everything I want to say. I'm scared, and at the same time I feel terrible about doing this to him. I'm oscillating between fear and pity. It makes me reticent in my answers, and I want it to stop: Set him free, I think, because I don't want to go on like this. I really can't bear it, and to end it I almost say, Leave it, judge. I'll take him with me.

But it's impossible, and it would be nonsense. My feelings confuse me. How can I be sympathetic to someone so evil? And in the same way I empathize with him. I empathize with Stijn, his lawyer. It must have been a terrible blow to him: me, always the confidante and liaison with Wim. Now I stand diametrically opposed to him. It makes me feel sick.

All these different emotions are killing me. The hearing is scheduled to go on the whole day, but by four o'clock, I'm exhausted—I can't keep my eyes from falling shut. The judge notices and decides to end the hearing. Many more will follow. How am I going to last? Maybe my therapist is right. Maybe I can't live with what I have done.

ESP (Extra-Security Prison)

2016

ON MARCH 3, A SPECIAL COMMISSION WILL DECIDE WHETHER WIM WILL have to remain in the ESP.

Leading up to that day, I become more and more convinced that his transfer to a less secure prison will reduce our chances of living. Under a regular regime, prisoners have free contact with one another. Wealthy detainees—always the worst criminals—enjoy special privileges with corrupt personnel: telephones in their cells, computers, and so on. They live in relative luxury, and that's how they get to have unimpeded contact with the outside world. Under those circumstances and with his natural dominance and charisma, he'll have no trouble finding someone he can use as a gunman—as our killer. I knew that his incarceration at the ESP wouldn't last forever, but I had hoped it would last as long as possible.

I'm sitting on the couch next to Sonja when John van den Heuvel, the crime journalist, calls. He says he heard that Wim's health is failing and that he has to have surgery again.

Sonja immediately replies it's one of his old tricks and that he'd done exactly the same to get out after his last transfer to the ESP.

What Sonja says is true. He himself had agreed to a medical and psychiatric evaluation, but he always remained in control. The ESP regime was not good for his heart. He stated that he was afraid to die in the ESP and therefore wanted to spend as much time as possible with his family, with us.

Our statements and recordings, in which—without ambiguity—he extorts Sonja and threatens to kill her, show that his story doesn't make sense. But he's had a lot of success with it, and he's using his medical condition again to take control of the situation. If he succeeds in getting out of ESP, the next step will be to organize our deaths.

I feel resistance to a possible change—to my disadvantage—boiling up in me.

It's too ridiculous for words. He would get more freedom, and I would be robbed of mine: having to avoid public places, stay alert constantly, looking over my shoulder at every step. It would restrict my life even more than it already has, and why? Why should I be in my own version of ESP so he can get out? Why should he receive privileges he will only abuse to get rid of us?

I call Piet, head of our security team, and ask him if Wim really is sick. I also warn him that this is a repetition of past history and that they should get a second medical opinion. Wim knows for a fact that a doctor cannot compromise his or her medical ethics by speaking about his condition, so he can tell the Justice Department whatever he likes.

It's the day the commission rules on the extension of his ESP detention, and I passionately hope that they will not have the wool pulled over their eyes. We are kept in suspense for hours.

We expect the result at four p.m., but it is not until four thirty that we get the liberating message: he'll remain in the ESP for the next six months.

What a relief.

Fort Knox

WOUT MORRA, OUR LAWYER, WHO'S BEEN WITH US SINCE THE MOMENT we had to decide whether we would go through with testifying, calls us and tells us that the security team wants to meet us. They want to make an announcement to Sonja, Peter de Vries, and me.

That can't be good. It can only mean one of two things: they have foiled an attempt to kill us, or they suspect he is planning one.

Piet gets started and tells us he's thought about this for a long time, how to tell us. Wim has managed to give the order to have us assassinated. He has ordered me to go first, then Peter, and then Sonja. I feel my blood pressure rise, and my head starts throbbing. I predicted this, but now that the time has come, I don't want to die. I can see the image of my beautiful grandchildren before my eyes, and I can hardly control my tears.

I don't want to cry in public, especially since I have always been the one to predict this. If I had wanted to avoid all this I shouldn't have started it in the first place. But it gets to me: my own brother wants to kill me.

Never before has the threat been so near.

"I would also like to point out the positive side to this story," Piet says.

"Yes, please do," I say wryly.

"This act means he really should never leave the ESP."

"I totally agree," I say. "He's provided the best reason for keeping him there. And his giving these orders confirms everything we've said in our statements about him."

Sure, that's a kind of silver lining, I suppose. But it doesn't cancel out the sadness of this story. Saddest of all is his predictability, that his only way to react is murder. Even now, his behavior is always dictated by revenge, an emotion that controls him and makes him careless.

Of course I am at the top of his list: he hates me most, and blames me for his situation.

Only now do I understand why Sonja never found him pitiful. I had only heard him issue death threats to her and others, but he'd never threatened me before. Now that he is, my pity for him is gone.

That, too, is positive.

In Fort Knox—my house—I feel safe, and today, the twelfth of March, I decide to stay in and not go outside at all. The risk of going down the stairs and walking the ten yards from my house to the car is too great considering the present concrete threat. I don't have to, and why should I tempt fate? I have to take care of a couple of things, but I can do that when people come to me.

Sandra arrives first. When I canceled our coffee appointment, she knew that something was going on, and she's coming right over. I tell her about the conversation Piet and I had and that she wasn't included because she wasn't mentioned in Wim's order. I do think she has the right to know, though, and I'm glad she came. The fact that he can issue orders, even from a maximum-security prison, is very disconcerting, and it's a reason for her to be alert, too.

"Yes," she says, as dry and emotionless as always, "I feel really sorry for you, but we knew this was going to happen, right? And I'm not going to believe he'll never take Mitri and me out. If he succeeds in eliminating one of you, he'll get greedy and I will be added to the list."

"I'm convinced of it. After one success, he'll only want more," I tell her. "He knows he'll never get out, so he doesn't care anyway. One life sentence or two; he'll just speed things up, even though that will mean the risk of discovery. He mustn't succeed, so I'll stay in for the time being."

"I think that's a good idea," Sandra says. "Did they say how they know all this?"

"No, they won't say."

That evening, the bell rings. It's Miljuschka. I have asked her to come and go over some papers with me. In case I do end up dying on the street, I want her to know what to do. Tears are standing in her eyes when I open the door.

"Don't cry," I say, "nothing's wrong. I will survive this, but I want you to know where everything is. Pretending there is no problem is nonsense; we have to be practical. So come on, don't cry."

Poor kid. I talk tough, but I'm crying on the inside. The thought of her and her two little ones punches a hole in my heart. I love those kiddies, and I'd hate to have them exposed to a death so early in their lives. I'm afraid they'll be traumatized.

"Can I take a bath?" Miljuschka asks. "Will you join me?"

We've been taking baths together ever since she was old enough to sit up. First in a tub, and after we'd outgrown that, I had a twin bathtub built. It's our quality time together. She asks me as if she were five years old.

"Of course," I say.

In the bath, the tears come back.

"Who's getting out first?" It is the question we always ask each other.

"I need to wash my hair," she says.

"Okay, I'll get out first."

Then she asks me, "Mom, can you wash my hair? Like you used to?"

She sounds like it might be the last time.

"Sure. Turn around," I say, so she can't see the tears running down my cheeks. I wash her thick brown hair, like I have always done, ever since she was born.

MARCH 13, 2016

Sonja is coming to dinner. I told her to wear her bulletproof vest, but when she arrives she's not wearing it. I ask her why.

"I don't think it's necessary."

"Why not?"

"I'm going everywhere anyhow."

"You want to make things easy for him?"

"Yes," she said decisively, "I'd rather have him kill me than you. At least you can take care of the children. I'm no good at it."

She says this in a bone-dry tone, as if she's already said goodbye to life. I can tell that she's absolutely serious, and it gives me the shivers.

"But I can't get along without you," I say. "Who's going to clean my house and get toilet paper? Without you, I'll drown in my own mess." I'm being totally honest, but what I mean to say is, I love you, sis. I can't live without your love.

And that's true. We have been through so much together, shared and withstood so much; she's the only one in the world I trust, and I wouldn't know what to do without her.

"Box, we will not let him win. Next time, you're wearing your vest, okay?"

MARCH 14, 2016

Since I'm at home, I make the best of it and call Francis to pick up my mother plus steaks, sandwich filling, and bread and fruit, to have lunch at my house, all of us together. Sonja and Richie are here, too; on Sonja's advice, I'm not having Miljuschka come over anymore, because they might mistake her for me.

Except for the way we act or move, we don't resemble each other, but that is exactly the reason they might confuse me with her. So I won't see my child or my grandchildren.

We haven't told my mother anything about the threat; she's eighty and couldn't bear the thought. What you don't know won't hurt you: innocently, she enjoys being with her children, grandchildren, and great-grandchild. We eat and drink together, and we're having fun. Seeing her enjoy herself makes me happy.

When they're getting ready to leave, she comes to me and says, "Francis is not herself. She's acting strangely. Do you know what's wrong with her?"

My darling mother. She knows Francis through and through. They have a special bond, and my mother notices at once when something's wrong with her.

"No," I lie, "just a bit of mother-daughter stuff with Sonja, but it will pass. Don't worry, Mom."

I see everybody out, and Fran embraces me at the door. She's crying softly.

"Why don't you start walking down, Mom, because it'll take you an hour." I send her on ahead so she can't see Fran crying.

"Don't cry, sweetie, it will be all right," I say, trying to comfort her. The poor girl, she, too, has been living her whole conscious life with the impending death of her loved ones. What a heavy burden for a child. "You don't believe I'm going to get myself killed by him? I don't think so!" I try again.

"He succeeded with Daddy, and I don't want to lose you as well," she cries.

"That's not going to happen. Have a little faith. Come on, go to Granny or she'll figure out something is going on."

"I love you," she sobs.

"I love you too, sweetie," I say with a lump in my throat, and I push her out just before the tears start welling again. I want to be strong for her sake.

So much misery.

MARCH 15

Ever since I've known that Wim has ordered me to go first, I've stayed home, but I can't go on like this for the rest of my life. I need to find a way to go out safely, and the only thing I can think of is that, since he has declared war on me, I must walk the streets in battle gear. I already wear a bulletproof vest to protect the most vital parts of my body, but I start searching the Internet for head and neck protection. Before long, I find the stuff I want. I pick out a helmet and a throat protector.

Richie and Sonja are with me that day, and Richie asks me what I'm doing. "I'm buying a bulletproof helmet so I can head back the bullets," I joke, to keep the conversation light. "And I'm getting a throat protector: two for one."

It's an insane subject to discuss with a young adult, but the kids know it could happen. It wouldn't be wise to order the helmet under my own name, because I might jeopardize the investigation. You never can tell who knows who, and if the information gets out on the street—that Astrid Holleeder is dressing against an attempt—it could tip off the gunman. I get someone else to pick up the helmet and collar, a very decent young man who won't make people suspicious. At five that afternoon, he rings my bell.

"Did it go okay?"

"Yes," he says, "I got them both, the helmet and the collar." He gives me a big blue bag.

"Perfect!" I say, and I take the helmet and collar straight out of the bag. "Let's hope it fits," I say, because the helmet only came in size L.

I jam it onto my head, hard, and a lump immediately forms.

It takes getting used to. After some practice and adjustments, I manage to strap the helmet on correctly.

The collar is easier to handle. It fits, but I look ridiculous. I stand out like an elephant in a bed of strawberries. I can't walk around like this, but, given the circumstances, I'll have to.

I pick out a big scarf and drape it around the helmet and the collar, as some sort of headscarf, to camouflage them.

"There," I tell myself, "that's better."

MARCH 17

I get a phone call that my street camera is on the blink, and the reason the security people give is that the wire must have been cut. That frightens me. Because if that's really the case, there is a chance I'm being watched by someone who doesn't want to be seen on camera.

I send a message to Piet, including the remark from the technical security people, and that I want him to know this, because I'm heading home now. Should something happen, they have to include that in their investigation.

I'm already wearing my vest. On my way home, my car starts sputtering. That's all I need! They didn't tamper with it, did they? First the camera, now the car. The fear feels like a knot in my stomach. I can't very well stop now, though.

I put on my collar and lay out my helmet. Let's hope my car keeps going. I take a route via a police station, so that if the car breaks down, help will be near. I intend to leave the car and run.

I'm being followed by a car now. Sweat is running down my head in streams. My heart is pounding in my throat. I check my mirrors constantly.

The car crawls along. I'm coming up to a roundabout, and I want to know if the car is following me, so I drive around twice.

It's a risk to keep driving in a sputtering car, but I have to make sure. I drive by all the exits on the roundabout, and fortunately the car behind me takes an exit.

I'm getting paranoid.

Annoyingly slowly, I make my way to my block. It's light here and it feels a bit better. I park the car, put on my helmet, and walk into my house.

I've always said: He'll get life, but I do, too. Though I don't expect my life to last as long as his.

The Confrontation

I HAD BEEN TOSSING AND TURNING AND SWEATING ALL NIGHT. I FELT feverish and took some aspirin, hoping to feel better.

I knew it was tension that was making me sick. In a few hours, I would be in the same space with the contractor of my murder. How am I going to do this?

Normally a human being runs or fights when in acute danger. I couldn't run, because the defense had a right to interrogate me, so I had to report to the judge. Fighting was impossible, because we were separated by glass and several clerks.

I had to calm down, control my anger, the way I'd been doing for two years, listening to his stories about extortion, threats, and the liquidation of Sonja, his denigration of Cor, putting down my mother, threatening the children—all those conversations that made my blood boil. In order to gather evidence, I had pretended to find what he said and did normal.

During the past two years, there have been moments when I was torn between my intelligence, ordering me to think ahead and wait for the Justice Department to take action, and my urgent desire to cut his throat then and there.

For years, I have listened to what he'd done to others or would do, and that alone made me furious.

Now it was about me.

How could I sit quietly in that worthless witness stand and answer questions as if he had not already ordered our killings? And not let on to him that I knew what he was up to with us, which would hamper the pending trial against him? I'd love to break through the glass wall to get at him and squeeze his throat. How was I to muster the strength to undergo this patiently?

I had to calm down before I got in the secure transport that would take me to De Bunker Courthouse. The only way not to flip out was to activate the survival mechanism from my youth and do what I did as a kid in overwhelming situations: I sat down "behind my eyes." I was physically present but mentally absent, as if I had left my body and was looking on from a distance. This numbed the emotion in my body and made me feel safe.

In that state, I arrived, with Wout, at De Bunker, where we were seen first by the district attorneys. They wished me strength and were sympathetic to the insane circumstances under which I had to testify.

I asked them if the judge conducting the witness hearing knew about the order Wim had given from the ESP. She did. I felt relieved, because she, too, would understand how difficult it was for me to be here with him.

The judge came in. "How are you doing?" she asked.

That simple, personal question broke my defensive wall, and I started crying: "Not so good. It's especially hard on the children."

"Yes," she said, "but you were expecting this, weren't you?"

"Yes," I said, "I knew this was going to happen—"

"But it doesn't make it any better!" Wout interrupted us.

"Well, then," she said, and her voice became businesslike as she continued, "what I really came for is to ask you to only answer the questions posed by Mr. Franken. That way we'll move through as quickly as we can."

It was the same as with my other hearing: before I even start,

I'm being muzzled. I wanted to stand up for myself. I had been silent long enough, and I should be able to answer as I saw fit. But I couldn't bear it now, not under these circumstances, not after this treatment. I felt the last bit of energy flow out of me. I was too tired to resist their ridiculous restriction. I would answer yes and no and wait out this misery, then go home.

I dragged myself upstairs to the witness stand. I felt his presence through the glass.

I cut myself off from my feelings and answered as briefly as I could, like a robot. I thought I'd finally satisfied the judge, but now Stijn Franken wasn't happy. As in the earlier hearings, we talked about the recordings of Wim I had made.

Apparently a clip had been broadcast on the talk show *Pauw*, a clip the defense didn't have.

"That's possible," I replied. "Maybe Peter's got it, or Sonja?"

"But you were repeatedly asked, and you testified that you handed over everything?"

"Yes, that's right, they asked, and I did testify that I'd handed it over. But that question was asked only to me, not to Sonja."

That answer gave Stijn Franken a reason to request the judge to suspend my hearing.

Wout and I were sent downstairs, where we took a seat and waited. After nearly two and a half hours, the door opened.

"Please come with me for a second, Mr. Morra?" the clerk asked. Wout got up, surprised, and walked to the door.

"What about me?" I asked.

"Not you," he said.

"Why not me? It's my hearing, right? I've been here for two hours, and I can't come? Listen, I want to know where I stand—I'm not going to wait any longer! Wout, you see to it that I get to hear what's happening."

But nobody told me anything. And again I was waiting in a locked room. I heard no one and saw no one. I was about to call 911 when I heard the sound of stumbling in the hallway. It sounded like my sister's footsteps. I heard more footsteps. The door swung open and the judge came in.

All my pent-up emotions about my brother trying to kill me, sitting at home for months, the grief of the children, the concern for my mother, and the fact that I'd been locked up for more than two hours came flooding out and landed on her. "What is going on?" I asked angrily. "You lock me up for two and a half hours without me knowing where I stand!? That's totally indecent. Couldn't you have taken the trouble to tell me what was going to happen?"

"Sorry," she said.

"'Sorry'?" I raged. "You're not pulling this on me again. I am a free witness, and I'm not going to be sitting in a locked room again. I'm leaving now."

"Just wait a while longer," she said. "I still have to question your sister in the next room."

"I'll give you ten minutes, and if this door is not open, I'll kick it in!" I shouted, totally out of control.

The judge left the room, locked the door, and shortly after that, I heard Sonja scream.

Now my blood really started to boil. What was happening next door? The door was still locked. I couldn't go anywhere, and I saw no other option but to draw attention by kicking the door forcibly. It worked. Within three minutes, there were three guards at the door. I knew them all.

"Take it easy, Astrid," one of them said.

"I hear my sister screaming," I said. "Where is she? We're getting out of here. You are not going to terrorize her. First she's been terrorized by him her whole life, and now by the Justice Department and the judiciary? It's not going to happen! Box, we're out of here. We quit!"

"No," said a guard, "that's impossible. We need to get the secure transport."

"I don't need transport. Open the door, we'll get home by ourselves!"

Sonja came into the room where I was, totally upset. "They sealed off my house and want to search it as if I'm the suspect. Stijn Franken wants them to look for the recordings at my place. But I've told them a million times I've lost them."

"What?" I say to the judge. "Have you lost your minds?"

"As, I'm out of here and I'm never coming back! He's done it again. He is totally in control. He wants to kill us, but we are being treated as suspects."

We understood there was very little sympathy for our situation. I had turned over some of the tapes to the Justice Department, but I had also given some to Sonja, and she'd lost them. Wim and his defense had demanded that the judge order a search of Sonja's house, but we knew he was just trying to stall. Even if we'd had them, we'd of course never keep them in the house—something Wim had taught us! He knew that. Something else was going on.

I mentally rewound all the hearings of the past months. So far, not one single question had been asked about the crimes Wim was suspected of. It had all been about the years prior to the killings and about the tapes. They were getting nowhere fast. Several hearings had been canceled, one hearing ended halfway through at the request of the defense, and this hearing went no further than five questions about the tapes.

He was stalling!

He was such a brilliant strategist! He had lulled everyone to sleep, including me. He was making sure to divert attention from what was really happening, slowing down the case so he had time to whack us before we were able to testify before the judge. It had to be said: Wim, hats off to you! You are the man.

The next day I called Peter de Vries, who had appeared on that episode of the *Pauw* news show. Together we reconstructed where the USB stick with that particular recording was and handed it over.

Tired

I FEEL SO TIRED. I TRY TO RALLY, BUT THE PAST FEW DAYS HAVE SUCKED the life out of me. I am so sick of all this dictating my days, my life, and my mood. I miss my old life, which I have given up for this thankless task. I react irritably to everyone, but no one around me can help it, me feeling so down. I go to bed and hope to wake up in a different mood.

I dream that I'm being called and I hear Wim's voice. He talks incoherently, almost gibberish, but he asks me nothing. Not to help him get out, nothing.

I wake up with a start, and the only thing I can think of is, I wish he were here and that everything was back to normal. I don't want all of this. I can't bear doing this to him.

How is it possible? He wants to kill me and I want to see him free.

I feel that I'm longing for death. This is no life. The burden is too heavy; it touches everything. Every time I go outside, I know it might be the last time. And at the same time, I know he will never go outside again.

Basically we're both already dead.

The peace death would bring is tempting.

I'm trying to look for the little things in life that make it worthwhile, but today I can't find any.

MARCH 29, 2016

We talk to the police about the fiasco during the hearings, and I hand them the tape that I'd also given to the judge. I comment on the contents of the recording and play them some segments. The tape is a classic example of his extortion methods.

But what I'd really hoped for, looked forward to, was that they would tell me more about my murderer. I'd like to know where to look so I can take action myself. But they don't want to say anything, and I respect that, obviously.

We talk about our hearings being canceled, and I ask the DA for the reason behind it. After a few minutes, I get my answer. The defense wants to postpone.

It feels like a slap in the face. I had thought the delay was due to them wanting to grant Sonja and me some rest after the nightmare of last time, but the delay was just another tactic at the instigation of the defense.

It feels like a race against the clock. It is killing me that they can't or won't see that this is Wim's strategy. I'm beat.

MARCH 30

My phone buzzes with a text message from Peter: "Three years and four months." I was torn from sleep so I don't understand right away. What is he talking about?

Then I get another message, from a colleague, with an image of clinking champagne glasses. Now it starts making sense: today was the verdict on appeal in the criminal case against Wim for threatening Peter de Vries. Initially he got off with three months, but now he gets three years and four months. Four months for threatening Peter, plus the completion of his suspended three-year sentence.

A justified sentence by the court, because he doesn't deserve a suspended sentence; he would only use the freedom to extort again, and more severely. This is a big boost in these hard times. It feels as if the court is finally starting to understand what a manipulator Wim really is, how subtly he toys with the judicial system, how he always dictates everything in the end.

No Limit Soldiers

IT'S EIGHT FIFTEEN A.M. WHEN I GET A TEXT. IT'S THE POLICE, ASKING whether they can call me.

I text back, "Of course," and wonder what's going on.

"Good morning, Astrid." I recognize the voice of one of the detectives.

"Good morning," I answer.

"We'd like to inform you that we charged your brother this morning on suspicion of ordering your murder, Sonja's, and Peter's."

I feel tears come to my eyes, and I can't hold them back. "Okay," I manage to say.

"We thought we'd better tell you in case there's a leak."

"Sorry, but I'm really upset. It's as if I realize only now that all of this is real. It's so dramatic—my own brother," I say through my tears.

"Yes, I know," the voice on the other end says.

"Thanks for telling me," I say.

"My pleasure," he says, and hangs up.

Tears are rolling down my cheeks.

I imagine his face as he's told why he is being arrested, and I suddenly feel so sorry for him. He must have been so startled by my betrayal, his omnipotence torn apart in every possible way. Everything he is used to doing unnoticed is being noticed. Good for us, but at the same time, sad for him. He's being dragged down more and more, and I don't see how he'll ever recover.

Wim denies the allegations and declares that if it were up to him, his family would not be hurt. "If I heard anything like that, I'd certainly warn them."

Now, where had I heard that before?

There have been situations twice before when Sonja and I supposedly "had our turn." This was the third time, but this case was different in that there was sufficient concrete evidence that the Justice Department could investigate.

The DAs explain that Wim had made contact with two members of NLS, which stands for No Limit Soldiers, an international group known for its drug trafficking and assassinations, with branches in the Netherlands. They are being held responsible for the murder of Helmin Wiels, leader of the biggest political party on the island of Curaçao (Pueblo Soberano).

The two members Wim approached have both been convicted of murder. Liomar W. is serving a twenty-four-year sentence for killing a Dutch couple. Edwin V. was sentenced for a shooting in which one person was killed. They are being held in the same facility as Wim—the most heavily secured prison in the country—because they tried to escape from prison on Curaçao.

Sonja and I look at each other in bewilderment. We hadn't expected this—Wim has tapped a network totally unknown to us. But these are no small potatoes. How could the authorities have let him spend time in the prison yard with them, exercising and cooking together?

According to Liomar W., Wim met him in a corner of the prison yard, out of sight of the cameras, to talk to them unseen and unheard.

Typical of Wim, I think immediately, and obviously the NLS guys are no amateurs, either; they, too, know how to communicate undetected.

Luckily the Justice Department was alert, and they picked up on two key details that tipped them off to Wim's plans. First, the fact that Edwin V. wanted to be transferred for no reason caught their attention. They suspected that Wim might want to get some distance from his fellow prisoner. Rightly so, because that's just the way he works: make sure you're not around when something is about to happen, so you can't be linked to it.

Second, the Justice Department noticed that Wim had been very chipper lately. I can see why: As soon as we were dead, he would have regained control over us, and that prospect would have cheered him.

The investigation started, and Edwin V. was caught passing a phone number that he didn't care to discuss. Asked by the police whether he'd ever heard of Holleeder wanting something to happen to his sisters, he didn't deny it, but he answered evasively:

EV: "It's none of my business. I am not going to comment. I'm not here to testify about his sisters. No, that's not my problem."

Liomar W., on the other hand, spoke in some detail about what Wim had asked them.

LW: "He told me and that other Antillean guy that he's mad at his sisters. He wants them dead. You know what it is? He wants those people who have testified against him, especially his sisters . . . he said to do them as soon as possible. Have them killed. That's the way he said it."

Wim wanted them to look for a gunman and had promised them a lot of money.

LW: "Either way, money is no object, that's what he says. Sixty thousand, seventy thousand, that's a lot of money, right? That's what he pays for killing people."

Wim wanted to pay thirty-five thousand per sister.

LW: "He said thirty-five thousand. So, seventy thousand. Those are very good figures. That's what he used to pay."

Liomar W. continued. Wim didn't have the means to take care of the murders himself. He asked the two fellow prisoners to organize the assassinations through their contacts outside.

LW: "Yeah, he just wants us to find him some people. What needs to be done? Well just eh... he wanted, you know... contract killer. That's what he wants."

The person who could do that had been identified, according to Liomar W.; he was a leader of NLS.

Wim had, as we were told earlier, a priority list. Number one on his to-do list was me. Rightly so. I would want to kill him, too, if he'd done to me what I've done to him.

But the sisters weren't the only ones on the list.

LW: "What I know, that is important, those sisters for sure, Peter R. de Vries, yes, he wants him and all that, he says, he puts a lot of pressure on his affairs. He talks: he just wants that asshole... that's what he says... just: that they die, too.

Those three that I know, that they are the most important
people: that's what he said to me and also to my partner."

Poor Peter. Wim had already said, "If I have to go in for even one
day, I will see to it that the same happens to him as happened to
Thomas."

His fellow detainees had promised him to take care of it, and an
advance had been paid and received.

LW: "To be honest, yes. We have told him it is possible. And we
have received money for it, but not that much. It was five
thousand euros, split in two. Through a middleman."

As for the reason why we must be killed:

LW: "He wants them dead, so they're not there anymore... I think
so they can't testify against him."

We had predicted all of this. We shouldn't be surprised that our
brother is prepared to take the risk of using strangers to silence
us before we can confirm our statements to the judge. But it does
sound very harsh when you hear someone else talk dryly about a
possible murder—yours. As if it's some carpeting job.

He came so close to arranging our deaths from the best high-
security prison in the Netherlands. What will be in store for us
when he moves to a lower-security prison?

Scooter Incident

I STILL LIVE ON THE STREET WHERE WIM USED TO COME TO MY DOOR, where he picked me up, where we'd walk and talk together, him always asking me, "Any news?" It's a street known for its many bars and restaurants, and it's popular with the criminal crowd.

The Justice Department has often advised me to move, but I've lived here happily for twenty-one years, and I'm not about to give it up because I'm testifying against Wim. I don't believe that moving out of my house will increase my safety. I know the store owners on the street, and I feel I benefit from that social safety net. I don't want to lose my community on top of everything else.

Even if I wanted to, I couldn't move. Being a witness has cost me a lot of money; moving is financially impossible unless I can find a house with more or less the same rent, and the chances of that are slim. So I stay put, at an address known to half the criminal world in Amsterdam.

Aware of the danger because everyone knows where I live, and also aware that leaving my house requires me to walk down some stairs, I am very careful. Before I go out in the daytime, I scan the street for suspicious people, put on my customized bulletproof vest, gather my courage, and get into my bulletproof car. First, I lock the car doors (because what good are bulletproof windows when the door opens), and I drive away.

I check whether I'm being followed, and if I'm not sure, I take a roundabout full circle or I turn around at once and continue in the opposite direction. I always maintain a gap of six yards between me and the vehicle in front of me, in case a scooter or a motorbike stops next to me. The distance to the vehicle gives me the opportunity to speed away, running over the bike if necessary; by then I wouldn't care anymore.

Getting back into my house is a bit more complicated. Driving down my street looking for a parking space is not wise. From a bar or a restaurant, someone can easily watch me; pick a position, wait till I turn on to my street, and then boom. I can drive down my street only after midnight, when the bars and restaurants are almost empty and I can be sure to find a parking space close to my house. That's why I often wait till twelve to head home. The downside is that when it's dark, I can barely see people coming, even in those few steps from my car to my house. When I have a bad feeling, I don't just wear my vest—I also put on my bulletproof helmet and collar and check the camera system on my phone to make sure no one is waiting for me in the stairwell. Then I run upstairs.

Sometimes I'm afraid to stay out late just because I might not be able to park my car in front of my door when I get home. So I go home early.

Tonight was such a night. It was eight thirty, and I had to go home. I put on my vest in the car. I checked carefully to see whether I was being followed, but I saw no one behind me. I drove around my house so I wouldn't have to turn on to my street and be seen there unnecessarily. I had decided to park in the first space available on Churchill-laan, the street perpendicular to mine, so I wouldn't have to circle around, risking being spotted.

Everything I needed was inside the car; I didn't have to open the trunk. I always made sure that I could get out very fast and be away from the car as quick as I can.

I parked the car and walked down Churchill-laan. A hundred yards away I saw a car, double-parked, a new model. Approaching the car, looking through the rear windshield, I saw no driver in the car, only a passenger.

Where is the driver? The question shot through my mind immediately, and I scanned the street. I got a weird feeling. I saw no one on the street and took into account that the missing driver might be waiting for me on one of the porches of the houses. I walked past the car and looked inside.

A young Antillean-looking man turned his head away from me and looked at his phone. I immediately thought, Is he signaling? Maybe he was just waiting for someone in one of the houses. It was possible. But then again, maybe not. I started walking faster. I had to get off this street as soon as I could. A hundred more yards and I'd be at the intersection.

I turned the corner and saw a group of skaters waiting for the traffic light. Pffft. I was relieved. With so much activity, nobody in his right mind would liquidate someone, but, still not reassured, I kept walking—fast.

I was past the shoe store when I caught sight of a scooter out of the corner of my eye. I was scared and looked back. On the scooter was a guy dressed in dark clothes, wearing a helmet. He had dark eyes and a thin mustache. We looked each other in the eye, and I felt this was going to be the end of me. It was a very strong sensation.

I went through my chances quickly. He was a house away from me and on a scooter, I was on foot and unable to get away. I saw him bend over to get something, and I thought, Why don't I just resign myself to this?

Instinctively, I backed away from him and he tried to prevent me by calling out, "Lady, can I ask you something?"

At first I felt I had to stay put out of courtesy—maybe he did just want to ask for directions, as my common sense told me? But then suddenly my instincts took over.

I shouted, "No, you can't ask me a damn thing!" and I started running. I ran as fast as I could, but it felt as if I was standing still. I didn't dare look over my shoulder, afraid of losing seconds. Getting distance from him seemed to take forever, and I thought, He's coming, he's coming, and I'm not fast enough. He's coming.

I ran upstairs and put the key in the lock, my hands trembling. I made it in, safely behind my steel doors. My heart was pounding, and my breath felt raw in my throat.

I ran to the window to see if he was still there, but nothing. He was gone. I called my security and told them the story.

"You have to get out of there," they replied.

I left the next day. My loss is almost complete: my work, my house—I've lost it all.

But I'm still alive.

We Celebrate Cor's Birthday

WE CELEBRATED COR'S BIRTHDAY ON AUGUST 18, 2016, AT ROYAL SAN'S, the restaurant where Cor had eaten last, just like every year. A new café had opened across the way, about two years before: Het Wapen (The Weapon). Cor would have seen the humor in it. On the site where he'd spent the last seconds of his life there was now a terrace full of people drinking beer. Cor couldn't have hoped for a better memorial.

Shortly before his death, he had gotten a beer out of the fridge, at eleven a.m. "Freddy Heineken has gotten to me," he joked to Francis.

It was true. Freddy Heineken had gotten to him: not through the beer he brewed, but through the curse attached to the Heineken ransom, the lost six million that had corrupted his relationship with Wim without him noticing it. And that was the reason for the first, second, and, finally, the fatal attempt on his life. The curse spread to everything and everyone connected with the ransom, directly or indirectly.

To Thomas van der Bijl, who stated that he had dug up the ransom and was silenced, partly because of it.

To Willem Endstra, who arranged for Willem to keep his bloody gambling halls, and who got caught up in a web he couldn't escape from alive.

And to Wim himself—the curse had driven him to commit the craziest crimes.

We are watching two guys with beer bellies having a lot of fun. "People with fat guts are fun to be with, Dad used to say," Frances commented.

"Yes, but he was always trying to lose weight," Sonja replied. "Remember he was taking those slimming aid pills, that Xenical? If he wanted to have an extra hamburger or two he would just take some extra pills. Or he took up exercising like a madman, like when he started playing tennis with his friend Kai."

Every year we bring up the same memories, because new ones aren't available.

"Remember that time when they were done playing tennis and a jealous woman had scratched HOER [whore] on Kai's car?" I say.

"Yes," Sonja says. "Kai was too embarrassed to drive it, so Cor took his key and scratched an A after HOER [hurrah] and said, 'Problem solved!'"

"Hurrah to you today, Cor," Sonja says. "Happy birthday!"

We raise our glasses.

Together forever!

Afterword

BROTHER,

It breaks my heart to have you locked up, but believe me when I say that I am in there with you. I will give you a life sentence, but I will have the same. A life full of fear, until the moment my time comes. Or, like you say, "When you see him running toward you with that piece, you still have a moment. A moment to think, 'I wish I hadn't done it.'" But I did it. I would have liked things to be different, but you left me no choice.

In 1996 you started hunting for Cor. You had Cor, Sonja, and Richie shot at, in front of their house, the house that you pointed out. I knew the hunt was over when I stood next to Cor's lifeless body in the mortuary in 2003. After two failed attempts, you told Sandra, you finally succeeded: Cor was dead.

In the following years, you wreaked death and destruction on everyone close to you. In 2006 you were arrested for extorting Willem Endstra and Kees Houtman, among others. Not for murdering Endstra or Houtman, just for extorting them. And that was wrong.

Still, when you went away to jail, at least we'd gotten room to breathe. But as soon as you were released in 2012, it started all over. That is why I have testified. Peter would have to go, just like Thomas, who you took care of on your first day inside. Sandra's son, he would have to go, because he knows people you have problems with. Your sister would have to go, since she wouldn't give you the money she made from the book about the Heineken kidnapping by Peter R. de Vries. Your sister, who has to flip a coin to decide which of her children will go first.

I have to testify, because I know you will execute your threats. Or, as you would say, "I don't threaten, I just tell you what to look out for." The message is clear: You don't threaten, you execute—that is, you have others execute; you never do it yourself. "You know what I'll do, right?"

Yes, we know what you'll do, and we know what you have done. Like the serial killer keeping his trophies, you'll never let us forget.

I know I'm the last one you expected to do this, just like I was the last to believe my big brother would harm his family so profoundly.

"We are the same," you often told me. And that is partly true. I can think like you, reason like you, and act like you. That is the reason you are in prison.

But those similarities don't make me the same as you. Because everything you do hurts other people. And that's exactly what I'm trying to avoid.

I know you trusted me. I have betrayed that trust. I don't like that about myself, but I did it deliberately. I feel I was justified, because you betrayed Cor, and many others.

Your unsuspecting victims let you into their houses and into your lives, let you spend time around their children and their families. And all along, you always had your own agenda. I have had one myself for the last couple of years. I've had conversations with you, for years, with only one aim: to document everything you've done in order to prove that you actually did tell me about your crimes.

Was it necessary to record conversations with you? Yes, because nobody would believe me otherwise. Everyone told me that if you denied the allegations, I wouldn't have a leg to stand on. So I did what Endstra had wanted to do for years but couldn't because in doing so he would have revealed his own criminal acts. I taped you.

You know enough now. You know this is the end of the road, because of everything you've told me.

You know you will go to prison for life.

To others, I still have to explain why you deserve that. I have tried by testifying against you, but those testimonies lack nuance. To understand who you are and what you have done—to me, to yourself, and to all of us—I would have to explain my life story.

And a whole life is much too complicated to write down in a few testimonies. No police interrogation, not even dozens of them, could capture our relationship, your complexity, or our common reality.

It's an insane reality.

With you, nothing is what it seems. When you don't talk on the phone or get visitors in prison, the police think this should be comforting for us. We, on the other hand, get really scared, because we know what that means. You are staying out of contact with the outside world, so that when we are out of the way you can play innocent: "But, Your Honor, I have not called anyone or seen anyone in prison. How could I have given an order to assassinate them?"

If you wonder, Wim, why I did this to you, this is my answer: for Cor. For Sonja. For Richie. For Francis. For all the children who have lost their fathers because of you. And for all the children I want to spare that suffering.

It's time to stop the killing.

That Sonja, Sandra, and I will have to pay with our lives for testifying against you, you know that. We know that. The only reason you're still alive is that you want to take our lives.

But despite that certainty, Wim, I still love you.

Acknowledgments

I would especially like to thank Peter R. de Vries. He was the first one we—my sister and I, but also the rest of the family—ever put our trust in and to whom we told our whole story. He has never betrayed that trust. He was there for us from the moment Cor was killed, and he supported us on the long road of making and disclosing our statements. Peter, thank you for your friendship, your reliability, your sincerity, your support, and your courage, on behalf of my mother, as well.

About the Author

Astrid Holleeder is a Dutch lawyer and writer. She is the sister of the criminal Willem Holleeder and was, together with her older sister and a former friend of Willem, a witness to his prosecution. Her memoir *Judas* sold half a million copies and became the best-selling book in the Netherlands in 2016. Her second book, *Diary of a Witness*, also became an instant bestseller.